INDIA'S BOOK OF FIRSTS

hachette
INDIA

First published in 2024 by Hachette India
(Registered name: Hachette Book Publishing India Pvt. Ltd)
An Hachette UK company
www.hachetteindia.com

1

Cover Image Credits:
Front Cover: National Rail Museum: by courtesy of Shubhali Chopra; Pratibha Patil: President's Secretariat/GODL–India; Virat Kohli: President's Secretariat/GODL–India; Arjan Singh: by courtesy of PIB; Vikram lander: Indian Space Research Organisation/GODL–India; A.R. Rahman: President's Secretariat/GODL–India; Saina Nehwal: Ministry of Youth Affairs and Sports/GODL–India; Sushruta: CCA–SA 3.0 Unported/Alokprasad at en.wikipedia – https://commons.wikimedia.org/wiki/File:Shushrut_statue.jpg; Digital: Canva studio/Pexels.com; Maize crops:Alejandro Barrón/Pexels.com; Sakshi Malik: President's Secretariat/GODL–India; **Back Cover**: Delhi Haat: Ministry of Culture/GODL–India; Rakesh Sharma: Indian Air Force/GODL–India; Museum: by courtesy of PIB; Manika Batra: President's Secretariat/GODL–India; Dhirubhai Ambani: India Post/GODL–India; **Spine**: PTI stamp: India Post/GODL–India; National War Memorial: Ministry of Defence/GODL–India; Gramophone: Oktay Köseoğlu/Pexels.com.
All other images are from the public domain.

The copyright details and credits for the photographs in the book are on pages 338–342.

Old place names (such as Madras, Calcutta and Bombay) may have been used to retain the historicity of the information as well as avoid confusion with earlier presidencies and provinces of the same name.

All information has been updated till 30 November 2023 unless stated otherwise.

Subsequent edition/reprint specifications may be subject to change, including but not limited to cover or inside finishes, paper, text colour, and/or colour sections.

ISBN 978-93-5731-203-5

Hachette Book Publishing India Pvt. Ltd
4th & 5th Floors, Corporate Centre
Plot No. 94, Sector 44, Gurugram – 122003, India

Typeset by Manmohan Kumar, Delhi

Printed and bound in India by Manipal Technologies Limited

CONTENTS

PUBLISHER'S NOTE

Human endeavour has always been to achieve and accomplish and then strive to better the same. There are people who continuously push the boundaries. While the world goes on to record the most, the largest, the highest, the tallest, as and when they are surpassed, there is only one category that stays absolute – the first! The first to achieve something has a special space in history; etching their names in the first place and everything that comes after, settles for second space. *India's Book of Firsts* – a first of its kind – presents a compilation of the many firsts of India and Indians. Bringing you a comprehensive list of these firsts across fields like governance, the arts, cinema and photography, sports, science and technology, and more, the book aims to both entertain and inspire. Featuring entries of India's firsts such as – the first woman photojournalist (Homai Vyarawalla), the first Nobel Prize winner (Rabindranath Tagore), the first dual-way elevated taxiway (IGI Airport, New Delhi), the first fully organic state (Sikkim) and more – the book presents a whole range of records. There are also personality profiles in the book that zoom in on pioneers in their respective fields. Most chapters feature an additional timeline at the beginning. Also, all entries (except in sports, where the records have been arranged according to tournaments) are arranged chronologically. There may be more firsts that we wish we could include but we had to be selective keeping certain constraints in mind. Nonetheless, we have covered all significant areas, including a number of quirky facts.

GOVERNANCE, POLITICS AND NATIONHOOD

TIMELINE

EARLY PERIOD

- 600 BCE – The 'Mahajanapadas' emerge
- 600 BCE–13 century CE – The kingdoms of Cholas, Cheras and Pandyas established
- 340–185 BCE – The Mauryan Empire is established
- 4th–6th centuries CE – The Gupta Empire is established; Touted as the 'golden Age of India'
- 1526–1857 – The Mughal Empire is founded by Babur with Bahadur Shah II as the last ruler. The reign was also interrupted by Sher Shah Suri in 1540
- 1612 – The East India Company signs a trade agreement with Mughal emperor Jehangir
- 1857 – The Sepoy Mutiny; Bahadur Shah Zafar deposed by the British East India Company

- 1862 – High courts are established in Bombay, Calcutta and Madras (now Mumbai, Kolkata and Chennai respectively)
- 1885 – Indian National Congress is formed

20TH CENTURY

- 1947 – India gains Independence
- 1948 – Assassination of Mahatma Gandhi
- 1950 – India declared a Republic
- 1952 – First general elections are conducted
- 1956 – States Reorganization Act is passed
- 1962 – India seizes Daman, Diu and Goa from Portuguese
- 1966 – Indira Gandhi becomes the first woman PM
- 1975 – The state of Emergency is declared
- 1977 – First non-Congress government elected
- 1984 – Operation Bluestar is conducted; Assassination of Indira Gandhi; Rajiv Gandhi takes over as PM
- 1991 – Assassination of Rajiv Gandhi
- 1998 – BJP forms a coalition government under Atal Behari Vajpayee as the PM

21ST CENTURY

- 2000 – Birth of the billionth Indian citizen
- 2004 – Return of Congress as Dr Manmohan Singh is sworn in as the PM
- 2005 – Right to Information launched
- 2007 – Pratibha Patil becomes the first woman President
- 2014 – Landslide victory for BJP. Narendra Modi is sworn in as the PM

EARLIEST REPUBLIC ON THE SUBCONTINENT

Vrijji, a *mahajanapada* ('republic' or 'kingdom') of ancient India, with its capital at Vaishali (present day region of Mithila in Bihar), dating to the sixth century BCE, is believed to be the earliest republic on the Indian subcontinent. Formed by the union of several clans, including the Lichchhavis, Jnatrikas and Videhas, it had no monarch, but a popular assembly of elders who carried on the business of state.

EARLY ADMINISTRATION

An elaborate machinery for taxation and administration was in place at the time of the Mauryan rulers (c. 322–180 BCE). The state maintained a vast bureaucracy with important functionaries called *tirthas*. The top administrators in this system were the minister (*mantri*), the high priest (*purohita*), the commander (*senapati*), and the prince (*yuvaraja*).

FIRST WOMAN RULER

Nayanika from the Satavahana dynasty (first century BCE) is considered the first woman ruler of India as she was queen regent to her son, Satakarni II. Razia Sultan of the Mamluk dynasty was the first and the only woman ruler of the Delhi Sultanate. She ascended the throne in 1236 CE and was the first woman ruler in India. There have been multiple portrayals of her character in mainstream media by actresses such as Nirupa Roy and Hema Malini.

A portrait of Dom Francisco de Almeida

FIRST COLONIAL RULE

Colonial rule began in India with the establishment of the first European trading centre in Quilon (now Kollam), Kerala, in 1502 by the Portuguese. In 1505, Dom Francisco de Almeida was appointed the first Portuguese viceroy in India by King Manuel I of Portugal. They established fortresses on the Malabar coast in Kerala and the presence of the Portuguese in India lasted till 1961.

FIRST POLITICAL ORGANIZATION

The Zamindari Association of Calcutta was the first recorded political organization in the country. An organization for landlords, principally organized by Radhakanta Deb and Prasanna Kumar Tagore, it was formally launched in 1838 and changed its name to Landholders' Association shortly after. It was set up to defend the landlords against pro-peasant policies of the government. It became defunct in 1851.

FIRST WAR OF INDEPENDENCE

An integral first step in India's struggle for Independence, the Sepoy Mutiny, was the first organized fight against the colonial British rulers. It is also known as the 'First War of Independence' and the 'Rebellion of 1857'. In 2007, the government of India celebrated the 150th anniversary of the mutiny.

An Illustration of the Sepoy Mutiny from the *Illustrated Times*

FIRST PENAL CODE

British historian and politician Thomas Babington Macaulay chaired the first law commission of India that was set up in 1862. It was on the basis of the recommendations of this commission that the Indian Penal Code (IPC) and the Criminal Procedure Code (CrPC) were drafted and introduced in Bengal (now West Bengal) in 1862.

FIRST BARRISTER-AT-LAW

On 21 June 1862, Gyanendramohan Tagore (1826–90) passed the barrister-at-law examination from Lincoln's Inn in England, the first Indian to do so. He enrolled into the Calcutta High Court in Bengal Presidency as the first Indian barrister in November 1865.

There have been 106 amendments to the Constitution of India till September 2023.

FIRST CENSUS

The first ever census across the country was conducted in 1872 in British India. The first regular census was conducted in 1881, and then every ten years. The last census was conducted in 2011. The census is conducted by the registrar general and the census commissioner under the Ministry of Home Affairs, Government of India.

FIRST PUBLIC PROSECUTOR

S. Subramania Iyer (1842–1924) was a jurist and freedom fighter and was appointed public prosecutor in Madras, Tamil Nadu, in 1887.

FIRST RENDITION OF THE NATIONAL SONG

In 1896, 'Vande Mataram', by Bankim Chandra Chatterjee was published in his work *Anandamath,* and was first sung at the Indian National Congress session in Calcutta. This was the first rendition of our national song. The poem has six stanzas and the first two stanzas have been adopted as the national song for India.

FIRST DESIGN OF THE NATIONAL FLAG

Our national flag was not always the tricolour we have now. The current design of the flag was adopted in 1947 as the flag of independent India. Forty years prior to that, on 22 August 1907, freedom fighter Bhikhaiji (or Bhikaji) Rustam Cama (1861–1936) from Bombay raised the 'Flag of Indian Independence' at the International Socialist Conference in Stuttgart, Germany. The flag featured three colours: green at the top, saffron in the middle and red at the bottom. There were eight lotuses on the top band to symbolize the eight provinces of British India and the middle band carried the words 'Vande Matram' in Devanagari. The band at the bottom had a crescent to represent Islam and the sun to represent Hinduism. It was based on one of the first unofficial flags of India, designed by Sachindra Prasad Bose and Hemchandra Kanungo which was hoisted on 7 August 1906 at Parsi Bagan Square in Calcutta and was known as the 'Calcutta flag'.

FIRST RENDITION OF THE NATIONAL ANTHEM

Composed by Rabindranath Tagore, 'Jana Gana Mana', India's national anthem, was sung for the first time on 27 December 1911 at the Calcutta session of the Indian

National Congress. The Constituent Assembly accepted the translation of the first verse in Hindi as the national anthem of India on 24 January 1950.

FIRST PANCHAYATS

Panchayats were first established in villages under the Panchayat Act in 1912. The model did not meet much success. It was in 1952 that a new Panchayat Act revived the system.

FIRST SATYAGRAHA

In 1917, Mahatma Gandhi organized the first satyagraha in Champaran, Bihar. This satyagraha, the first of many more to follow, was organized against British laws that governed the cultivation of indigo.

A satyagraha is a determined resistance coupled with non-violence.

FIRST WOMAN PRESIDENT OF A NATIONAL PARTY

Annie Besant (1847–1933), a woman's rights activist and a British socialist was elected president of the Indian National Congress in 1917 and was the first woman to head the party.

FIRST WOMAN LEGISLATOR

Dr S. Muthulakshmi Reddy (1886–1968) was a pioneer for women empowerment. She was a social worker, physician and an educationist and worked towards the emancipation of women. In 1926, she became the first woman legislator (Madras Legislative Council member). In 2019, the Tamil

Nadu government announced the celebration of her birthday on 30 July as 'Hospital Day'.

FIRST WOMAN CABINET MINISTER

Vijaya Lakshmi Pandit (1900–90), born in Allahabad in British India to Motilal Nehru and Swaruprani Thussu was a pioneering Indian woman. Inspired by Sarojini Naidu and Annie Besant, she became the first woman cabinet minister and was elected as the minister for local government and health in 1937. She was ambassador to the erstwhile USSR from 1947 to 1949, becoming the first woman ambassador of India. She also served as ambassador to the US and Mexico (1949–51) and in Ireland (1955–61). Her longest tenure was in London, as high commissioner to the UK, serving from 1954 to 1961. Her last posting as ambassador was in Spain. In September 1953, she also became the first woman president of the United Nations General Assembly and the first and only Indian to hold that post. The same year she was also a candidate for Secretary General of the United Nations. She later also served as governor of Maharashtra from 1962 to 1964 and as member of the Lok Sabha from 1964 to 1968. An integral part of the Quit India Movement (1942–45), she was jailed multiple times as well. However, it did not deter her strong resolute to bring about change. She was also actively involved in helping the

Vijaya Lakshmi Pandit

victims of the Bengal famine of 1943 and worked towards the reformation of inheritance laws for Hindu widows.

FIRST PRIME MINISTER

Jawaharlal Nehru (1889–1964) was declared the first prime minister of independent India in 1947. He was later elected for the position in 1952, 1957 and 1962. He was also the prime minister for the Interim government pre-independence from 2 September 1946. Unfortunately, he was the first prime minister to die in harness on 27 May 1964 serving for 17 years.

FIRST DEPUTY PRIME MINISTER

Sardar Vallabhbhai Patel (1875–1950) was the first deputy prime minister of India. He was sworn in on 15 August 1947 in the first cabinet of independent India. Often referred to as the 'Iron Man of India', the world's tallest statue is dedicated to him. The 'Statue of Unity' in Gujarat, stands tall with a staggering height of 182 metres.

FIRST REPUBLIC DAY PARADE

After gaining independence on 15 August 1947, India became a sovereign and democratic republic on 26 January 1950, which is celebrated as Republic Day. The first republic day parade was held on the same day at Irwin Stadium (now Major Dhyan Chand National Stadium) with Dr Sukarno,

Dr Rajendra Prasad (in the carriage) on his way to take part in the first Republic Day Parade

the then President of Indonesia as the chief guest. It is amusing that the first Republic Day parade at Rajpath (now Kartavya Path), New Delhi, actually took place five years later in 1955, which became its permanent venue.

FIRST CHIEF JUSTICE OF INDIA

On 26 January 1950, Justice Sir Harilal J. Kania (1890–1951), was appointed as India's first Chief Justice. He held the position till 6 November 1951.

FIRST CHIEF ELECTION COMMISSIONER

Sukumar Sen (1898–1963) was India's first chief election commissioner from 21 March 1950 to 19 December 1958. The Election Commission of India conducted the first two general elections during 1951–52 and 1957 under his leadership. One can only imagine the enormity and importance of the mammoth task to conduct the first ever elections for a massive electorate.

FIRST GENERAL ELECTION

The first ever elections in the country were organized during 1951–52, with a total of 401 constituencies. Among these, 314 constituencies were with one seat, 86 constituencies were with two seats, and one was with three seats. There were 14 recognized multi-state political parties and 39 state parties. Votes were casted in ballot boxes allotted to the respective candidates by people aged 21 and over. The Indian National Congress witnessed a landslide victory and formed the government.

FIRST PRESIDENTIAL ELECTION

The first presidential election in the country was held in 1952 when Dr Rajendra Prasad (1884–1963) was declared the first president of India with 507,400 votes. He went on to win the second presidential election held in 1957 as well.

> There were 4,056 electors in the first presidential elections.

FIRST PRESIDENT

Dr Rajendra Prasad won the first presidential elections in 1952 to become the first president of independent India. He held the position for two sessions and remains till date the only one to complete two complete terms.

FIRST VICE PRESIDENT

Dr S. Radhakrishnan (1888–1975) was the vice president of India during 1952–62. He was the also the first to serve this office twice consecutively, which is effectively the longest tenure as vice president. This feat was repeated by Hamid Ansari, who held office from 2007–17.

FIRST SESSION OF PARLIAMENT

A parliament session is summoned by the President and is usually conducted three times in a year. The first session of parliament that was held in free India was summoned on 13 May 1952 by Dr Rajendra Prasad as the president and Jawaharlal Nehru as prime minister.

FIRST CABINET

The First cabinet with Jawaharlal Nehru as the prime minister and Dr Rajendra Prasad as the President consisted of the following members:

Minister	**Portfolio**
Jawaharlal Nehru	Prime minister, External Affairs and Commonwealth Relations and Scientific Research
Sardar Vallabhbhai Patel	Deputy prime minister, Home Affairs and States and Information and Broadcasting

R.K. Shanmukham Chetty	Finance
B.R. Ambedkar	Law
Baldev Singh	Defence
John Matthai	Railways and Transport
Maulana Abul Kalam Azad	Education
Dr Rajendra Prasad	Food and Agriculture
Syama Prasad Mukherjee	Industries and Supplies
Jagjivan Ram	Labour
C.H. Bhabha	Commerce
Rafi Ahmed Kidwai	Communications
Amrit Kaur	Health
Narhar Vishnu Gadgil	Works, Mines and Power
K.C. Neogy	Relief and Rehabilitation
N. Gopalaswami Ayyangar	No portfolio assigned
Mohanlal Saxena	No portfolio assigned

FIRST SPEAKER OF THE LOK SABHA

'Dadasaheb' G.V. Mavalankar (1888–1956) was the first Speaker of the Lok Sabha and held the position from 15 May 1952 to 27 February 1956.

FIRST DEPUTY SPEAKER OF THE LOK SABHA

Madabhushi Ananthasayanam Ayyangar (1891–1978) was elected on 30 May 1952. He also later served as the fifth governor of Bihar.

The expenditure ceiling (maximum expenditure allowed to candidates) currently ranges between ₹28–40 lakhs for assembly constituencies and ₹75–90 lakhs for parliamentary constituencies.

FIRST WOMAN MAYOR

Padma Bhushan Tara Cherian (1913–2000) was appointed Mayor of Madras, Tamil Nadu in 1957.

FIRST USE OF INDELIBLE INK

Indelible ink, more commonly referred to as the election ink, was first used in the third Lok Sabha elections in 1962. Mysore Paints and Varnish Ltd, based in Mysore (now Mysuru), Karnataka, currently owned and operated by the Government of Karnataka, was authorized to manufacture the ink. The company continues to supply this ink to this date and is the sole manufacturer. They also export the ink to many other countries for their elections. The 1962 elections were also the first to use single ballot paper and a single ballot box. In the two elections that took place before that, there used to be separate ballot boxes kept for each candidate.

FIRST WOMAN CHIEF MINISTER

Freedom fighter Sucheta Kripalani (1908–74) was elected as the chief minister of Uttar Pradesh in 1963. With her swearing in, she became the first woman chief minister of the country. She served in this position up till 1967.

FIRST AND ONLY WOMAN PRIME MINISTER

Indira Priyadarshini Gandhi (1917–84), took up office in 1966 and served until 1977. She was elected again in 1980 and served in office until her assassination in 1984. She was the first and only woman prime minister.

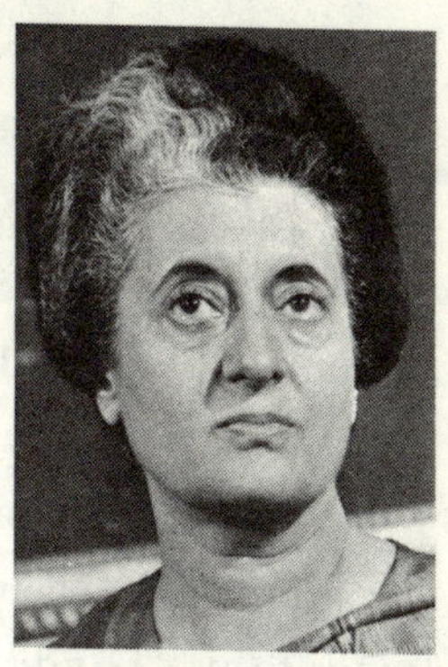
Indira P. Gandhi

FIRST LOK SABHA DISSOLUTION (UNTIMELY)

In a first for the history of the Indian Parliament, the fifth Lok Sabha session in 1971, was untimely dissolved by Indira Gandhi. The second such Lok Sabha dissolution was under the presidency of Charan Singh in 1979 and the third in 1991 under Chandra Shekhar. The Lok Sabha has been untimely dissolved three more times since then. The Lok Sabha is dissolved after a period of five years, however, it can also be dissolved irrevocably by the President on the recommendation of the Prime Minister any time within that tenure.

FIRST WOMAN IPS OFFICER

Kiran Bedi (b. 1949) was the first woman to join the Indian Police Service (IPS) on 16 July 1972. She retired in 2007 and was later the lieutenant governor of Puducherry (May 2016–February 2021). In 1994, she became the first Indian woman to win the Ramon Magsaysay award in government service. She also became the first woman and first Indian to head the United Nations Police in 2003.

FIRST USE OF HINDI AT UNITED NATIONS (UN)

Atal Bihari Vajpayee

Atal Bihari Vajpayee (1924–2018), as India's minister for external affairs presented his speech in Hindi at the United Nations General Assembly in 1977, becoming the first person to use Hindi at UN and the first Indian leader to use Hindi at an international platform. An Indian diplomat translated the speech to English.

FIRST PRIME MINISTER TO RESIGN

Morarji R. Desai

After assuming office on 24 March 1977, Morarji Ranchhodji Desai (1896–1995) became the first prime minister of India to resign from the office. He resigned from his post on 28 July 1979, after a split from the Janata Party. He was also the first non-Congress prime minister.

FIRST ELECTRONIC VOTING MACHINES

Electronic voting machines (EVMs) are used to conduct the voting electronically. Ballot papers are not issued and voters can vote by clicking on the button next to their desired candidate. They were used for the first time in the assembly by-elections in Kerala in April 1982. The machines were introduced by the Electronics Corporation of India Ltd (ECIL), headquartered in Hyderabad (now in Telangana).

FIRST CHIEF MINISTER ELECTED ABROAD

M.G. Ramachandran (1917–87), popularly known as 'MGR' was elected as the chief minister of Tamil Nadu in absentia, while he was admitted in a hospital in New York. The first instance of such an election, his nomination papers were flown in from the US and he was sworn in on 10 February 1985, forty-three days after the election. He was the first film star to become a chief minister.

India's constitution is the longest written constitution in the world.

FIRST TEENAGE VOTE

In 1989, the Constitution of India underwent the 61st amendment to lower the voting age in the country for Lok Sabha and state legislatures from 21 years to 18 years. As a result, 35.7 million voters in the age group of 18–21 years cast their votes.

FIRST HUNG PARLIAMENT

When no single political party has majority of seats in the parliament, it is termed as a hung parliament. In the history of the Indian general elections, this situation first arose in 1989.

FIRST WOMAN CHIEF JUSTICE

Justice Leila Seth (1930–2017) was appointed the chief justice of Himachal Pradesh on 5 August 1991, becoming India's first woman chief justice of a high court.

FIRST WOMAN PRESIDENT

Pratibha Patil

Pratibha Devi Singh Patil (b. 1934) took office as the 12th President of India from 2007 to 2012, thereby, becoming the first woman president of the country.

FIRST NOTA OPTION

The 2014 general elections were the first to offer the option of choosing 'None of the Above' (NOTA), also known as the 'against all' or a 'scratch' vote internationally. It provides a neutral vote to those voters who do not wish to vote for any candidate on the electoral ballot. Around 1.04 per cent of voters polled NOTA in the 2019 elections. It may be noted that even if maximum votes are cast for the NOTA option, the candidate with the most votes will be declared as the elected candidate. The general elections of 2014 also marked a landmark move by including a third gender category of voters, called 'Others'. As many as 28,314 voters enrolled in this category in 2014 and 38,970 voters in 2019.

FIRST TRANSGENDER LAWYER

Sathyasri Sharmila, a lawyer in the Bar Council of Tamil Nadu and Puducherry, became the first transgender lawyer in India. Completing her degree in 2007, she enrolled as an advocate after the National Legal Services Authority of India (NALSA) judgment of 2014, which recognized the third gender.

FIRST TRANSGENDER JUDGE

Joyita Mondal Mahi, India's first transgender judge, was appointed as a judge in the Lok Adalat in West Bengal in 2017.

FIRST INDIAN WOMAN ON THE UNITED NATIONS LAW BOARD

Neeru Chadha (b. 1955) was the first Indian to be appointed to the International Tribunal for the Law of the Sea (ITLOS), being elected to the UN body in June 2017.

FIRST EVMS/POSTAL BALLOT PAPERS WITH PHOTOGRAPHS OF CANDIDATES

For the 2019 general elections, the EVMs/postal ballot papers carried the photographs of all the candidates in the constituency. This enabled the voters to correctly identify the candidates they wanted to vote for and avoid confusion.

FIRST TRANSGENDER ELECTION AMBASSADOR

Gauri Sawant, a transgender activist from Mumbai, Maharashtra, was appointed as the first transgender election ambassador in the country in 2019. She was appointed by the Election Commission of India along with 11 other election ambassadors from the state.

FIRST PAPERLESS BUDGET

The Union budget for 2021 was presented on a 'Made-in-India' tablet on 1 February 2021 by Finance Minister Nirmala Sitharaman, doing away with the long-standing tradition of printing the budget papers and also the convention of carrying them in a briefcase.

FIRST CITIZEN TO HAVE A 'NO CASTE, NO RELIGION' CERTIFICATE

M.A. Sneha Parthibaraja, from Tirupattur, Tamil Nadu, became the first Indian citizen to win the right to not have a caste or religion, on 5 February 2021. It was a nine-year-long legal struggle to attain the certificate.

The Supreme court museum was inaugurated on 6 April 2004 and is an apex location to soak in the judicial heritage of our country.

FIRST WOMAN RAJYA SABHA MEMBER FROM NAGALAND

S. Phangnon Konyak from Dimapur, Nagaland, became the first woman member of the Rajya Sabha from the state of Nagaland in March 2022. She holds the distinction of being the second woman from the state to be member of the Lok Sabha, Rajya Sabha or the State Assembly after Rano M. Shazia. She achieved yet another milestone when she presided over the upper house on 25 July 2023.

DEFENCE

TIMELINE

EARLY PERIOD

- Mid 17th–mid 18th century – The Marathas established a naval wing of their armed forces which was practically the first Navy in India
- 1612 – East India Company's Marine is established
- 1824 – The Naval Arm is renamed Bombay Marine and participate in the first Anglo-Burmese War
- 1840 – Her Majesty's Indian Navy (renamed in 1834) participates in the Opium War and later the Second-Anglo Burmese War (1952)
- 1895 – The Indian Army is established along with the presidency armies of the East India Company

20TH CENTURY

- 1914–18 – Indian soldiers were deployed as adjunct to the forces of the British Empire in the First World War
- 1932 – The Indian Air Force established under the British Rule
- 1939–45 – Indian soldiers were deployed as adjunct to the forces of the British Empire in the Second World War
- 1942 – Indian National Army is formed by Subhas Chandra Bose

- 1947 – First Kashmir War with Pakistan
- 1948 – Operation Polo to successfully annex Hyderabad
- 1949 – K.M. Cariappa takes over as the first Indian Chief of Army Staff
- 1950 – Current service Indian Army, India Air Force (IAF) and Indian Navy is established
- 1950–53 – Troops sent against the North Korean invasion of South Korea
- 1961 – Operation Vijay launched to annex Diu, Goa and Daman from the Portuguese
- 1962 – Sino-India War
- 1965 – India and Pakistan War
- 1967 – Sino-India conflict over the invasion of Sikkim
- 1971 – Bangladesh Liberation War or India–Pakistan war of 1971
- 1979 – Smiling Buddha – India's first nuclear test
- 1984 – Siachen Conflict with Pakistan known as Operation Meghdoot
- 1999 – Kargil War with Pakistan – Operation Vijay (Army), Operation Safed Sagar (IAF) and Operation Talwar (Navy)

21ST CENTURY

- 2001–02 – India–Pakistan stand off
- 2002 – Test-fire of nuclear capable ballistic missile – Agni
- 2006 – Nuclear agreement with the US
- 2007 – Nuclear agreement with Pakistan
- 2016 – Surgical strikes on Pakistan-administered Kashmir
- 2017 – China-India border standoff over Doklam
- 2019 – Balakot Airstrike

FIRST CANTONMENTS

Lord Clive, in 1765, initiated the building of cantonments for British troops when they were stationed. This was to keep them 'cantoned' in one place and maintain sanitised environments for them and enforce the discipline of the military life. Bhatinda, Punjab is the largest cantonment, out of the 62 cantonments built across the country.

FIRST INDIAN PILOTS

During the First World War, Lieutenant Indra Lal Roy (1898–1918) from Calcutta (now Kolkata), West Bengal, was the first Indian pilot to be part of the Royal Flying Corps and later the Royal Air Force. He died in action aged 19 and was posthumously awarded the Distinguished Flying Cross. The only other pilots from India that were known to have flown in the First World War were Sardar Hardit Singh Malik, Lieutenant S.G. Welingkar, Lieutenant Errol Sharat Chandra Sen and Lieutenant Naoroji.

A stamp commemorating Lieutenant Indra Lal Roy

FIRST VICTORIA CROSS

Presented for valour in the 'presence of the enemy', the Victoria Cross is the highest honour in the British honours system. The first Indian to be awarded this honour was Sepoy (later Subedar) Khuda Dad Khan of the 129 Baluchis for his act of bravery at Hollebeke, Belgium on 31 October 1914 in the First World War.

FIRST AIRCRAFT

The Westland Wapiti, a biplane aircraft with a maximum speed of 362 km/hr was inducted into the Indian Air Force on 1 April 1933. The aircraft could carry a load of 263 kg and was fitted with two machine guns. Four such planes formed the A Flight of 1 Squadron.

Westland Wapiti

FIRST COMMISSIONED OFFICER

Major General K. Bhagwati Singh (ID 1-0-No.1) passed out of the Indian Military Academy (IMA) in 1934, with his batchmate (and later field marshal) Sam Manekshaw, becoming the first commissioned officer. Interestingly, his son, Admiral Madhvendra Singh was the chief of Naval Staff of the Indian Navy from December 2001 to July 2004.

The Agnipath Scheme launched by the government in June 2022 for youth recruitment received 54 lakh applications.

FIRST GEORGE CROSS

In 1935, Britain's prestigious George Cross, awarded for gallantry, not in the presence of an enemy was awarded to an Indian. Havildar Nandlal Thapa of Gurkha Rifles received it for his courage and devotion to duty.

FIRST ACTIVE OPERATION (IAF)

The 1 Squadron operated from Miranshah in North Waziristan (now in Pakistan) against hostile tribesmen in September 1937.

FIRST NAVAL PILOT

Lieutenant Y.N. Singh serving the Royal Indian Navy was deputed to England in 1941 for basic training. He later obtained his wings in Canada in 1944 and served in the escort carriers of the Royal Navy in the Second World War.

FIRST ARMY HEADQUARTERS

Army Headquarters were first housed in Red Fort, Delhi, in 1947. However, it was shortly relocated. Currently the Army has its headquarters in the Integrated Defence

Headquarters, Ministry of Defence, New Delhi. In April 2023, the Indian Army announced plans for a new 'Thal Sena Bhavan' opposite the Manekshaw Centre in Delhi cantonment, slated to be completed in 2025.

FIRST INDIAN COMMANDER–IN–CHIEF (ARMY)

General (later field marshal by special investiture on 15 January 1986) K.M. Cariappa (1899–1993) took over the position of C-in-C on 15 January 1949 and held office till 14 January 1953. The only other C-in-C was General M. Rajendra Sinhji Jadeja and after that the post was abolished.

FIRST FIGHTER JET

India introduced fighter jets with the induction of the British single-seat Vampire in 1948. The first Vampire built indigenously, under a licenced agreement between De Havilland Aircraft Company Ltd, UK and Hindustan Aeronautics Ltd (HAL) was flown on 21 February 1952. However, they were all phased out by 1975.

FIRST CHIEF OF AIR STAFF

Air Marshal Subroto Mukerjee (1911–60) was the first Indian chief of air staff and succeeded Air Marshal Sir G.E. Gibbs on 1 April 1954. At that time the position was only equivalent to that of a lieutenant general of the Army. The IAF got its first air chief marshal with the appointment of Air Chief Marshal Arjan Singh in 1966.

FIRST DEFENCE ACADEMY

Inaugurated on 16 January 1955, the National Defence Academy at Khadakwasla, Maharashtra, was set up to give its students a military orientation and prepare them to join any of the three uniformed services of the Indian armed forces.

A stamp commemorating the National Defence Academy

FIRST INDIAN CHIEF OF NAVAL STAFF

Vice Admiral Ram Dass Katari (1911–83) was appointed as the first Indian chief of naval staff in 1958.

There has been no one appointed to the post of 'Admiral of the fleet' in the Indian Navy till date.

FIRST CHIEF OF FOREIGN AIR FORCE

Air Commodore K. Jaswant Singh (1915–63) took charge as the air chief of the Ghana Air Force on 25 March 1959. He was sent there to plan and establish the force.

FIRST STRIKE OF THE INDIAN NAVY

During the Goan Liberation Struggle, on the night of 17–18 December 1961, the Indian Navy conducted its first operation, called Operation Vijay. The IN ships demolished the Portuguese airstrip and sank three vessels.

They received 12 decorations (three posthumous) for this operation. In 1971, Operations Python and Trident were the first operations conducted in a war.

FIRST HELI–LIFTED BATTALION

Raised in 1762 as 10 Battalion of the Coastal Sepoys, the First Guards (2 Punjab) was heli-lifted during the counter-insurgency operations in Nagaland during 1969–70.

FIRST NAVAL ACADEMY

In January 1969, a Naval Academy was established at Cochin (now Kochi), Kerala and the first batch of cadets graduated in December 1970, with Commander Ramdas as the first officer-in-charge. Prior to this, all cadets were trained in the United Kingdom.

FIRST SUBMARINE BASE

INS *Virbahu* was commissioned near Vishakhapatnam in Andhra Pradesh on 19 May 1971. This was the Indian Navy's first submarine base. This was later followed by INS *Vajrabahu* (1996) and the announcement of INS *Varsha*, which is currently under development.

FIRST FIELD MARSHAL

In 1973, S.H.F.J. (Sam) Manekshaw (1914–2008), was promoted from General to Field Marshal. He was part of the first intake of the Indian Military Academy in Dehradun and later went on to become the seventh chief of Army staff. He received the Padma Bhushan in 1968 and the Padma Vibhushan in 1972.

FIRST MISSILE

The Indian Defence boasts of a range of exemplary missiles. On 25 February 1988, *Prithvi*, the first tactical surface-to-surface missile was test-fired.

FIRST WOMEN IN THE ARMY

The Indian Army commissioned a batch of 25 women on 6 March 1993 at the Officers Training Academy in Madras (now Chennai), Tamil Nadu. Inducted in non-combat departments, such as legal, logistics, education and supply, this was the first time they were inducted outside the Army Medical Corps (AMC).

FIRST WOMEN IN THE AIR FORCE

Twelve women trainees were inducted into the Air Force in non-technical branches in July 1992. It was the first service to do so. On 21 June 1993, after the 48-week training programme, they were commissioned as Pilot Officers and received their badges. They were accorded a short service commission for five years and a regular service tenure based on performance.

FIRST UNIFIED THEATRE COMMAND

Admiral Arun Prakash (b. 1944), then Vice Admiral, took over as the first Commander-in-Chief of the Andaman and

Nicobar Command in 2001. This gave him operational control of all the three services and the Coast Guard in the Andaman and Nicobar theatre.

FIRST CHIEF OF INTEGRATED DEFENCE STAFF

Lieutenant General Pankaj Joshi was appointed the first Chief of Integrated Defence Staff (CIDS) in the country on 1 October 2001. A three star rank officer from the three services in rotation is appointed to the post.

The Armed Forces Veterans' Day is celebrated on 14 January.

FIRST INDIGENOUS EQUIPMENT

The ministry of Defence invests in the research and development of indigenous military equipment. The table below showcases some of the indigenous equipment across the three services:

ARMY

Name of the equipment	Type of Equipment	Date of Commissioning/ Inauguration
Vijayanta	Tank	12 December 1965
Yukthirath Mine Protected Vehicles (MPV)	Mine Protected Vehicles	30 October 2009
Rudra	Weaponised helicopter	8 February 2013

NAVY		
INS *Nilgiri*	Modern warship	3 June 1972
INS *Shalki*	Submarine	February 1992
INS *Kora*	Missile corvette	10 August 1998
INS *Bangaram*	Fast attack craft	10 February 2006
INS *Vikrant*	Aircraft carrier	12 August 2013
INS *Kamorta*	Anti-submarine corvette	12 July 2014
INS *Astradharini*	Torpedo Launch Vehicle	6 October 2015
AIR FORCE		
HF-24 *Marut*	Fighter aircraft	17 June 1961
Lakshya	Pilotless drone	September 1992
LCH *Prachand*	Multi-role combat helicopter	October 2022

FIRST TRI–SERVICES AFFILIATION

Bengal Sappers of the Indian Army have been affiliated with the Indian Navy and Indian Air Force since 2002. Originally called the Bengal Sappers and Miners, they are headquartered in Roorkee (now in Uttarakhand), and have won 80 battle honours and 11 theatre honours.

FIRST NUCLEAR SHELTER

In 2002, the Defence Research and Development Organisation (DRDO) introduced an integrated battlefield shelter for the three services. This shelter can withstand strikes that are nuclear or chemical for up to 96 hours. Measuring 28 m in length and with a diameter of 2.5 m, the portable shelter has chemical toilets, water tanks, two power generators and pumps for sewage disposal. It can accommodate 30 people and has the capability to be used as a command post, a communication centre and an observation post.

FIRST IAF MARSHAL

Air Chief Marshal Arjan Singh (1919–2017) was given the rank of Marshal on 26 January 2002. This post was

Air Chief Marshal Arjan Singh

equivalent to a field marshal of the Army. He also received the Distinguished Flying Cross.

FIRST WOMAN TO COMMAND A PASSING OUT PARADE

The 77th passing-out parade at the Officer's Training Academy (OTA), Chennai, on 20 March 2004, was commanded by Lieutenant Rashmi Narayan, making her the first woman in the Indian armed forces to command a passing-out parade.

FIRST WOMAN LIEUTENANT GENERAL

The first woman to reach a three-star rank across the three services was Dr Punita Arora when she was promoted to the rank of Lieutenant General on 1 September 2004.

FIRST WOMAN AIR MARSHAL

Air Marshal Padmavathy Bandopadhyay, AVSM, VSM, (b. 4 November 1944) has a lot of firsts to her credit. A pioneering woman, she joined the Indian Air Force as a medical officer. She became the first to attend the Defence Services Staff Course in 1978. She then went on to become the first woman in the continent to specialise in aerospace medicine. During 1989–90, she visited the North Pole, becoming the first woman to do so. In 1995, she was awarded the Indira Gandhi Priyadarshini Award for her work in high altitude and aerospace medicine and cold physiology. By 2002, she was the first woman to reach the rank of vice marshal and subsequently was promoted to Air Marshal. On 1 October 2004, she took over as the director general of medical services (Air). Married to Sati Nath Bandopadhyay, together they became the first IAF couple to receive honours from the president in the same investiture ceremony. She was awarded the Padma Shri in 2020.

Air Marshal Padmavathy Bandopadhyay (left)

FIRST NAVAL CHIEF OF STRATEGIC FORCES

Vice Admiral Vijay Shankar (b. 30 September 1949) became the first Naval officer to head the Strategic Forces Command for the tri-services which administers India's nuclear weaponry. Earlier the command was headed by IAF officers. He was appointed in 2006 and he retired in 2009.

FIRST DISTANCE LEARNING PROGRAMME FOR SOLDIERS

e-Gurukul, launched by the Corps of Signals in 2007 was the first distance learning programme to keep soldiers up to date with technology even in inaccessible counter-insurgency areas. Along with live videos, officers can also interact with the instructors via chat or voice applications. Tests are also conducted online and assessments are carried out individually. Inaugurated by Major General K.J.S. Oberoi, this reduces the need for troop movement, making them available for active service, besides saving time and expenses.

FIRST FOREIGN RESCUE OPS

Reportedly, 1,632 US military personnel went missing in the regions comprising Northeast India, China and Myanmar. In 2008, the US military started the first search operation in Arunanchal Pradesh with the assistance of the Indian Air Force. The operation was called off in 2010.

FIRST WOMEN OBSERVERS

The first batch of women cadets training to be Observers was inducted in the Naval Academy in April 2011 in Kochi, Kerala. After their graduation, the cadets would be involved in planning tactical operations in the maritime reconnaissance stream to serve in multiple-crew aircraft.

FIRST WOMEN COMBAT PILOTS

In October 2012, Flight Lieutenants Alka Shukla and M.P. Shumathi were trained to fly the twin-engine Mi-8 at the Yelahanka station. The first to fly a utility and assault helicopter, they were trained for airdropping troops, bombing, search and rescue missions, rocket attacks and other heliborne operations. Prior to this, women only flew the non-combat Chetak and Chetan helicopters.

FIRST CITIZEN OF INDIAN ARMY

A special celebration was held at the headquarters of the Western Command of the Indian Army when Lieutenant Colonel Kartar Singh was felicitated as the 'First Citizen of the Indian Army' and a Super Veteran on 1 April 2013, his 100th birthday. He was commissioned into Licters British Infantry Unit in 1937 and served India in Egypt and Sudan in the 1940s during the Second World War. He was appointed as the first Indian Commanding Officer of 1 Mahar Regiment which he led from 1947 to 1951. During the 1947–48 Indo-Pak operations in Jammu & Kashmir, his battalion earned the first Maha Vir Chakra.

FIRST DEDICATED MILITARY SATELLITE

The GSAT-7 satellite, launched by the Indian Space Research Organization (ISRO) on 30 August 2013 was the first dedicated military satellite. The multi-band communication satellite, named Rukmini, is mostly used for the communication requirements of the Indian Navy among its warships, submarines, and land and aircraft systems. This was followed by the launch of GSAT–7A (Angry Bird) in 2018 that caters services to the Indian Air Force. In March 2023, the Ministry of Defence announced their deal with NewSpace India Limited (NSIL) to develop GSAT–7B, for the exclusive use of the Indian Army.

FIRST RECRUITMENT APP

Army Calling, a mobile application launched by the Indian Army in May 2015 was the first such application in the world to recruit Army personnel. It was developed by Voobr and can be downloaded from the Google Playstore. The app seeks to make information simpler and more accessible.

A new branch has been approved by the government for the Indian Air Force in 2022. The Weapons Systems Branch will unify all weapon system operators into one entity.

FIRST WOMEN FIGHTER PILOTS

While women have been flying helicopters and transport aircraft for the armed services since 1991, it was only on

18 June 2016 that three women were commissioned as fighter pilots at the Air Force Academy in Dindigul, Telangana. Flying Officers Avani Chaturvedi (b. 27 October 1993), Bhawana Kanth (b. 1 December 1992) and Mohana Singh (b. 22 January 1992) were selected from a batch of 130 flight cadets that included 22 women. They were cleared for flying fighter aircraft and trained with the batch at the Indian Air Force base in Hakempet. Their duties initially remained limited to protecting Indian skies in combat air patrols and did not extend to flying over enemy territory.

Mohana Singh (left), Avani Chaturvedi (center) and Bhawana Kanth (right)

FIRST 'GREEN' SHIP

In February 2017, INS *Sarvekshak*, a survey vessel based at the Southern Naval Command in Kochi, Kerala, became India's first naval ship to go green by installing a zero-maintenance solar power system. The system generates 5.4 kW of electricity using the razor-thin solar panels that line the canopy of the retractable helicopter deck and are maintenance-free for 24 years.

INS *Sarvekshak*

FIRST USE OF AIR CAVALRY

During exercise Vijay Prahar that was carried out in Suratgarh, Rajasthan, in May 2018, Indian troops worked on their first use of air cavalry. In an air cavalry operation, weaponized helicopters carry out coordinated attacks with the tanks and mechanized ground forces. Precise coordination is required to carry out such attacks.

FIRST NATIONAL WAR MEMORIAL

Proposed in 1960, but actualized on 25 February 2019, the national war memorial was inaugurated near India Gate, New Delhi. Covering over 40 acres and designed by the Chennai-based WeBe Design Lab, it has the names of Indian soldiers martyred in 1947–48 (Kashmir), 1961 (Goa), 1962 (China), 1965 and 1971 (Pakistan), 1987 (Siachen), 1987–88 (Sri Lanka), 1999 (Kargil) and other operations. The memorial is designed with concentric circles, with the Amar Chakra (Circle of Immortality) and an Eternal Flame in the centre. It is surrounded by the Veerta Chakra (Circle of Bravery), which is a gallery depicting iconic battles and the Rakshak Chakra (Circle of Protection). The circles represent *chakravyuh* or traditional Indian war formation.

National War Memorial, New Delhi

FIRST WOMEN IN MILITARY POLICE

In a landmark move, the Indian Army on 25 April 2019, issued a formal notification inviting women applicants for the post of soldier–general duty. This is the first time that the army presented women with an opportunity to apply for positions for personnel below officer rank. The portfolio included investigating offences like molestation, rape and theft along with assisting civil police and preventing breaches of regulation by army personnel.

FIRST SPECIAL OPERATIONS DIVISION

The Special Operations Division, India's first such organisation was announced on 15 May 2019. Drawing personnel from the IAF's Garud force, the Indian Navy's MARCOS commondo unit and the Army's special forces, the division would have around 3,000 commondos at its peak. The first chief of the division was Major General A.K. Dhingra.

FIRST CHIEF OF DEFENCE STAFF

On 31 December 2019, General Bipin Rawat (1958–2021) was appointed India's first Chief of Defence Staff (CDS). The post was designed to serve as a chief for the three services and a military adviser to the minister of defence on all matters related to the three services.

General Bipin Rawat

FIRST INDIAN PEACEKEEPER TO WIN THE UNITED NATIONS MILITARY GENDER ADVOCATE AWARD

Major Suman Gawani, an officer of the Indian Army, won the UN (United Nations) Military Gender Advocate of the Year award on 29 May 2020 in a virtual ceremony. She became the first Indian peacekeeper to receive the honour. She served as a peacekeeper in a UN mission in South Sudan (UNMISS) in 2019.

Border Roads Organization's (BRO's) first carbon nuetral habitat was inagurated in October 2022 at Hanle, Ladakh.

FIRST WOMEN DEPLOYED AT SIACHEN

Captain Shiva Chauhan became the first Indian woman to be operationally deployed at Kumar Post, Siachen glacier. She was delployed in January. By December, Captain Geetika Koul became the first woman medical officer to be deployed at Siachen and Captain Fatima Wasim became the first woman medical officer to be deployed at an operational post at Siachen.

FIRST WOMAN OFFICER TO COMMAND A NAVAL WARSHIP

Lieutenant Commander Prerna Deosthalee was the first to command a naval warship deployed in December 2023.

STATES AND UNION TERRITORIES

FIRST STATE (PRE–1947)

The division of the Bihar and Orissa province in 1936, into present day Odisha (then Orissa) was the first state that was formed on a linguistic basis.

FIRST STATE–CONTROLLED ROAD TRANSPORT SYSTEM

Inaugurated on 31 July 1948, the Calcutta State Transport Corporation was the first state-controlled road transport system in the country.

FIRST STATE UNDER PRESIDENT'S RULE

The resignation of the congress ministry under Gopi Chand Bhargava (1889–1966) led to the imposition of President's Rule on Punjab from 20 July 1951 to 17 July 1952, making it the first Indian state under President's rule.

FIRST LINGUISTIC STATE (POST–1947)

On 1 October 1953, the Telugu-speaking Andhra state was carved out of Madras state, with its capital at

Kurnool. Later on 1 November 1956, it was merged with the Telugu-speaking areas of Hyderabad state to form Andhra Pradesh.

FIRST STATE TO SET UP FAMILY COURT

The Family Courts Act 1984 aimed at promoting conciliation and speedy settlements of disputes related to marriage and family matters. The functioning of these Family Courts lies with the state government in consultation with their respective High Courts. Rajasthan was the first state to set up a Family Court and was closely followed by Maharashtra in 1989. As of June 2023, as many as 762 Family Courts are operational in the country.

FIRST STATE/UT TO ACHIEVE 100 PER CENT LITERACY

India has 28 states and 8 union territories.

Kerala was declared a 100 per cent literate state, the first of all, on 18 April 1991. It also happened to be the 81st birthday of Dr Malcolm S. Adiseshiah, the doyen of adult education in India.

FIRST STATE WITH A CLIMATE CHANGE DEPARTMENT

A climate change department was opened at the sub-national level in Gujarat in 2009. It became the first state in India and Asia and also the fourth in the world to have a dedicated department for climate change. The department is responsible for undertaking actions on mitigating climate change and adapting to it as well. The organization is headed by the chief minister of the state.

FIRST STATE TO UNVEIL A RETAIL POLICY

In January 2016, the Andhra Pradesh government became the first state to unveil a retail policy. To give a boost to ease of doing business, they offered greater flexibility in working hours in the retail sector. They also included food and grocery as part of the Essential Services Maintenance Act (ESMA) to deter enterprises and stakeholders of strikes. Stock limits for essential commodities were removed and retailers were allowed to keep staff part-time on hourly basis.

FIRST FULLY ORGANIC STATE

On 18 January 2016, Sikkim was declared India's first fully organic state. About 75,000 hectares of Sikkim's agricultural land has been successfully converted into certified organic land by implementing practices stipulated by the National Programme for Organic Production.

Digital media*

FIRST DIGITAL STATE

Kerala was declared a digital state on 27 February 2016 by the then

*Representative image

President Pranab Mukherjee. With nearly 100 per cent mobile phone density, high e-literary level (75 per cent), two government data centres, highest digital banking rate and a state-wide area network (KSWAN) that connects over 3,000 government offices, Kerala is equipped for the digital age.

FIRST STATE TO HAVE A 'HAPPINESS' DEPARTMENT

In August 2016, with the setting up of the Rajya Anand Sansthan, Madhya Pradesh became the first state to have a 'happiness' department. The department's functions include, identifying and defining yardsticks of happiness and well being, preparing and publishing a comprehensive happiness report for the state and working as a knowledge center for resources on the subject of happiness.

FIRST STATE TO HAVE A SINGLE EMERGENCY NUMBER

On 28 November 2018, Himachal Pradesh became the first state to launch a single number for all emergency calls. The emergency number '112' connects to the fire, police, health and other helpline numbers through an Emergency Response Centre (ERC).

FIRST STATE/UT TO ENACT A LAW ON CONTRACT FARMING

Tamil Nadu passed a law on contract farming in February 2019, titled the Agricultural Produce and

Livestock Contract Farming and Services (Promotion and Facilitation) Act. Contract farming enables transparency and legally safeguards the interests of farmers, producer companies and purchasers.

FIRST STATE/UT TO REGULATE CROPS

Telangana became the first state in the country to regulate its crops. It will be the first state that will stipulate for its farmers when and how much of which crops to grow. As the Kharif season began in 2020, the state regulated the cropping pattern with a detailed cropping map and a seed regulation authority. These measures were taken to match supply to the market demand.

Maize crops*

*Representative image

FIRST STATE TO HAVE A POLICY ON AI, BLOCKCHAIN AND CYBER SECURITY

With the introduction of the Tamil Nadu Block Chain Policy 2020, the Tamil Nadu Cyber Security Policy 2020 and the Tamil Nadu Safe and Ethical Artificial Intelligence Policy 2020, the state became the first to introduce such policies. The policies are aimed at augmenting the IT and IT-es sector in the state, protecting the government's databases and websites, and improving government workflows and processes, among others.

FIRST FULLY ORGANIC UNION TERRITORY

In 2021, Lakshadweep became the first union territory to be certificated 100 per cent organic in the country. Certified under the PGS–India, a participatory Organic Guarantee Programme of the Department of Agriculture and Farmer's Welfare, all farming activity in the UT is carried out without the use of synthetic pesticides and fertilisers.

FIRST STATE TO RUN THE FIFA FOOTBALL FOR SCHOOLS PROGRAMME

Kalinga Institute of Social Sciences in Bhubaneswar, Odisha launched the first FIFA Football for Schools Programme in the country. On 27 October 2021, the programme was virtually inaugurated by Naveen Patnaik, the chief minister of the state. The programme run by Fédération internationale de football association (FIFA) is an overarching approach towards education, development and empowerment of children.

FIRST STATE TO HAVE ITS OWN INTERNET SERVICE

The Kerala Fiber Optic Network (KFON) is an intensive IT infrastructure project of the state and is aimed to ensure internet connectivity to all citizens of the state. The scheme is also envisaged to provide free internet services to families below the poverty line. Announced in 2022, the KFON network goal is also in alignment with the recommendations of the United Nations.

FIRST 'SMOKE–FREE' STATE

Himachal Pradesh achieved the status of becoming the first 'smoke-free' state in the country in 2022. This essentially means that all households in the state have Liquid Petroleum Gas (LPG) connections. Since traditional methods stressed plantation and also caused pollution, the shift to LPG connections has been a welcome one. The central government's, Pradhan Mantri Ujjwala Yojana and the state government's Himachal Grihini Suvidha Yojana contributed to this effort.

FIRST STATE/UT TO BE 'HAR GHAR JAL' CERTIFIED

Goa became the first state, while Dadra and Nagar Haveli and Daman and Diu, became the first union territory to be declared 'Har Ghar Jal' certified in August 2022. This includes 2.63 lakh households in Goa and 85,156 households of Dadra and

The youngest state in the country is Telangana, having been formed in 2014.

Nagar Haveli and Daman and Diu. This is part of the Jal Jeevan Mission that aims to provide potable water to every household in the country by 2024.

FIRST STATE TO HAVE A DIVYANG DEPARTMENT

With a fund allocation of ₹1,143 crores, the Maharashtra government has announced a dedicated and separate 'Divyang' department for the welfare of people with disabilities. The first state to have such a department, it was announced on 3 December 2022, marking the International Day of Persons with Disabilities. Sections under the Social Justice and Special Assistance that looked after the issues related to people with disabilities were clubbed to make a dedicated department.

FIRST STATE TO ACHIEVE 100 PER CENT RAILWAY ELECTRIFICATION

The state of Haryana, became the first state to have a fully electrified railway network in March 2023. 1,710 kms of the broad gauge rail network in the state has now been 100 per cent electrified.

FIRST STATE TO IMPLEMENT 'RIGHT TO HEALTH'

On 4 April 2023, after a series of protests and backlash, Rajasthan became the first state to implement 'Right to Health' for all its citizens. The act applies to public hospitals and designated private hospitals. Under the provisions of the act, all citizens of the state will be provided free emergency services without pre-payment, and healthcare would not be denied on the basis of police clearance among other details.

EDUCATION

TIMELINE

EARLY PERIOD

- 5000 BCE – Gurukul's were the ancient traditional system of education.
- 1500–600 BCE – The Vedas such as the Rig Veda are believed to be written. Early education involved teaching and learning the tenets taught in the Vedas and the Upanishads
- 600–200 BCE – The *Dharmasutras* and *Brahmanas* form basis of teaching and learning
- 500 BCE – The *Upanishads* encouraged the teacher and the student to be explorers in the search of knowledge
- 2nd century BCE–3rd century CE – *Arthashastra* by Chanakya is placed in this era
- 2nd century BCE–2nd century CE – The *Charaka Samhita*, a compendium of Indian Ayurveda is believed to have been written and formed the base for early medical education along with the *Sushruta Samhita* that covered more on medicine and surgery
- 6th–13th century CE – The Nalanda Mahavihara is established in the Gupta Empire

- 12th–13th century CE – Temple Schools were established such as the Nataraja Temple in Chidambaram
- 945 CE – Rashtrakuta dynasty established buildings with Royal patronage with arrangements for educators and scholars
- 1542 – Jesuits introduced India to European learning and the printing of Books
- 1820s – Establishment of missionary schools
- 1835 – Madras Medical College is established; English Education Act was passed
- 1854 – The Wood's despatch stipulated reforms in the Education system
- 1857 – Earliest universities are set up

20TH CENTURY

- 1951 – First IIT is established
- 1961 – National Council for Education Research and Training (NCERT) was formed
- 1995 – Mid-day meal scheme is launched
- 1956 – University Grants Commission is set up under the UGC Act
- 1968 – First National Educational Policy is announced

21ST CENTURY

- 2001 – Sarva Shiksa Abhiyaan launched
- 2009 – Right to Education Act was passed; Rashtriya Madhyamik Shiksha Abhiyan is launched
- 2020 – New National Educational Policy is introduced

EARLIEST UNIVERSITY

Nalanda Mahavihara, functioned uninterrupted from sixth century BCE (around Buddha's time) up to the 13th century CE when it was destroyed by the mughal ruler, Muhammad bin Bakhtiyar Khilji. Located about 95 km south-east of present-day Patna in Bihar, the curriculum at the university then included subjects such as logic, medicine, metaphysics, grammar and the sciences. An exclusively postgraduate and doctoral institution was started in Rajgir, Bihar, in 2014 to emulate the great centre of learning.

FIRST SANSKRIT UNIVERSITY

The Sampurnanand Sanskrit Vishwavidyalaya in Varanasi, Uttar Pradesh, believed to be established in 1791 was the first Sanskrit university in India. It was opened as a Sanskrit college during Company rule. There are now 628 affiliated colleges with this university across India.

FIRST MODERN COLLEGE

The Hindu College of Calcutta, Bengal (now Kolkata, West Bengal) is believed to be the first college to offer modern education in India. Established in 1817, with David Hare as the principal, it was renamed Presidency College in 1855 and later Presidency University on 7 July 2010.

FIRST MODERN UNIVERSITY

The first missionary college was opened by William Carey, a British Christian missionary, at Serampore, Bengal (now

Srirampur, Hooghly District, West Bengal) in 1818. In 1829 it was granted the status of a university.

A sketch of William Carey

FIRST TECHNICAL UNIVERSITY

India's first technical university was the Thomason College of Engineering, established in 1847 at Roorkee (now in Uttarakhand). It has now become the Indian Institute of Technology (IIT) and its civil engineering department is the oldest one.

FIRST MODERN INDIAN UNIVERSITIES

The first modern Indian universities in the country were modelled after the London University. The universities of Calcutta (now University of Calcutta), Madras (now University of Madras) and Bombay (now University of Mumbai), were established as non-teaching examining bodies in 1857. The university of Punjab and Allahabad (now Prayagraj) were the next to follow, but after a gap of three decades.

FIRST POSTGRADUATE DEGREE

The first postgraduate Master of Arts (MA) degree was conferred by Calcutta University in Calcutta, Bengal in 1862.

FIRST COLLEGE FOR WOMEN

Set up in 1849, the Bethune School of Calcutta, Bengal, was merged with the Banga Mahila Vidyalaya. In 1879, classes in Bethune College started with one student, Kadambini Bose.

The PRASHAST mobile app that can screen up to 21 disabilities in school children was launched in 2022.

Bethune College, Kolkata

FIRST VETERINARY COLLEGE

In 1882, the first college of veterinary science was established at Lahore (now in Pakistan). Until this college was set up, lectures in veterinary science were given to civilians at the Agricultural College at Saidapet, Madras (now Chennai, Tamil Nadu) and at the College of Sciences in Poona (now Pune), Maharashtra.

FIRST WOMEN GRADUATES

Kadambini Ganguly née Bose (1861–1923) and Chandramukhi Basu (1860–1944) passed the BA examination from Calcutta University in 1883 and became the first women graduates in the country.

FIRST COLLEGE ALUMNI ASSOCIATION

The Madras Christian College, Tamil Nadu became the first college to have an alumni association. Dr William Miller, the then principal of the college formed the first alumni association in 1891.

Anderson Hall in the campus of the Madras Christian College, Tamil Nadu

FIRST INSTITUTE TO TEACH MODERN ARCHITECTURE

The first taught course in architecture in India can be traced to a draftsman's class at the Sir J.J. School of Art, Bombay (now Mumbai, Maharashtra) in 1896. Later in 1913, the course was reorganized, which gave rise to an independent Department of Architecture.

FIRST UNIVERSITY ACT

The first set of educational reforms that instructed universities to offer more teaching courses and also present students with research opportunities along with exerting more control over affiliated colleges was initiated by the Indian Universities Act, 1904.

FIRST TO OBTAIN A DOCTORATE

The first doctorate in the country was awarded by the University of Allahabad, when in 1904, Annoda Prasad Sircar received his DSc.

FIRST RESIDENTIAL UNIVERSITIES

The Banaras Hindu University (BHU) was established in 1915 as a teaching and residential university. Many other universities followed suit shortly after, like the

The recommended pupil-teacher ratio in primary classes for special education is one special education teacher per 10 students with disabilities and for upper primary level it is one special education teacher per 15 students with disabilities.

Universities of Mysore (1916), Patna (1917) and Osmania (1918), and Aligarh Muslim University (1920).

FIRST WOMEN'S UNIVERSITY

With D.K. Karve (1858–1962) as the first principal and Dr R.P. Paranjpye as the vice chancellor, The Shreemati Nathibai Damodar Thackersey (SNDT) Women's University was established on 5 July 1916 in Poona, Maharashtra.

FIRST INTERMEDIATE COLLEGES

Intermediate colleges offering courses for the duration of two years between high school and degree college, were first established in the Universities of Punjab and Allahabad in 1917, as proposed by the Sadler Commission. The Sadler Commission was appointed to analyse and suggest measures for the betterment of higher education especially in the University of Calcutta.

FIRST COLLEGE OF PHYSICAL EDUCATION

Established in 1920, the YMCA College of Physical Education in Madras, Tamil Nadu was Asia's first college for physical education. Founded by Harry Crowe Buck from Pennsylvania, US, the college is now affiliated to the Tamil Nadu Physical Education and Sports University.

FIRST MILITARY SCHOOL

The Rashtriya Indian Military School (RIMC) in Dehradun, Uttarakhand, established as the Prince of Wales Royal Indian

Military College on 13 March 1922. Prince Edward VIII, the then Prince of Wales, set up the school to provide training to Indians (only boys) to become officers for the armed services. By 2021, women were also allowed admission to the institute.

The National Achievement Survey (NAS) saw participation from 3,401,158 students from 1.18 lakh schools.

FIRST SCHOOL OF MINES

The Indian School of Mines and Applied Geology opened on 9 December 1926 in Dhanbad, Jharkhand. It was renamed the Indian School of Mines in 1957 and in 2016, it became an Indian Institute of Technology (IIT).

FIRST STATISTICAL INSTITUTE

In 1931, the Indian Statistical Institute (ISI) was established in Calcutta, Bengal (now Kolkata, West Bengal), by scientist and statistician P.C. Mahalanobis.

FIRST HOME SCIENCE COLLEGE

The first home science college in the country was Lady Irwin College, established in 1932 in New Delhi.

FIRST MINISTER OF EDUCATION

Maulana Abul Kalam Azad (1888–1958) became independent India's first minister of education during

1947–58. He was fondly called Maulana Azad, wherein Azad was his chosen pen name. He was a freedom fighter and an activist. In his youth he composed poetry in Urdu and went on to write journalistic pieces that were critical of the colonial government. He also was one of the founding committee members of the Jamia Milia Islamia University in Aligarh. He is credited for establishing the first Indian Institute of Technology (IIT), the School of Planning and Architecture (SPA), the University Grants Commission

Maulana Abul Kalam Azad

(UGC), the Indian Institute of Science (IISc), the Sangeet Natak Akademi, the Sahitya Akademi, the Lalit Kala Akademi and the Indian Council of Cultural Relations. He was the youngest president of the Indian National Congress and his birthday (11 November) is celebrated as National Education Day across the country.

FIRST INDIAN INSTITUTE OF TECHNOLOGY (IIT)

The Indian Institute of Technology (IIT) are centrally-funded technical institutes under the Ministry of Education, government of India. The first IIT was established at Kharagpur, West Bengal, in 1951, at the site of the Hijli Detention Camp. There are currently 23 approved IITs across the country and Uttar Pradesh is the only state to have two IITs.

FIRST NATIONAL EDUCATION COUNCIL

The first national council for education was the All India Council for Secondary Education (AICSE) which was set up in 1955.

FIRST INSTITUTE FOR POPULATION SCIENCES

To prepare students for administrative, research, consultancy and teaching careers in population sciences, the Demographic Training and Research Centre was established in 1956 in Bombay, Maharashtra. It was renamed the

International Institute of Population Sciences in 1970. Apart from being the first such institute, it also serves a sizeably larger region than the other centres by serving the United Nations Economic and Social Commission for Asia and the Pacific (ESCAP) region.

Vidyanjali is a school volunteer initiative by the government and110,874 volunteers had signed up on the online portal by the end of 2022.

FIRST INDIAN SCHOOL ABROAD

The first Indian educational institute set up outside the borders of the country was the Indian High School, Dubai, which was set up in 1957.

FIRST NATIONAL AWARD FOR TEACHERS

Instituted in 1958, the National Award for Teachers were set up to celebrate the contribution of teachers who have worked towards the enhancement of the quality of school education and added to the lives of their students. Conducted by the Ministry of Education the award is given to selected teachers from primary, middle and secondary schools. It is presented by the President or the Vice President annually on 5 September (National Teacher's Day).

FIRST NATIONAL INSTITUTE OF MANAGEMENT

On 17 November 1961, the government of India in collaboration with the government of West Bengal, the

Ford Foundation, the MIT Sloan School of Management, US and many other Indian industries came together to set up the Indian Institute of Management Calcutta (IIM–C) in Calcutta. The IIMs are funded by the central government to teach degree, doctoral and executive courses in business management.

FIRST CORRESPONDENCE COURSES

The first introduction to non-formal education was done by the University of Delhi when it introduced the first correspondence courses in 1962.

Faculty of Arts, University of Delhi

FIRST YOGA UNIVERSITY

The first of its kind yoga university was the Bihar Yoga Bharati in Munger, Bihar. An institute for advanced studies in yoga, it was set up in 1964.

FIRST INSTITUTE OF MASS COMMUNICATION

The Indian Institute of Mass Communication (IIMC) was the first institute in the country to provide formal education in mass communication. An autonomous institution under the Ministry of Information and Broadcasting, it was set up in 1965 in New Delhi. It has been shifted to the Jawaharlal Nehru University (JNU) campus in New Delhi.

FIRST INSTITUTE OF OCEANOGRAPHY

Founded on 1 January 1966, the CSIR–National Institute of Oceanography (CSIR–NIO), is an autonomous research organization that is tasked to undertake scientific research and studies of special oceanographic features of the northern Indian Ocean. The main campus is in Dona Paula, Goa and its regional centres have been set up in Mumbai, Kochi and Vishakhapatnam. It is one of the 37 constituent laboratories of the Council of Scientific and Industrial Research (CSIR).

FIRST NATIONAL POLICY ON EDUCATION

India's first national policy on Education was announced in 1968. The policy focussed on expanding educational opportunities, to elevate the quality of education in all stages, develop science and technology and cultivate moral and social values. A second National Educational Policy was announced in 1986 which was modified in 1992. On 29 July 2020, the new National Educational Policy (NEP 2020) was announced by Prime Minister Narendra Modi.

> As per the AISHE 2021–22, there are 75 female teachers per every 100 male teachers.

FIRST NATIONAL INSTITUTE FOR THE VISUALLY IMPAIRED

The National Institute for the visually impaired was established in 1979 in Dehradun, Uttarakhand.

FIRST LAW UNIVERSITY

The National Law School of India University (NLSIU) in Bangalore (now Bengaluru), Karnataka was set up as the first law university in the country in 1986. It was notified in the official gazette on 29 August 1987. The university's chancellor is the Chief Justice of India. Now, there are 23 national law universities across the country.

National Law School, Bengaluru

FIRST INSTITUTE OF FASHION TECHNOLOGY

The National Institute of Fashion Technology (NIFT), Delhi, was set up by the Ministry of Textiles, Government of India on 24 August 1987. The institute was designed to train professional human resources for the textile industry. Currently there are 18 NIFT campuses across the country.

FIRST RURAL UNIVERSITY

The Mahatma Gandhi Chitrakoot Gramoday University, in Chitrakoot, Madhya Pradesh, was set up in 1991 to promote rural education.

FIRST COLLEGE FOR THE HEARING-IMPAIRED

Affiliated to the University of Madras, the St Louis Institute for the Deaf and Blind opened on 8 September 1993. It offers graduate degrees and is the first college for hearing-impaired students in the university.

FIRST TECHNICAL UNIVERSITY FOR WOMEN

The first technical university in the country was set up in 1847 and it was after 51 years that the first technical university for women was founded. The Indira Gandhi Delhi Technical University for Women (IGDTUW) was set up in 1998 in New Delhi.

FIRST UNIVERSITY FOR THE DISABLED

The Jagadguru Rambhadracharya Handicapped University in Chitrakoot, Uttar Pradesh, was established on 27 September 2001 as a private university. It aimed to provide higher and professional education exclusively to persons with disabilities in four categories: the visually impaired, the hearing-impaired, the mobility impaired and the mentally impaired, as defined in the Persons with Disability Act, 1995.

FIRST RADIO JOCKEY TRAINING ACADEMY

In July 2003, the Academy of Broadcasting was set up in Chandigarh and was the first academy to train radio jockeys.

FIRST UNIVERSITY FOR THE STUDY OF OUTER SPACE

The Indian Institute of Space Science and Technology (IIST) located in Thiruvananthapuram, Kerala, is the first university in India and Asia to be solely dedicated to the study and research of outer space. Established in 2007 by the Indian Space Research Organization (ISRO), the institute offers degree and doctoral programmes with a focus on topics such as space science, space technology, geoinformatics, earth system sciences and their applications.

FIRST METRO TECHNOLOGY INSTITUTE

The Institute of Metro and Rail Technology (IMRT) was established in October 2013 in Hyderabad, Telangana. The institute offers both, short and long-term courses to design, build and manage modern-day rail systems.

There are 17 universities in the country that are exclusively for women.

FIRST SOLAR-POWERED SCHOOL

The first fully solar-powered educational institute was the Sri Aurobindo International Centre for Education in White Town, Puducherry in 2014. It was originally set up in 1943 by Mirra Alfassa, the spiritual collaborator of Sri Aurobindo.

FIRST GENDER-NEUTRAL CERTIFICATE

The first gender-neutral graduation certificate was issued by the National Academy of Legal Studies and Research (NALSAR), Hyderabad, Telangana, in June 2015.

FIRST COLLEGE FOR SANITATION WORKERS

In August 2018, the Harpic World Toilet College, located in Aurangabad in Maharashtra, was founded. Students are trained in the required skills and the courses also make them aware of the occupational hazards. Run by the British company Reckitt Benckiser, the institute has trained more than 3,200 sanitation workers.

FIRST RAILWAY UNIVERSITY

The National Rail and Transport University was established on 5 September 2018 at the Pratap Vilas Palace in Vadodara, Gujarat. Subsumed by the Gati Shakti Vishwavidyalaya, it became a central university as of July 2022. The institute offers degrees in transport management, transportation technology, rail systems, rail infrastructural engineering, and communication engineering.

TRANSPORT

TIMELINE

EARLY PERIOD

- 2300 BCE – The first tidal dock is believed to have been established at Lothal (present-day Gujarat)
- 16th century – The existing Grand Trunk Road is re-built by the Sur Empire, Mughal Empire and the British empire
- 1850s – The work on the Grand Trunk Road nears completion
- 1853 – First Railway line established and first railway service began
- 1873 – The first horse-drawn tramway operates in India

20TH CENTURY

- 1911 – Aviation begins in India
- 1932 – The civil aviation sector takes off in India
- 1934 – Indian Roads Congress is formulated
- 1942 – Department of War Transport is established to look after the demands of transport in war time
- 1943 – The first road development plan (the Nagpur Plan) is worked out

- 1972 – International Airports Authority of India (IAAI) is established
- 1986 – National Airport Authority is established; six national waterways established by the Inland Waterways Authority of India; Computerized ticketing and reservation services are introduced in Indian Railways at Delhi
- 1987 – The Bureau of National Civil Aviation Security is formed after the first tragic crash in India (Air India Flight 182)
- 1988 – The National Highways Authority of India (NHAI) is established under the NHAI Act
- 1999 – The Mountain Railways of India are designated as UNESCO World Heritage Site

21ST CENTURY

- 2004 – Chhatrapati Shivaji Maharaj Terminus is declared a UNESCO World Heritage Site
- 2009 – Ministry of Road Transport, Shipping and Highways is bifurcated into Ministry of Shipping and Ministry of Road transport and Highways
- 2019 – The Vande Bharat Express is flagged off
- 2020 – Delhi metro's magenta line becomes completely driverless
- 2022 – First surety bond Insurance for infrastructure products is launched
- 2023 – First dual-way elevated taxiway of the country inaugurated in Delhi

FIRST HIGHWAY

The historic Grand Trunk Road, that runs for 2,400 km, links Central Asia and the Indian subcontinent. The route was re-constructed in the reign of Sher Shah Suri in the 16th century. The first steps towards the metalling work for the road were undertaken during the tenure of Lord William Bentinck, the then Governor General of India (1828–35).

FIRST STEAMBOAT

Diana was the first steamboat to bc built in India in 1819 by Jessop & Co. Ltd in Calcutta (now Kolkata, West Bengal), and it was launched on 12 July 1823.

FIRST REGULAR PUBLIC TRANSPORT

The first public road transport for regular long-distance travel was introduced between Aligarh and Kanpur in Uttar Pradesh in November 1841.

FIRST RAIL CONSTRUCTION COMPANY

In 1844, R.M. Stephenson (1808–95), a British railway engineer, formed the East Indian Railway (EIR) Company to construct the railways. On 17 August 1849, the EIR and the Great Indian Peninsula (GIP) Railway Company, England, signed a contract authorizing the construction and operations of

R.M. Stephenson

railway lines in major cities like Calcutta and Bombay (now Mumbai).

FIRST RAILWAY STATIONS

The first railway stations in the country were Bori Bunder, Byculla, Sion and Thane stations on the Bori Bunder–Thane line in Maharashtra. They were built for the inaugural run of the first passenger train in 1853.

Bori Bunder station, Maharashtra in 1853

FIRST PASSENGER TRAIN

The first passenger train in India started from Bori Bunder station (later renamed Victoria Terminus and then Chhatrapati Shivaji Maharaj Terminus) in Bombay to Thane, Maharashtra, on 16 April 1853. Three locomotives, namely Sindh, Sultan and Sahib, were used to pull the train with 400 passengers in 14 railway carriages.

Indian Railways now runs 11,000 trains everyday out of which 7,000 are passenger trains.

FIRST INDIGENOUS RAILWAY CARRIAGES

Steward and Company, and Seton and Company were the first coach-building firms in the country. The first indigenous coaches were employed for the first train journey in Calcutta on 15 August 1854 from Howrah to Hoogly.

FIRST TRAMS

The first tram in the country ran from Sealdah to Armenian Ghat in Calcutta, covering a 3.9 km distance on 24 February 1873. This was a horse-drawn tram. The service was dicontinued shortly and was re-introduced in 1880. The service celebrated its 150th anniversary in 2023.

FIRST TRAFFIC POLICE

With 17 sepoys in its ranks, the first Traffic Department of Calcutta Police in Calcutta, came into force in 1874.

FIRST IMPORTED CAR

In 1892, the then Maharaja of Patiala, reportedly imported the first motor car, a De Dion Bouton car.

FIRST SHIPPING COMPANY

The Swadeshi Shipping Company was set up by Freedom fighter V.O. Chidambaram Pillai at Tuticorin (now Thoothukudi), Tamil Nadu, in 1906.

FIRST DOUBLE-DECKER TRAIN

The Flying Ranee, a superfast train was India's first double-decker train. It ran between Bombay Central and the Surat station and began its operations in 1906. In 1939, its services were halted owing to the Second World War and it resumed in 1950 for a regular daily service.

An advertisement for the Flying Ranee

FIRST SHIP TO SAIL FROM INDIA

SS *Loyalty*, the first ship carrying the flag of an Indian shipping company, the Scindia Steam Navigation Company set to sail on 5 April 1919 with passengers from Bombay to the British Isles. *Loyalty* was originally a hospital ship and was converted into a vessel for passengers.

The day that SS *Loyalty* took its first voyage, 5 April, is now celebrated as National Maritime Day.

FIRST ELECTRIC TRAIN

On 3 February 1925, the first electric train operated in India on the Harbour branch of the Great Indian Peninsula Railway from Victoria Terminus to Kurla in Bombay covering a distance of over 16 kilometres.

FIRST MOTOR BUS

On the Afghan Church–Crawford market route, the first motor bus was introduced on 15 July 1926. It had a cruising speed of 20 km/hr and carried 24 seated and a few standing passengers.

FIRST PILOT LICENCE

Jehangir Ratanji Dadabhoy Tata (1904–93), an aviator, entrepreneur and chairman of the Tata Group, became the first licensed pilot in India when he received his pilot licence No. 1 in 1929. His accomplishments are innumerable and across industries. He joined the Tata Group after his return to India and then founded India's first commercial airline, Tata Airlines, in 1932. In 1953, the airline was nationalized and renamed Air India. As irony would have it, the Tata Group bought the airline back when it was disinvested by the government in 2022. Being the first licensed pilot in the country, J.R.D. Tata also flew the first commercial mail and the first flight in Indian history in 1932. He received the title of Honorary Air Commodore of India and was also known as the 'Father of Indian civil aviation'.

J.R.D. Tata

He is credited for founding many enterprises such as the Tata Consultancy Services, Tata Motors, Tata Salt, and Voltas among others. He was awarded the Padma Vibhushan in 1955, the

French Legion of Honour in 1982 and the Bharat Ratna in 1992.

FIRST DELUXE TRAIN

The Deccan Queen was the country's first deluxe train. Its route ran between Victoria Terminus, Bombay and Poona (now Pune), Maharashtra. First operated on 1 June 1930, it had 61 first-class, 156 second-class and 19 attendants' seats.

FIRST STATE TRANSPORT SYSTEM

- The Nizam's State Railways Transport Department (NSRTD), in Hyderabad (now in Telangana), set up a road transport service in June 1932. As many as 27 buses operated through three depots for a 24 km route and could seat up to 25 passengers each.
- On 31 July 1948, the Calcutta State Transport Corporation, headquartered in Calcutta was introduced and it was the first state-controlled road transport system in the country.

The total length of national highways in the country was 146,145 km by the end of 2023.

FIRST AIR-CONDITIONED TRAIN

The Frontier Mail (now renamed the Golden Temple Mail) that ran between Bombay and Amritsar was the first air-conditioned train to run in India in 1934. Prior to this, some coaches had double lined walls with lead-zinc sheets that were filled with ice to keep the passengers cool.

FIRST INDIAN CAR MANUFACTURERS

Registered in 1942, Hindustan Motors Ltd, manufactured vehicles and it was followed by Premier Automobiles (1944) and Standard Motor Products of India Ltd (1948). The first Indian-built car, Hindustan 10, although not fully indigenous was made in 1946.

FIRST OVERSEAS CARGO SERVICE

The Scindia Steam Navigation Company inaugurated a continental line for overseas cargo between India and European countries on 3 February 1948, as the cargo steamship SS *Jalabala* shipped off from Bombay (now Mumbai), Maharashtra.

SS *Jalabala*

FIRST LOCOMOTIVE FACTORY

In 1950, the first locomotive factory was set up at Chittaranjan in Paschim Bardhaman District, West Bengal. The first manufactured diesel locomotive, with an imported engine was manufactured at the Varanasi Diesel Locomotive Works, Varanasi, Uttar Pradesh, on 4 January 1964.

FIRST TROLLEY BUS

Trolley buses were imported to replace tramcars on the Gowlia Tank–Mazagon route in Bombay on 11 June 1962. They were later withdrawn in 1971 for buses.

FIRST SUPERFAST TRAIN

With an average speed of 130 km/hr, the Rajdhani Express, was commissioned on 3 March 1969, to run between New Delhi and Howrah, West Bengal.

FIRST NATIONALIZED TRAMWAY COMPANY

In 1880, the Calcutta Tramway Company was registered in London, UK. It was later nationalized by the government in 1976.

FIRST METRO

The first metro ran 16.3 km underground between Dum Dum and Tollygunge in Calcutta on 24 October 1984. The metro had the capacity to carry 1.73 million passengers in a day.

FIRST INDIGENOUS HOVERCRAFT

The Scientific Instrument Co. Ltd, Allahabad (now Prayagraj), Uttar Pradesh, made a twin-engine, air-cushioned hovercraft, in 1987. It had a 55 HP thrust engine for propulsion and an 8 HP engine for lift, with a payload capacity of 500 kg and a speed of 45 km/hr.

Two new lighthouses were inaugurated at Dhanuskhodi, Tamil Nadu and Kelshi, Maharashtra on 14 May 2022.

FIRST BATTERY–BUS FLEET

The Delhi administration introduced 76 battery-operated buses to ply on 11 routes in Delhi in 1987, through the Delhi Energy Development Agency. Each bus had the cruising speed of 40 km/hr and a maximum speed of 60 km/hr.

FIRST WOMAN TRAIN DRIVER

In 1988, Surekha Yadav Bhosale became the first woman to drive an Indian Railways train. She joined the Indian Railways as a trainee assistant driver in 1986. She drove the first 'Ladies Special' local train, which started in April 2000 in Mumbai, Maharashtra.

FIRST ZERO–EMISSION ELECTRIC CAR

The Reva Electric Car Company, Bengaluru, Karnataka in a joint venture with the Amerigon Inc. of California, US and the Maini group of Industries, Bengaluru manufactured REVAi, the first zero-emission electric car. It was first flagged off in March 1988 in Delhi and then sold worldwide by 2011 in over 26 countries. Mahindra and Mahindra acquired it in May 2010.

The Reva NXR, a concept car displayed at the Frankfurt show, US

FIRST HOVERCRAFT FERRY

The first hovercraft ferry service began in Gujarat between Surat and Ghogha Port. A diesel hovercraft service began on 10 December 1992, linking the two ports, 55 nautical miles (102 km) apart, in two hours.

FIRST PRIVATE SECTOR PORT

The Pipavav Port in Gujarat was inaugurated in November 1996 and was the first private sector port in the country.

FIRST CORPORATIZED PORT

The Ennore Port (now Kamarajar Port Ltd) on the Coromandel Coast, Chennai, Tamil Nadu, was a public company before it became a corporatized port in 1999.

FIRST SATELLITE NAVIGATION SYSTEM

Launched on 15 February 1999, SANJAY, is a navigation system that uses a global positioning system (GPS) receiver and mapping software. One may install it in the vehicle and access Delhi's road map and get audio information about routes. It was designed by the L.B. Saxena Design lab in New Delhi and uses 24 satellites.

An MoU was signed in 2022 between the government of Madhya Pradesh and NHAI to construct ropeways at 14 sites in the state.

FIRST COMPRESSED NATURAL GAS (CNG) AUTOS

The first Compressed Natural Gas (CNG) autos debuted in Delhi on 29 May 2000. Launched by Bajaj Auto Ltd, they had a 3 kg CNG Tank and a standby tank with 3 litre petrol. It is powered by a 175 cc engine and it meets the Bharat–II emission norms.

FIRST GREEN RAIL CORRIDOR

The Southern Railways inaugurated the Manamadurai–Rameswaram route as the country's first green corridor in July 2016. Bio-toilets that were developed by Indian Railways and the Defence Research and Development Organization (DRDO) were installed in 150 coaches of 13 pairs of express and passenger trains. The have a zero human waste discharge.

FIRST FULLY SOLAR–POWERED RAILWAY STATION

Assam's Guwahati railway station became the country's first fully solar-powered station. It was commissioned in 2017 and has 2,352 solar panels on the roof. A step towards making the railways more environmentally responsible, the project is aimed at reducing their carbon footprint. On an average, the solar panels have the capacity to generate 2,048 kWh power per day.

FIRST ELECTRIC BUS

- Reportedly commenced in Himachal Pradesh, the first electric bus service was for Rohtang Pass at an altitude of 3,962.4 m in 2017. Developed by Goldstone Infratech and the Automobile Research Association of India. It can carry up to 30 passengers and cover a distance of 200 km on a full charge.
- The first electric double-decker bus in India was launched at the Y.B. Centre in Mumbai, Maharashtra on 19 August 2022. The Switch EiV 22 would be run by the Mumbai civic transport body. Two new electric buses, including the first air-conditioned double decker is also slated to join the Brihanmumbai Electric Supply and Transport Undertaking (BEST).

FIRST VISTADOME TRAINS

On 16 April 2017, the Indian Railways introduced special seven coach vistadome trains on the Visakhapatnam–Araku route in Andhra Pradesh. It has see-through glass on all sides, including a glass roof, LED lights, a GPS-based information system and an observation lounge to observe panoramic views throughout the journey.

> *Fairy Queen* is the oldest functioning steam engine in the world.

FIRST ELECTRIC CABS

Inaugurated on 26 May 2017, Nagpur, Maharashtra became India's first city to have an electric mass mobility system. With a fleet of 200 electric vehicles including taxis, buses, e-rickshaws and autorickshaws, owned by cab aggregator Ola, the multi-modal electric vehicle project is the first of its kind.

FIRST ROLL-ON-ROLL-OFF FERRY SERVICE

A roll-on-roll-off ferry service began from 22 October 2017 between Ghogha Port and Dahej in Gujarat. Covering a distance of 31 km, the service reduces the travel time between the two towns by around six hours. Earlier it would take almost 7–8 hours to cover the same distance that the ferry service covers in just over an hour. It can carry 1,000 passengers and 150 vehicles.

FIRST SOLAR FERRY BOAT

Aditya was the country's first solar-powered boat and it was launched in December 2017. Constructed by the NavAlt Solar and Electric Boats Pvt. Ltd, it has 78 rooftop solar panels and sails at a maximum speed of 7.5 knots. The seating capacity of the boat is 75 passengers and operates on the Vaikom–Thavanakadavu route in Kerala, covering a distance of 2.5 km.

FIRST 'DRIVERLESS' METRO

The Delhi metro has a 'driverless' metro line on its Magenta line, that began operations on 25 December 2017. The line initially covered a distance of 12.64 km and connects Kalkaji Mandir, New Delhi to Botanical Garden, Noida, while halting at nine stations. By May

Magenta line, Delhi Metro

2018, the line was extended to Janakpuri West metro station by 24.34 km. Initially, it was run by an operator, with high levels of automation based on the Communication Based Train Control technology and by 2020, it was completely driverless.

FIRST WOMAN MARINE PILOT

Reshma Nilofer Naha (b. 4 February 1989) is the first and only Indian woman marine pilot in the country. Joining the Kolkata Port Trust in 2011, she became a trained marine pilot in January 2018. As a river pilot, she guides ships in and out of Sagar, and Haldia and Kolkata ports through the River Hooghly.

FIRST INDIGENOUS PAYMENT ECOSYSTEM FOR TRANSPORT

The National Common Mobility Card (NCMC) was launched in Ahmedabad, Gujarat on 4 March 2019. It is based on the 'One Nation, One Card' model and allows users to pay across multiple platforms from a single card. It was launched by the Ministry of Housing and Urban Affairs, Government of India.

FIRST FULLY ELECTRICAL SUV

The Kona Electric by Hyundai is India's first fully electric SUV. It was launched on 9 July 2019 and can cover up to 452 km on a single full charge. The company introduced four drive modes in the car: Eco, Eco+, Comfort and Sport.

FIRST CORPORATIZED TRAIN

The Tejas Express, launched on 4 October 2019, is India's first corporatized train. While the infrastructure is owned and run by the Indian Railway Catering and Tourism Corporation (IRCTC), a subsidiary of the Indian Railways, the on-board services are outsourced to private contractors. These services include catering, housekeeping, ticketing, and refund, among others. Shuttling between Lucknow and New Delhi, the train only has two halts – Kanpur and Ghaziabad. Running all week, except Tuesdays, it is contracted under the public-private partnership model.

FIRST UNDERWATER METRO

India's first underwater metro under the Kolkata Metro Rail Corporation underwent a trail run in April 2023. The metro line will connect Salt Lake to Howrah via Kolkata with a 520 m stretch below the River Hooghly. The tunnels are built 33 m below the riverbed. The metro service is expected to be operational in 2024.

FIRST DUAL-WAY ELEVATED TAXIWAY

On 14 July 2023, the country's first dual-way elevated taxiway was inaugurated at the Indira Gandhi International Airport, New Delhi. The elevated taxiway reduces taxi distance for aircraft by 7km and annual carbon dioxide emissions by 53,000 tonnes. The Eastern Cross Taxiway is 2.1 km long and 44 m wide to allow the safe passage of two big aircraft.

STRUCTURES

EARLIEST TREATISE ON GEOMETRY

The four *Shulba Sutras* – Baudhayana, Apastamba, Katyayana and Manava – dating back to sixth century BCE, describe geometric altar constructions in the shape of falcons, tortoises, circles and rhombus, among others. The Baudhayana indicates knowledge of the Pythagoras Theorem.

FIRST ARCHITECT

The first architect on record was Maha Govinda, who was mentioned in the Buddhist work *Dhammapada*. He designed several Indian cities in northern India in the fifth century BCE. The *Mayamata*, was another treatise on housing architecture from the same period and was authored by the 'divine' architect Maya.

FIRST KNOWN EXAMPLE OF ANCIENT HYDRAULIC ENGINEERING

Remains of a large rectangular brick tank, an exemplar example of ancient hydraulic engineering was found near a first century BCE site in Singraur (Sringaverapura) near Allahabad (now Prayagraj), Uttar Pradesh. Water from the River Ganga was brought into a silting chamber through a feeding channel and clean water flowed out of the silting chamber into the main tank.

FIRST GARDEN TOMB

Built during 1517–18, the tomb of Sikandar Lodi (r. 1489–1517) of the Lodi dynasty, was built by Ibrahim Lodi, the son of Sikandar Lodi. Located in Lodi Gardens, New Delhi, the tomb is built in the Indo-Islamic architectural style.

FIRST UNMANNED LIGHTHOUSE

The first unmanned lighthouse was situated near Tellicherry (now Thalassery) in Kannur District, Kerala. Built in 1835, it has an altitude of 27 m from the mean sea level and a range of 8 km. It was renovated in 1924.

FIRST HOUSEBOAT

Victory, a houseboat built in 1888, stationed at the Dal Lake in Srinagar, Jammu and Kashmir, was the first houseboat.

FIRST ELEVATOR

The first elevator in the country was installed at Raj Bhavan, Calcutta (now Kolkata), West Bengal in 1892. The lift was the first designed electric lift by Otis.

FIRST HYDROELECTRIC PROJECT

In 1902, the Shivanasamudra in Chamarajanagar District, Karnataka, was opened and it involved harnessing the Kaveri Falls to supply electrical energy to the Kolar goldfields.

FIRST ROCK GARDEN

The Rock Garden in Chandigarh was started by Nek Chand in 1957. He was a government official who began working on the garden secretly in his spare time. The garden is primarily a sculpture garden built with industrial and home waste and recycled items. Spread over 12 acres, the garden has sculptures, plants, a staging area and a nursery.

Prime Minister Narendra Modi with the President of France at the Rock Garden, Chandigarh, during a visit

THE FIRST SKYSCRAPER

The twenty-six storeyed, Usha Kiran, an apartment building in Bombay (now Mumbai), Maharashtra was the first skyscraper in the country. Built between 1964 and 1967, the building was 80 m high.

FIRST UNDERGROUND MARKET

Palika Bazaar, at Connaught Place in New Delhi was set up in 1978 and is the first underground market in the country.

FIRST INDIAN WINNER OF THE AGA KHAN AWARD FOR ARCHITECTURE

The Aga Khan award for architecture is one of the most prestigious awards in the industry. Presented in three-year cycles, beginning in 1978, with a prize money of 1 million USD (approx. ₹8.25 crore), the prize recognizes projects, stakeholders, buildings and teams that translate aspirations of the Muslim society through design and architecture. The first Indian winner of the award was the Mughal Sheraton Hotel, Agra in 1980. Here is a list of all the Indian winners of the prize:

Awardee	Location	Award cycle
Mughal Sheraton Hotel	Agra, Uttar Pradesh	1978–80
Entrepreneurship Development Institute of India	Ahmedabad, Gujarat	1990–92
Aranya Community Housing	Indore, Madhya Pradesh	1993–95
Vidhan Bhavan	Bhopal, Madhya Pradesh	1996–98
Slum Networking of Indore City	Indore, Madhya Pradesh	1996–98
Lepers Hospital	Lasur, Maharashtra	1996–98

FIRST FLOATING RESTAURANT

An eight room restaurant, part of a tourist complex in Sirhind, Punjab, was the first floating restaurant. It was set afloat on the Bhakra Canal in 1979.

FIRST BAHA'I HOUSE OF WORSHIP

Famously called the 'Lotus Temple', the Baha'i House of Worship in Kalkaji, New Delhi, is the first of its kind structure in India and Asia. It was built between 1980 and 1986 on 26 acres of land. Designed as a blossoming lotus: the main structure has three folds of nine concrete petals and each of these petals are made of Grecian marble. The temple is surrounded by several pools of water and rises to 35 m in height.

FIRST UNESCO WORLD HERITAGE SITES

The United Nations Educational, Scientific and Cultural Organization (UNESCO) began the listing of world heritage sites from 1978 with 12 sites announced in the first list. The sites are chosen using 10-point criteria so that a framework may be provided for their preservation and are deemed as sites of universal value. The Taj Mahal, the Agra Fort in Agra, the Ajanta caves and the Ellora caves in Aurangabad were the first Indian sites to be declared as part of the list in 1983.

India currently has 42 sites inscribed on the world heritage list (34 cultural, seven natural and one mixed).

Taj Mahal, Agra

FIRST AMUSEMENT PARK

Appu Ghar, was opened at Pragati Maidan as the first entertainment centre for the whole family in 1984. The entertainment park was named after the mascot of the Asian Games, Appu the elephant. In 2008, it was shut down and reopened in Gurugram, Haryana. It is spread across 12 acres and is the country's first amusement park.

FIRST REVOLVING RESTAURANT

The first revolving restaurant was the Neelkanth Patang in Ahmedabad, Gujarat, located 67.4 m above ground level. The restaurant was inaugurated in 1984 and had a 90-minute rotation. The rotation would unfold a view of the old and the new city of Ahmedabad.

FIRST CABLE-STAYED ROAD BRIDGE

Built in 1988, the Akkar Bridge in Jorethang, Sikkim that runs over the River Rangit is a cable-stayed road bridge, the first of this kind in India. The all-concrete bridge is

1.5 km wide and nearly 20 m deep. The bridge has two 77 m spans that are symmetrical and are supported from a single pylon. With 17 pairs of cable stays, the 21 m decking above the riverbed is supported by the 55 m high pylon.

FIRST WATER PARK

Shankarbhai Chaudhary opened Shanku's Water Park on the Ahmedabad–Mahesana Highway in Gujarat in 1993, on a 75-acre campus. The water park, included a giant speed slide, a spiral water ride, a simulated wave pool and a corner just for kids.

FIRST PERMANENT CRAFTS MARKET

Dilli Haat in Delhi was opened in 1994 with 62 stalls selling handicrafts from all over the country, and

Handicrafts displayed at Dilli Haat, New Delhi

25 food stalls. The stalls are rented on subsidised prices to promote handicrafts. The second Dilli Haat was opened in Pitampura and a third one in Janakpuri (both in Delhi). The Haats are run by the Delhi Tourism and Transportation Development Corporation (DTTDC).

FIRST ECO–HOTEL

The first hotel to get an eco-friendly certification in India and Asia was 'The Orchid' in Mumbai, Maharashtra. It was opened in 1997.

FIRST IGLOO STAY

Vikas Kumar and Tashi Dorje opened the Keylinga's Manali Igloo Stay near Sethan Village, about 16 km from Manali in Himachal Pradesh, in 2017.

FIRST INDIAN TO WIN THE PRITZKER ARCHITECTURE PRIZE

Dr Balkrishna Vithaldas Doshi (1927–2023), from Pune, won the famed Pritzker Architecture Prize on 12 March 2018. He was the first Indian to win the award in the 40-year-old history of the award.

The Pritzker Prize is referred to as the Nobel Prize in architecture. Dr Doshi has also been felicitated with the Padma Shri, Padma Bhushan and the Padma Vibhushan.

Dr B.V. Doshi has featured as himself in films like *O Kadhal Kanmani* and *Ok Jaanu*.

BUSINESS AND ECONOMY

TIMELINE

EARLY PERIOD

- 500 BCE – The Mahajanapadas issue punch-marked silver coins
- 2nd century BCE – 3rd century CE – The *Arthashastra* by Chanakya is written
- 1st millennium BCE – Silk Road trade in India
- 14th century CE – Maritime trade is carried out between South India and Southeast and west Asia
- 1640 – First mint is set up in India by the East India Company
- 1813 – The charter of 1813 removed restrictions of International trade
- 1875 – First stock exchange established

20TH CENTURY

- 1947 – First Union budget announced
- 1950 – Planning commission is set up to oversee planning, allocation of resources and implementation and appraisal of the five-year plans

- 1950s–1991 – Nationalization of various companies across sectors
- 1955 – The Indian Insurance sector is nationalized; LIC is established; The Essential Commodities Act is passed
- 1957 – Mundhra Scandal, the first big financial scam of Independent India
- 1964 – Unit Trust of India (UTI) is established
- 1966 – Devaluation of the Indian Rupee; The Amul 'Utterly Butterly' topical ad campaign begins
- 1969 – 14 private banks are nationalized
- 1981–82 – India borrows from the International Monetary Fund (IMF)
- 1988 – Securities and Exchange Board of India (SEBI) is established
- 1991 – Economic Liberalisation announced by the then PM Narasimha Rao
- 1992 – Infamous Securities scam takes place
- 1998 – Amartya Sen wins the first Nobel Prize in Economics

21ST CENTURY

- 2000 – Conception of Special Economic Zones
- 2016 – Demonetization of ₹500 and ₹1000 notes is announced
- 2017 – Goods and Services Tax (GST) launched
- 2018 – Nirav Modi Scam is brought to light
- 2019 – Abhijit Banerjee wins the Nobel Prize in Economics with wife Esther Duflo and American economist Michael Kremer

FIRST FACTORY

A dye manufacturing unit was the first factory in India and it was set up by the East India Company in Surat in 1609. This was permitted by the then Mughal emperor Jehangir and marked the beginning of colonialism.

FIRST MINT

The first mint in India was set up by the East India Company in 1640 at Fort St. George, Madras (now Chennai), Tamil Nadu. In 1671, a letter of patent issued by King Charles II of England was installed in Bombay (now Mumbai), however, it was only in 1678 that the first coin was minted.

FIRST BANK

Established in 1770 by Alexander and Co. of Calcutta (now Kolkata), The Bank of Hindostan was the first bank to be set up in India. It survived three economic crises before shutting down in the 1830s.

FIRST KNOWN 'ADVERTISEMENTS'

- The *Hicky's Bengal Gazette*, the first printed newspaper from the 1780s marked the beginning of advertising in India. A series of simple messages that were 'classified' into different categories for easy reference or a list of the latest merchandise from England were the contents of these advertisements.
- The *Bombay Courier* carried what may be called as the first true advertisement in 1802 in Marathi.

FIRST FOREIGN COLLABORATION

In 1833, the first foreign collaboration took place with the setting up of Carr, Tagore and Company under the Charter Act of 1833. There were four partners in this firm, namely, W. Carr, Dwarakanath Tagore, D.M. Gordon and William Prinsep. It was closed down in 1847.

FIRST COMPANIES

Name of the company	Industry	Year of Establishment
Triton Insurance Company	General Insurance	1850
Alubari Tea Company (under the Kurseong and Darjeeling Tea Company)	Commercialized Tea	1856
Bombay Mutual Life Assurance Society	Life Insurance	1871
Tata Power Company Ltd	Private sector power	1910
Imperial Tobacco Company	Commercialized cigarettes	1910
Malankara Rubber and Produce company	Rubber estate	1910
Dunlop Rubber Company	Tyre company	1926
Hindustan Motors Limited	Car assembling; Car manufacturing	1942; 1948

Joy Ice Creams Pvt. Ltd	Ice cream manufacturing and marketing	1948
Automobile Products of India (API)	Scooter manufacturing	1949

FIRST FOREIGN BANK

The first foreign bank in India was the Chartered Bank that was established in 1853 in Madras. A merger with the Standard Bank in London, UK, in 1969, led to the incorporation of Standard Chartered Bank.

FIRST COMMERCIAL PRODUCTION OF IRON AND STEEL

At Porto Novo (now Parangipettai) in Tamil Nadu, a unit was set up to produce iron in 1830 without success. Three years later, the East India Iron Company set up blast furnaces in South Arcot and Coimbatore districts in Tamil Nadu. These were later shut down by 1858. The 1857 establishment of the Barakar Iron Works in Bengal (now West Bengal) produced pig iron. Steel production was started in 1892 at the Metal and Steel Factory at Cossipore (now Kashipur), Bengal and the factory was later moved to Ichapore (now Ishapur) in 1905.

India ranked 63rd (out of 190 countries) in the Ease of doing business index, released by the World Bank.

FIRST BUDGET

James Wilson presented the first Indian budget on 18 February 1869 in colonial India. A finance member of the Council of India, Wilson, founded *The Economist* magazine later and was also an advisor to the Indian viceroy.

FIRST ORGANIZED STRIKE

Following a wage cut in 1877, labourers went on strike at the Empress Mills in Nagpur, Maharashtra. This was the first organized strike in the country.

FIRST INDUSTRIAL ASSOCIATION

At the annual conference held at Poona (now Pune), The Industrial Association of Western India was formed in 1890.

FIRST STEAM–POWERED PLANT

A steam-powered plant was set up in 1899 at Calcutta. The Calcutta Electric Supply Corporation (CESC) marked the beginning of thermal power generation in the country.

FIRST ELECTRIFICATION

The first electrification took place in Calcutta, when it received current in 1899 after the setting up of the first thermal power plant by the Calcutta Electric Supply Corporation Limited.

FIRST GOVERNMENT BANKING AGENCY

Seal of the Imperial Bank

Founded in 1921, the Imperial Bank of India was formed by merging the Presidency banks of Bengal, Bombay and Madras. It later became the State Bank of India (SBI) on 1 July 1955.

FIRST LABOUR DAY

Malayapuram Singaravelu Chettiar (1860–1946) organized the first International Workers' Day celebrations on 1 May 1923 in Madras.

FIRST LEGISLATION FOR WOMEN

The first legislation for working women was the Bombay Maternity Benefit Act in 1929. The Equal Remuneration Act was passed in 1976.

FIRST STOCK EXCHANGE

A group of stockbrokers formed the Native Share and Stock Brokers Association in 1874 with Premchand Roychand, a cotton and bullion trader as the founder. Their building near Horniman Circle became the Bombay Stock Exchange (BSE) and the street came to be called 'Dalal street' (broker street) in 1930. BSE Ltd was Asia's first exchange. The Government of India recognised the BSE under the

Securities Contracts Regulation Act on 31 August 1957, making it the first recognised stock exchange. Built in the 1970s, the BSE Towers were renamed Phiroze Jeejeebhoy Towers after Sir Phiroze, who served as chairman of the BSE from 1966 to 1980. On 2 June 2004, they closed over 6,000 for the first time. BSE was also the first stock-exchange to introduce mobile-based trading on 21 September 2010.

A stamp commemorating the Bombay Stock Exchange

FIRST FULL–SERVICE INDIAN ADVERTISING AGENCY

Sista Advertising and Publicity Services opened in 1934 by Venkatrao Sista in Bombay as the first Indian advertising agency. It offered creative work and space selling in the media.

FIRST INDIAN GOVERNOR OF THE RESERVE BANK OF INDIA

Sir Chintaman Dwarakanath Deshmukh was the first Indian governor of the Reserve Bank of India (RBI). At RBI he was appointed the government's liaison officer in 1939 and he was appointed governor of RBI in 1943.

C.D. Deshmukh

FIRST AD ASSOCIATION

The Advertising Agencies Association of India (AAAI) was registered as a society on 21 September 1945 in Calcutta. It shifted its headquarters in 1961 moved to Bombay.

FIRST LABOUR LEGISLATION

The Industrial Employment (Standing Orders) Act of 1946 was the first labour legislation. It was followed by protective regulations, such as the Minimum Wages Act and the Factories Act in 1948. To protect unorganized labour, the Coal Mines Provident Fund and Bonus Schemes Bill was introduced and became an act in 1948.

FIRST INDIAN BANK TO OPEN A BRANCH OVERSEAS

A branch of The Bank of India was opened in London, UK, in 1946 and was followed by a branch in Paris, France in 1974, making it the first Indian bank to open a branch outside India.

FIRST DEMONETIZATION

Demonetization is the process of removing a currency note or coin as legal tender. India has undergone three cycles of demonetization. The first instance took place in 1946, when the ₹1,000 and ₹10,000 currency notes were removed from circulation. They were both reintroduced in 1954 along with the ₹5,000 and ₹1,500 notes. Morarji Desai, the then prime minister took the ₹1,000, ₹5,000 and ₹10,000 notes out of circulation in 1978. The latest instance of demonetization took place on 8 November 2016 when the ₹500 and ₹1,000 notes were declared invalid. New notes for ₹500, ₹200 and ₹2,000 were introduced along with new designs for the existing 10-, 20- and 100-rupee notes.

FIRST UNION BUDGET

On 26 November 1947, the then finance minister, R.K. Shanmukham Chetty presented the first Union budget of independent India. It was mostly an economic review, and no new taxes were levied as the union budget for 1948–49 was a quarter away. Eventually, budgets for short periods were called 'interim' budgets. Conventionally the union budget was presented at 5 p.m. on the last working day of February as per the British practice. The first aberration from this norm happened in 1999, when Yashwant Sinha, the then finance minister presented the budget at 11 a.m. In 2017, Arun Jaitley presented the budget on 1 February merging the railway budget, which was up till then separate from the union budget. In 2021, the budget went paperless.

R.K. Shanmukham Chetty

FIRST PLANNING COMMISSION

Under the chairmanship of Jawaharlal Nehru and with Gulzari Lal Nanda as the Deputy Chairman, the first Planning Commission was set up in 1951.

FIRST FIVE-YEAR PLAN

With a total outlay of ₹2,378 crore, the first five-year plan of free India was launched in 1951.

FIRST INTERIM BUDGET

To enable government expenditures to continue until the regular budget came out, an interim budget was presented in 1957 by the then finance minister T.T. Krishnamachari.

FIRST WOMAN BANK MANAGER

In 1962, Shanta Kumari became the manager of the Syndicate Bank, Bangalore (now Bengaluru), Karnataka.

FIRST DOMESTIC MUTUAL FUND

The first domestic mutual fund in the country was the Unit Trust of India's (UTI) scheme launched in 1964.

FIRST ANNUAL PLANS

For an interim period in 1966, the first annual plans replaced the full five-year plan. These plans continued till 1969 and were launched again in 1990–92.

FIRST COMMERCIALS ON RADIO

Vividh Bharati broadcasted the first commercial in 1967.

Hindustan Motors Ltd's Ambassador was the first car to be exported in 1975–76. It was sent to Guyana in South America.

FIRST ADS ON TV

The first advertisement on TV was for Gwalior Suitings in January 1976 and the first colour TV ad was for Bombay Dyeing in 1982, the same year that colour TV came to India.

FIRST CREDIT CARD ISSUED BY AN INDIAN BANK

The Central Card issued by the Central Bank of India in 1980.

FIRST WOMAN TO HEAD A FOREIGN BANK IN INDIA

Naina Lal Kidwai became the first woman to lead a foreign bank when she worked at ANZ Grindlays, where she worked from 1982 to 1994. The first Indian woman to graduate from Harvard Business School (1982), she won the Padma Shri in 2007 for her contributions in trade and industry.

FIRST BANK TO ESTABLISH A MUTUAL FUND

The SBI Mutual Fund was launched by The State Bank of India in July 1987. It was established under the provisions of the amendments of the Banking Regulations Act 1949 and was managed by its subsidiary, SBI Capital Markets Ltd.

FIRST AUTOMATED TELLER MACHINE FACILITY

Automated teller machines (ATM) with a 24-hour banking facility were installed at Bombay office of The Hong

Kong and Shanghai Banking Corporation (HSBC) on 4 September 1987.

FIRST CREDIT RATING AGENCY

Commencing operations in 1988, Crisil was the first credit rating agency in India. It was set up jointly by the LIC, ICICI, GIC and other financial institutions. N. Vaghul was the first Chairman and Pradip Shah was the first Managing Director of the firm.

FIRST WOMAN CHAIRPERSON – PUBLIC SECTOR UNDERTAKING

Laxmi Menon, was appointed the managing director and chairperson of Hindustan Teleprinters Ltd in 1989, making her the first woman chairperson of a public sector undertaking (PSU) in the country.

FIRST WOMAN PRESIDENT OF A STOCK EXCHANGE

Omana Abraham was made the president of the Cochin Stock Exchange in Cochin (now Kochi), Kerala, in 1991.

FIRST PSU TO GO PUBLIC

On 16 November 1992, Indian Petrochemicals Corporation Ltd (IPCL) went public with a ₹320 crore equity issue.

Infosys was one of the first companies to introduce Employee Stock Options (ESOs).

FIRST DEPOSITORY

The National Securities Depository Limited (NSDL) started operations in August 1996. It was jointly promoted by the IDBI, UTI and NSE, with C.B. Bhave as the first managing director.

FIRST INDIAN BANK LISTED ON THE NEW YORK STOCK EXCHANGE

ICICI Bank was listed on the New York Stock Exchange (NYSE) on 22 September 1999 with its American Depository shares priced at $9.80. It was the first Indian and the second Asian bank listed on NYSE.

FIRST INDIGENOUS PAYMENT CARD

The RuPay debit card by the National Payments Corporation of India (NPCI) was introduced on 26 March 2012 in Mumbai, Maharashtra. Some of the first banks to offer these cards were, the Bank of India, the State Bank of India, the Bank of Baroda and the Union Bank of India.

FIRST GOVERNMENT-OWNED ALL-WOMAN BANK

On 19 November 2013, Bharatiya Mahila Bank (BMB), opened its first branch at Nariman Point in Mumbai, Maharashtra, becoming India's first government-owned all-woman bank. Later, it was merged with the State Bank of India in April 2017.

FIRST TO WIN THE WHARTON SCHOOL DEAN'S MEDAL

Dhirajlal Hirachand Ambani (1932–2002), popularly known as Dhirubhai Ambani, started his entrepreneurial journey before the liberalization of 1991. He founded Reliance Industries in 1958. Liberalization provided the much needed boost to Reliance Industries Ltd as it opened avenues to global financial markets. In 1992, it became the first company to raise a round of investments by issuing global depository receipts (GDR) and by 1996 the company became the first Indian company to issue Yankee bonds. These bonds had a maturity period of 50 years. And if that sounds bizarre, the company came up with 100 year Yankee bonds just in a few months. This only went on to show the global trust in Dhirubhai's vision. On 15 June 1998 he was awarded the Wharton School's Dean's Award, becoming the first Indian to win it. He was also awarded the Padma Vibhushan posthumously in 2016.

A stamp commemorating Dhirubhai

FIRST WOMAN MANAGING DIRECTOR AND CHIEF FINANCIAL OFFICER OF WORLD BANK GROUP

On 12 July 2019, Anshula Kant was appointed as the Managing Director (MD) and Chief Financial Officer (CFO) of the World Bank. She was earlier a financial officer for the State Bank of India. Hailing from Roorkee, she completed her Bachelors in Economics from Lady Sri Ram College for Women and Masters in Economics from Delhi School of Economics.

FIRST INTERNATIONAL BULLION EXCHANGE

The India International Bullion Exchange (IIBX) was inaugurated on 29 July 2022 in Gandhinagar, Gujarat. The third such exchange in the world, it will sell physical gold and silver. Jewellers can register as trading partners with a minimum net worth of ₹25 crores to buy and sell the precious metals. Jewellers abroad have to follow certain instructions to avail the services after registering with the International Financial Services Centre Association (IFSCA).

FIRST OFFICIAL DIGITAL CURRENCY

The e-Rupee (e₹) also known as Central Bank Digital Currency (CBDC) was launched on 1 December 2022 by the Reserve Bank of India. The pilot project was launched in Delhi, Mumbai, Bengaluru, Chandigarh and Bhubaneswar. The sovereign currency is accepted legal tender by the Government of India and will push forward the digital revolution in India.

SCIENCE, TECHNOLOGY AND SPACE

TIMELINE

EARLY PERIOD

- 900 BCE – earliest Indian astronomical text, *Vedanga Jyotisa* is believed to have originated
- 800 BCE – The *Shulba Sutras* believed to be written by Baudhayana are from this time
- 6th–2nd century BCE – Earliest atomistic theory is brought forward by Kanada in the *Vaisheshika Sutra*
- 3rd–2nd century BCE – Pingala described the system of binary numbers in his book, *Chandahsastra*
- 5th century CE – Aryabhata uses trigonometric functions of sine and versine
- 15th century CE – The Kerala School of Astronomy and Mathematics worked on the expansion of trigonometric functions
- 448 CE – Inscriptions found from the Gupta Empire indicate the usage of decimals

- 598–668 CE – Bhramagupta was one of the first mathematicians to treat 'zero' as a number

20TH CENTURY

- 1930 – C.V. Raman wins the Nobel Prize in Physics
- 1954 – Homi J. Bhabha sets up Trombay, the atomic energy establishment
- 1963 – Vikram Sarabhai establishes the country's first rocket launching station at Thumba
- 1969 – Indian Space Research Organization (ISRO) is established
- 1972 – The Space Commission and Department of Space is set up
- 1974 – First nuclear test is conducted
- 1975 – First satellite, Aryabhata, is launched
- 1981 – Indian Antarctic Programme is kickstarted
- 1984 – First Indian man in Space, Rakesh Sharma spends seven days in space as part of the Intercosmos programme
- 1988 – Centre for Cellular and Molecular Biology sets up DNA fingerprinting technology
- 1991 – PARAM, the first indigeneous supercomputer is developed

21ST CENTURY

- 2009 – Venkatraman Ramakrishnan wins the Nobel prize in Chemistry
- 2013 – Mars Orbiter Mission launched
- 2023 – Chandrayaan 3 lands near the lunar South Pole; Aditya L1 launched

THE FIRST ASTRONOMERS

Lagadha, who lived in Srinagar, Jammu and Kashmir around 900 BCE was the first to systematize astronomy and the first to complete a text – *Vedanga Jyotisha* or *Jyotishavedanga* – on astronomy. Later, Aryabhata became the first astronomer to deduce that the earth rotates on its own axis to cause day and night and that the earth is round.

FIRST TO UNDERSTAND THE IDEA OF 'ZERO'

Brahmagupta (c. 598–668 CE) was the first mathematician to treat zero as a number and present its mathematical operations. Bhaskara I (c. 600–80 CE) was the first mathematician to understand the properties of both zero and infinity, and to state that any number divided by zero equals infinity.

FIRST STUDY OF INFINITE SERIES

The Kerala school of astronomy and mathematics, founded in 14th century by Madhava of Sangamagrama (c. 1340–1425 CE) was responsible for contributions to the study of infinite series, algebra, geometry, trigonometry and calculus. The infinite series for circular and trigonometric functions was one of the many results laid by Madhava that were later repeated in Europe.

FIRST MANUAL ON THE ASTROLABE

Mahendra Suri (c. 1340–1400 CE), an astronomer, wrote a manual on the astrolabe in Sanskrit under the patronage of ruler Firuz Shah Tughlaq of the Tughlaq dynasty. The astrolabe is an instrument for measuring the altitude of stars.

FIRST KNOWN RECORD OF AN ASTROLABE

The Yantraraja, with a 276 mm diameter, was designed and built in 1607 in Ahmedabad, Gujarat for astronomer Damodara during the reign of the Mughal ruler Jahangir.

FIRST CHAIN OF OBSERVATORIES

Sawai Jai Singh II (1686–1743), the ruler of the kingdom of Amber, Rajasthan built a chain of observatories in Mathura, Delhi, Varanasi and Jaipur from 1719 to 1737.

A painting of Sawai Jai Singh II

FIRST ASTRONOMICAL OBSERVATORY

William Petrie, an officer of the East India Company, made the first astronomical observations and calculated the latitude and longitude of the Masulipatnam Fort on 5 December 1786 from his private observatory. The first modern astronomical observatory was the Nizamia Observatory that was set up in 1908 in Hyderabad (now in Telangana).

FIRST MODERN CATALOGUE OF STARS

Based on his observations of the night sky in Madras (now Chennai), T.G. Taylor, an astronomer of the British East India Company created the Madras or Taylor catalogue in 1844. The catalogue had the positions of 11,015 stars.

The Samrat Yantra is the world's biggest sundial built by Sawai Jai Singh II, with its gnomon rising to 22.6 m.

FIRST ZOOLOGIST

In 1876, Rama Brahma Sanyal (1850–1908) joined the Calcutta Zoological Gardens in Calcutta (now Kolkata). He went on to write research papers on birds and sea snakes, and books on biology.

FIRST OFFICIAL INDIAN GEOLOGIST

Pramatha Nath Bose joined the Geological Survey of India (GSI) as an officer in 1880. He is known to have mapped the Vindhya Range and also the igneous rocks of Raipur and Balaghat areas.

FIRST TO OBSERVE A NOVA

A transient astronomical event, a nova causes a sudden appearance of bright or seemingly new stars that slowly fade away in a week or over months. The first Indian astronomer to observe a nova was Radha Gobinda Chandra (1878–1975) from Jessore (now in Bangladesh). He sighted the nova on 7 June 1918 in the Aquila constellation. He was also one of the first international members of the American Association of Variable Star Observers.

FIRST INDIAN DIRECTOR OF THE INDIAN INSTITUTE OF SCIENCE

C.V. Raman

Born in Tirucchirapalli (in present day Tamil Nadu) on 7 November 1888 in British India, Sir Chandrashekhara Venkata Raman (1888–1970) was a prodigy and a true pioneer who brought many accolades to the country. He completed his graduation at just 16 and at 19, he was an officer of the Indian Finance Services in Calcutta and served for a decade before he took up the position of the Palit Professor of Physics at the University of Calcutta in 1917, the first to hold this post. Although he was recruited in 1914, his appointment was delayed owing to the First World War. He also was the one to explain the blue colour of the sea! He won the Nobel Prize in Physics in 1930 for the discovery of the light scattering effect that came to be known as the Raman effect. The Raman effect was discovered on 28 February 1928, which is now celebrated as National Science Day in India. With this win he also became the first Asian to win a Nobel Prize in Science. Among the many awards and honours awarded to him, he was elected a fellow of the Royal Society in 1924, won the Matteucci medal in 1928 (first Indian to win it), The Knight Bachelor and the Hughes Medal in 1930, and the Lenin Prize in 1958 (first Indian to win the award). He was appointed as the first Indian director of the prestigious Indian Institute of Science in 1933. He started the Department of Physics at the institute and led it as a pivotal area of teaching and research.

FIRST CHAIN OF NATIONAL LABORATORIES

The Council of Scientific and Industrial Research (CSIR) approved five premier national laboratories on the proposal of Sir S.S. Bhatnagar. The National Physical Laboratory was the first to be founded in 1947 in Delhi and was followed by the National Chemical Laboratory in Poona (now Pune), in 1950.

FIRST DIGITAL COMPUTER

The HEC-2M, a British-built computer was installed at the Indian Statistical Institute in Calcutta in 1955. The first indigenous computer, ISIJU–1

As per the Global Innovation Index, India was at the 40th rank in 2023.

was later developed by the Jadavpur University and the Indian Statistical Institute in 1964.

FIRST OPTICAL FIBRE

The optical fibre was invented by Narinder Kapary from the Imperial College, University of London, UK, in 1955. Optical fibres are a thin and long fibre of glass through which light can travel without hindrance, whether it is bent or not.

FIRST NUCLEAR REACTOR

In 1956, Apsara, the first nuclear reactor, went critical at the Bhabha Atomic Research Centre (BARC) in Bombay (now Mumbai), Maharashtra. It was the first such Asian reactor and was shut down in 2009.

FIRST ANALOGUE COMPUTER

Biswaranjan Nag (1932–2004), built the first indigenous analogue computer in 1957. Formerly he was a professor of radio physics and electronics at the Institute for Radio Physics and Electronics (IRPE), Calcutta.

FIRST UNIVERSITY TO TEACH ASTRONOMY

The first educational institute to teach astronomy and astrophysics at postgraduate and research levels was the Osmania University, based in Hyderabad in 1959.

A stamp commemorating Osmania University

FIRST NUCLEAR IMPLOSION

At Pokhran in Rajasthan on 18 May 1974, India imploded its first nuclear device codenamed, 'Smiling Buddha' the test was conducted at a depth of 107 m. It yielded energy equivalent to 8-10 kilotonnes of TNT, and produced a 47 m wide and 10 m deep crater.

FIRST OCEANOGRAPHIC RESEARCH VESSEL

Commissioned on 1 December 1975, RV *Gaveshani,* was the first oceanographic research vessel. It carried teams of scientific personnel to their various expeditions for days and months on end.

FIRST ANTARCTIC EXPEDITION

A 21-member team left from the Mormugao Harbour in Goa on 6 December 1981, aboard MV *Polar Circle* and reached Antarctica on 9 January 1982. The expedition team returned on 21 February 1982 after having built Dakshin Gangotri, the first Indian scientific research base station in the Queen Maud Land area in Antarctica.

> Department of Science and Technology was established in May 1971.

FIRST WOMEN TO VISIT ANTARCTICA

Sudipta Sengupta (b. 20 August 1946), a structural geologist and Aditi Pant (b. 5 July 1943), a marine biologist became the first Indian women to visit Antarctica, as part of the third Indian expedition to Antarctica from 3 December 1983 to 25 March 1984. The expedition was aimed at studying atmospheric, biological, earth, chemical, and medical sciences in the region.

FIRST NATIONAL GENE BANK

The National Gene Bank was established in Delhi in 1985 by R.S. Paroda (b. 1942), director general of the Indian Council of Agricultural Research, Delhi.

FIRST TO MEASURE OZONE IN THE ATMOSPHERE

M. Vivekananda and R.S. Arora from the Raman Research Institute, Bangalore (now Bengaluru), were the first to measure the density and height distribution of ozone in the atmosphere over the city by a simple ground-based technique using radio waves in 1985.

FIRST TOKAMAK

A tokamak is essentially a magnetic bottle that has the capability to maintain conditions present inside the sun using energy generated from nuclear fusion reactions. The first Indian tokamak, Aditya, was installed in 1986 at the Institute for Plasma Research, Gandhinagar, Gujarat.

FIRST DISCOVERY OF AN ASTEROID

Through the optical telescope at Kavalur, Tamil Nadu, R. Rajamohan (b. 1944) and his team discovered an asteroid (No. 4130) in 1988.

FIRST SUPERCOMPUTER

Supercomputer Cray XMP-14 was installed at the National Centre for Medium Range Weather Forecasting in New Delhi on 25 March 1989. It was installed to facilitate medium-range weather forecasting and agrometeorology (agricultural meteorology) programmes.

FIRST INDIGENOUS CHIP

Developed by the Centre for Development of Advanced Computing (C-DAC), the Graphics and Intelligence-based Script Technology (GIST) was introduced in the market in the 1990s. Initially designed for the land records departments based in different climatic zones, it was also used by public information systems and industries.

FIRST INDIGENOUS SUPERCOMPUTER

PARAM 8000, developed by C-DAC in Pune, Maharashtra, in 1991 was capable of one billion calculations per second. This project was conducted in the supervision of Dr Vijay P. Bhatkar (b. 11 October 1946) who is considered to be the architect of India's national initiative in supercomputing.

India holds the 60th rank in terms of Network Readiness Index (NRI) 2023 report.

FIRST INDIGENOUS PALMTOP COMPUTER

The first indigenous palmtop computer was built in 1995 by a team of engineers working for Signals and Systems

India Private Ltd, headquartered in Gurugram, Haryana. It was suitable for a variety of field and industrial applications.

FIRST POWERFUL INDIGENOUS SUPERCOMPUTER

In 1998, under the supervision of Dr Vijay P. Bhatkar, C-DAC developed PARAM 10000. It was the first powerful indigenous supercomputer, capable of 100 billion calculations per second. It is housed at the National PARAM Supercomputing Facility (NPSF) at C-DAC, Pune, Maharashtra.

FIRST HUMAN ORGAN REGENERATION

Dr Balakrishna Ganpatrao Matapurkar from Maulana Azad Medical College, New Delhi, received US Patent No. 6227202 (from 1995) in 2001 for enabling regeneration of mammalian organs in the body at the site of old and diseased organs. He used unique stem cells in the body to regenerate organs like the uterus, urethra and ureters in animals, and large tendons in the human abdomen.

FIRST POWERFUL COMMERCIAL COMPUTER

Tata Consultancy Service (TCS) commissioned the 64-bit z-Series e-Server from IBM in 2001 and became the first organization in South Asia to adopt the latest technology at the time for mainframe computing.

FIRST INDIAN TO RECEIVE THE CHEMICAL LANDMARK PLAQUE AWARD

Prafulla Chandra Ray (1861–1944) became the first ever awardee outside Europe of the Chemical Landmark Plaque. The Royal Society of Chemistry honoured his life and work in 2011.

P.C. Ray

FIRST BIOLOGIST TO WIN THE LINNEAN MEDAL

Dr Kamaljit Bawa (b. 1939), president of the Ashoka Trust for Research in Ecology and the Environment (ATREE), and distinguished professor of biology at the University of Massachusetts, Boston, US, was awarded the Linnean Medal in 2018. He was awarded the prestigious medal for his pioneering research in the field of conservation biology.

FIRST ROBOTIC TELESCOPE

The country's first robotic telescope became operational on 12 June 2018 at Hanle, Ladakh. GROWTH–India is part of a collaborative effort of multiple countries called Global Relay of Observatories Watching Transients Happen (GROWTH) to observe the transient events of the universe.

As per the directory of R&D institutions in the country, there are 7,888 institutions in the country as of 2021.

FIRST WOMAN PRESIDENT OF THE ASTRONOMICAL SOCIETY OF INDIA

The Astronomical Society of India elected its first woman president, Dr G.C. Anupama, a senior professor and dean at the Indian Institute of Astrophysics in Bengaluru, Karnataka in 2019. She has projects such as the Himalayan Telescope at the Hanle Observatory in Ladakh to her credit and is a member of an international team setting up a 30 m telescope (TMT) in Hawaii, US.

FIRST AND LARGEST LIQUID-MIRROR TELESCOPE ONLY FOR ASTRONOMICAL OBSERVATIONS

The country's first liquid mirror telescope was set up in March 2023, atop a Himalayan mountain at the Devasthal Observatory Campus of the Aryabhatta Research Institute of Observational Sciences (ARIES) in Nainital, Uttarakhand. The largest such telescope in Asia, it will be used to track and observe Supernovae, gravitational lenses, space debris and asteroids and many more celestial objects. Created by astronomers from Belgium, Canada and India, the telescope collects and concentrates light through a revolving mirror with 4 m diameter and a thin layer of mercury. In addition to this is a thin translucent layer of Mylar is also part of the apparatus to protect the liquid from wind. A multi-lens optical corrector reflects light to create clear pictures using a large-format electronic camera, positioned at focus to capture images. The telescope collects over 10

GB data every night and will contribute immensely to our understanding of the universe.

SPACE

FIRST SPACE VENTURE

A Nike-Apache rocket supplied by NASA was launched on 21 November 1963 from the base in Thumba near Trivandrum (now Thiruvananthapuram), Kerala, kick-starting thc Indian space programme. Some parts of this sounding rocket were transported to the Thumba base on a bicycle! Owing to the proximity to the magnetic equator, the St Mary Magdalene Church in Thumba is a preferred site for rocket launches. The church also houses the Vikram Sarabhai Space Centre (VSSC) space museum.

FIRST INDIAN SPACE ORGANIZATION

In 1972, the Department of Space, Government of India executed India's space programme. Projects were executed in space sciences, technology, and activities through the Indian Space Research Organization (ISRO), headquartered in Bangalore, Karnataka.

FIRST SATELLITE CENTRE

Established in 1972, ISRO's Satellite Centre (ISAC), conducts research in satellite technology. Aryabhata, Bhaskara I and II, and Rohini and APPLE satellites, were all designed and built at ISAC.

FIRST SATELLITE

In 1975, Aryabhata, the country's first indigenous satellite was launched from a Russian facility. Since this pioneering launch, ISRO has launched 129 Indian satellites and 342 foreign satellites.

The image of the Aryabhata satellite featured on the reverse of the two rupees banknote between 1976 to 1997.

FIRST WEATHER–CUM–COMMUNICATIONS SATELLITE

Launched on 10 April 1982 on an American Delta–3920 launch vehicle, the Indian National Satellite INSAT-1A was India's first satellite employed for meteorological observations over India and the Indian Ocean. It was also to be used for domestic telecommunications, including nationwide direct TV broadcasting, TV programme distribution and meteorological data distribution.

FIRST IN SPACE

Squadron Leader Rakesh Sharma (b. 13 January 1949) flew aboard spacecraft Soyuz T-11 that was launched on 2 April 1984, as part of the Intercosmos programme and spent over seven days orbiting Earth. He was the first Indian to travel to space. Dr Kalpana Chawla (1962–2003), from

Rakesh Sharma seated on the far left end

Karnal, Haryana was an American cosmonaut who became the first woman of Indian origin in space. Onboard space shuttle Columbia, that took off on 19 November 1997 on a 16-day scientific mission, along with five fellow astronauts, she returned to Cape Canaveral on 5 December 1997. In 2003, Chawla died in space along with six other crew members when the shuttle Columbia tragically disintegrated while re-entering Earth's atmosphere.

Kalpana Chawla

India signed the Artemis Accord on 21 June 2023.

FIRST REMOTE–SENSING MISSION

On 17 March 1988, IRS-1A, the first of a series of indigenous remote-sensing satellites, was launched into a polar sun-synchronous orbit from the Soviet Cosmodrome at Baikonur. It carried LISS-I and LISS-II, cameras with a swathe width of 140 km during each pass over India.

FIRST INDIGENOUS SATELLITE SERIES

INSAT–2A, designed and built by ISRO was launched from Kourou, French Guiana on 10 July 1992 by the Ariane launch vehicle. INSAT–2B was launched on 23 July 1993 also by the Ariane. The third in the series, INSAT–2C was launched on 7 December 1995 and put into operation in February 1996.

FIRST INDIGENOUS SATELLITE LAUNCHER

ISRO developed the PSLV-D3, the first indigenous satellite launcher. On 21 March 1996, the 930 kg Indian remote-sensing satellite (IRS-P3) was sent into an orbit of 807 km from Earth, 17 minutes after it shot into space.

FIRST FLIGHT OF PSLV

The Polar Satellite Launch Vehicle (PSLV) is a four-stage vehicle (two solid and two propellant stages) with a lift-off weight of 294 tonnes and stands at a height of 44.4 m. Its first operational flight was on 29 September 1997 and put the IRS-1D into a polar sun-synchronous orbit, from ISRO's Sriharikota High Altitude Range (SHAR) centre in Sriharikota, Andhra Pradesh.

FIRST OCEANOGRAPHIC SATELLITE

The first satellite built for ocean applications was the IRS-P4 (OceanSat), and was launched into a polar sun-synchronous orbit, 720 km high, by the PSLV on 26 May 1999 from SHAR, Sriharikota. Weighing 1,050 kg, the satellite orbited the earth in 99.31 minutes and completed its mission on 8 August 2010.

FIRST FLIGHT OF GSLV

The Geosynchronous Satellite Launch Vehicle (GSLV-D1), the first of its kind in India, took off from the Satish Dhawan Space Centre, SHAR, Sriharikota on 18 April 2001. The three-stage vehicle carried GSAT-1, a 1,540 kg experimental communication satellite to be placed in the geosynchronous transfer orbit.

FIRST LUNAR PROBE

Launched by ISRO aboard the PSLV-XL rocket, Chandrayaan-1 was India's first lunar probe. Launched on 22 October 2008 from the Satish Dhawan Space Centre, SHAR, Sriharikota, Andhra Pradesh, it operated until August 2009. The mission included a lunar orbiter and an impactor.

FIRST INTERPLANETARY MISSION

On its 25th flight on 5 November 2013, PSLV-C25, launched Mangalyaan, the Mars Orbiter Mission (MOM) spacecraft, from SHAR, Sriharikota, Andhra Pradesh. The mission was aimed at observing the physical features of Mars and its atmosphere. This mission, made ISRO the fourth space agency in the world to reach Mars. India also became the first Asian nation to reach the Mars orbit and the first nation in the world to achieve this in its first attempt.

On 24 September 2021, the Mars Orbiter Mission completed seven years in space, although it was designed only for a six month mission life.

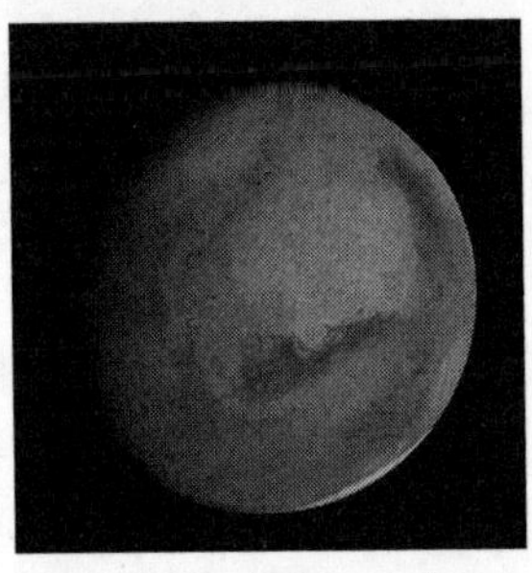

Mars as seen from the Mars Orbiter Mission

FIRST PRIVATE SATELLITE LAUNCHED

The first private satellite launched by Indians was the Exseed SAT-1 which was built by Exseed Space Innovations Private Ltd. The organization founded by scientists Kris Nair and Asshar Farhan, launched an amateur (ham) radio satellite on the Elon Musk-led company SpaceX's Falcon 9 rocket on 4 December 2018.

FIRST MISSION TO LAND A ROVER ON THE MOON

Chandrayaan-2 mission was ISRO's plan to land a rover near the unexplored lunar south pole. The mission consisted of an orbiter, a lander and a rover. It was launched on 22 July 2019 and was expected to land on 7 September 2019. The mission was however, unsuccessful as communication with the Vikram lander was lost a mere 2.1 km away from the moon's surface. NASA'S Lunar Reconnaissance Orbiter (LRO) camera detected debris from the Vikram lander on 3 December 2019 after being prompted by Shanmuga Subramanian, a mechanical engineer in Chennai, who spotted the debris.

FIRST DEDICATED COMMERCIAL SATELLITE MISSION

On 28 February 2021, PSLV-C51 successfully launched the satellite Amazonia-1, developed by Brazil, along with 18 co-passenger private satellites, from SHAR, Sriharikota, Andhra Pradesh. The first dedicated commercial mission of NewSpace India Ltd (NSIL), under the Department of

Space, Government of India, it was part of space reforms aimed at increasing the participation of private companies in the space sector.

FIRST PRIVATE SECTOR SPACE LAUNCHES

The Indian Space Promotion and Authorization Centre (IN-SPACe) authorized Dhruva Space Pvt. Ltd, Hyderabad, Telangana, and Digantara Research and Technologies Pvt. Ltd, Bengaluru, Karnataka, to launch their payloads on 24 June 2022, thus marking the beginning of private sector space launches in India. Dhruva Space's Dhruva Space Satellite Orbital Deployer (DSOD 1 U), a technology payload, along with Digantara's ROBust Integrating Proton Fluence Meter (ROBI), a proton dosimeter payload, were carried onboard the PSLV Orbital Experimental Module (POEM).

FIRST PRIVATELY BUILT ROCKET

On 18 November 2022, Vikram-S, India's first privately built rocket was launched from ISRO's launchpad, the Satish Dhawan Space Centre in Sriharikota, Andhra Pradesh. Developed by Skyroot Aerospace, a Hyderabad-based space-tech start-up, the rocket was named after Vikram Sarabhai as a tribute. This was the first rocket launched after private enterprises were invited to participate in this sector. The mission was fittingly termed, 'Prarambh' meaning 'the beginning' and carried two domestic and a foreign client's payload.

FIRST TO LAND A ROVER NEAR THE LUNAR SOUTH POLE

With the thundering success of Chandrayaan-3, India became the first country in the world to land its lunar rover near the south pole of the moon. Chandrayaan-3 was launched on LVM3-M4 rocket on 14 July 2023 from the Satish Dhawan Space Centre in Sriharikota, Andhra Pradesh. The lander entered the lunar orbit on 5 August 2023 and in a thrilling countdown, the lander touched down on the lunar surface on 23 August 2023. This also made India, the fourth country in the world after the erstwhile USSR, US, and China to land on the moon.

Image of the Vikram Lander taken by the Pragyan rover

FIRST SATELLITE TO STUDY THE OUTER ATMOSPHERE OF THE SUN

ADITYA-L1 is India's first satellite dedicated to studying the outer atmosphere of the sun. Indigenously developed by ISRO it was launched on 2 September 2023. It will stay approximately 1.5 million km away from Earth, which is about 1 per cent of the distance between the sun and Earth. The primary objective of the mission is to understand the magnetic field, heat, radiation and other elements of the sun's outer atmosphere and their impact on Earth.

MEDICAL SCIENCE

EARLIEST TREATISE ON MEDICINE

The earliest known treatise on human diseases and medicine is the Atharva Veda (c. 1500–1200 BCE).

FIRST MEDICAL SYMPOSIUM

Bharadwaja, a vedic sage, who is believed to have founded the Indian Ayurvedic system of medicine, presided over the first-ever symposium on medicinal plants in the seventh century BCE, possibly in the Himalayan region.

EARLIEST CATARACT SURGERY

Ancient Indian physician Sushruta (sixth century BCE) had diagnosed that cataract was a disease of the eye lens as was characterized by its opacity that resulted in impaired vision. He prescribed that cataract surgery was the only remedy for the same. It was performed with a curved needle used to loosen the lens and push the cataract out of the field of vision. After the surgery, the eye was soaked with warm butter and bandaged. Sushruta is considered the 'father of plastic surgery' and he pioneered the advancement of medicine in ancient India. His teachings of anatomy, pathophysiology and therapeutic strategies, featured in his *Sushruta Samhita*, were far ahead of his time.

Sushruta statue at Haridwar

EARLIEST TREATISE ON ETHICAL CODE FOR DOCTORS

Charaka, born around the 3rd century BCE is known to be one of the principal contributors to Ayurveda (a system of lifestyle and medicine from Ancient India). The *Charaka Samita* contains his contributions to the field of medicine. The *Charaka Samita* is divided into eight books amounting to a total of 120 chapters and discusses various aspects of diseases and treatment, emphasizing on the teamwork from a doctor, a nurse and the patient. It is recognized as one of the first texts to lay down the ethical code for doctors by blending in moral and scientific concerns.

FIRST HOSPITAL

The first modern hospital was established at Fort St. George, Madras (now Chennai), Tamil Nadu, in 1664.

Fort St. George

FIRST MEDICAL COLLEGE

Set up on 28 January 1835, Calcutta Medical College (now renamed Medical College and Hospital, Kolkata) was the first medical college to be established in India and Asia.

FIRST DISSECTION

In 1836, Pandit Madhusudan Gupta, the first Indian doctor of western medicine, also became the first to perform human dissection in Asia.

AYUSH, an acronym for the medical systems being practiced in India, stands for Ayurveda, Yoga & Naturopathy, Unani, Siddha and Homeopathy.

FIRST DOCTORS

Men: The first qualified Indian doctors were Bholanath Basu, Gopal Chandra Sheel, Dwarakanath Basu and Surajit Chakrabarti in 1839.

Women: Kadambini Ganguly (1861–1923) graduated from the Calcutta Medical College in 1888 as the first South Asian female physician trained in Western Medicine.

FIRST WOMAN NURSE

Bai Kashibai Ganpat from Thane, Maharashtra, was the first Indian woman to undertake training at a hospital of Jamsetjee Jeejeebhoy Group in Bombay (now Mumbai) in 1891 to become a nurse.

FIRST WOMAN SURGEON GENERAL OF INDIA

Mary Poonen Lukose (1886–1976) from Kerala graduated in 1909 from the University of Madras, Tamil Nadu, and studied medicine in the UK. In 1938 she became the first woman surgeon general of India in 1938 and was awarded the Padma Shri in 1975.

FIRST BLOOD BANK

In September 1939, Upendranath Brahmachari (1873–1946) set up a blood bank in Calcutta (now Kolkata), West Bengal.

Upendranath Bhramachari

FIRST RECONSTRUCTIVE SURGERY FOR LEPROSY

The first reconstructive surgery for leprosy in the world was conducted at Christian Medical college and Hospital, Vellore, Tamil Nadu in 1948 by Dr Paul Wilson Brand.

FIRST NEUROSURGEON

Dr Jacob Chandy (1910–2007) started the department of neurology and neurosurgery at Christian Medical College and Hospital, Vellore, Tamil Nadu in 1949. The first training programmes in neurosurgery were initiated in 1958 and in neurology in 1962.

FIRST CARDIOLOGIST

Men: Dr S. Srinivas from Bihar was the first cardiologist of India when he started his medical practice in 1950. He was trained by Dr Paul Dudley White and also became the first to bring the Electrocardiogram (ECG) machine to India.

Women: Dr Sivaramakrishna Iyer Padmavati (1917–2020) was the first woman cardiologist of India and also a woman of many firsts. She established the first cardiology clinic and catheter lab in 1953. Sometime later, as an examiner with the Medical Council of India, she introduced the first Doctor of Medicine (MD) in cardiology in India. In 1962, she established the first Indian medical school-based cardiology department, and India's first heart foundation. At 102, she was the director of the National Heart Institute, New Delhi, and the founder president of the All India Heart Foundation.

India is the largest exporter of the recombinant Hepatitis B vaccine.

FIRST AIIMS

The All India Institute of Medical Sciences (AIIMS) is a group of medical universities that were established as institutes of national importance under the act of the Parliament, with an objective to nurture excellence in all aspects of healthcare and develop the training patterns and education for students at the undergraduate and postgraduate level to showcase the high standards of medical education in the country. The first AIIMS was opened in 1956 in New Delhi.

AIIMS Delhi

FIRST TO RECEIVE THE LASKER AWARD

Rustom Jal Vakil (1911–74) was the first Indian to receive the International Albert Lasker Award of the American Public Health Association in 1957. The Lasker Awards are awarded annually to a living person who is considered to have the greatest contribution to medical science.

FIRST OPEN-HEART SURGERY

Dr Reeve H. Betts, an American missionary, started the first department of thoracic and cardiovascular surgery in 1948 at the Christian Medical College and Hospital, Vellore, Tamil Nadu. Cardiac surgical work at the hospital began in 1950. Along with Dr N. Gopinath, he performed the first successful open-heart surgery on a 12-year-old patient, Beulah, in 1961.

FIRST SEPARATION OF CONJOINED TWINS

On 11 August 1962, Dr J. Dalal, paediatrics and neonatology specialist, surgically separated a set of conjoined twins (also known as Siamese twins) born to one Mrs Kambli at Bhatia Hospital, Bombay, Maharashtra.

FIRST WOMAN NEUROSURGEON

Dr Thanjavur Santhanakrishna Kanaka (1932–2018) was the first female neurosurgeon in Asia. She also performed chronic electrode implants in the brain, being the first to do so and performed deep brain stimulation as early as 1975.

FIRST DISEASE ERADICATED

On 5 July 1975, smallpox was eradicated from India.

FIRST CORPORATE HOSPITAL

Founded by Dr Prathap C. Reddy, Apollo Hospitals was the first corporate hospital in the country. It was opened in 1983 in Madras , Tamil Nadu.

The longest drone flight under the i-Drone project delivered 3,525 units of medical supplies from Mokokchung to Tuensang in Nagaland (approx. 40 km).

FIRST IVF BABY

Born to Mani and Shyami Chawda on 6 August 1986, baby Harsha was the first baby born by the in vitro fertilization and embryo transfer (IVF-ET) method. This technique was used after three years of research by Dr Indira Hinduja of King Edward Memorial Hospital and Seth Gordhandas Sunderdas Medical College, Bombay, Maharashtra.

FIRST BREAST MILK BANK

Asia's first human milk bank was established at the Lokmanya Tilak Municipal General Hospital in Bombay, Maharashtra in November 1989. Dr Armida Fernandez was the one to pioneer this establishment.

FIRST SPERM BANK

A sperm bank was opened in Bombay, Maharashtra, by Dr Aniruddha Malpani and Dr Anjali Malpani in 1990 to help infertile patients. Facilities to store sperm for people who were critically ill to be used for implantation later were also provided.

FIRST HOSPITAL ON WHEELS

Flagged off from Victoria Terminus, Bombay (now Chhatrapati Shivaji Maharaj Terminus, Mumbai), Maharashtra, on 16 July 1991, the Lifeline Express or Jeevan Rekha Express is the world's first hospital train.

Jeevan Rekha Express

FIRST SUCCESSFUL HEART TRANSPLANT

On 3 August 1994, Dr P. Venugopal and his team of doctors at the All India Institute of Medical Sciences (AIIMS), New Delhi, performed a successful heart transplant surgery in five hours.

FIRST SUCCESSFUL LIVER TRANSPLANT

The first successful liver transplant was performed on 19 January 1996 at the Stanley Medical College in Chennai, Tamil Nadu. The first two attempts were performed at Apollo Hospital, Chennai and AIIMS, New Delhi respectively, but in both cases the patients died within a few days.

FIRST HEART–SHRINK SURGERY

Cardiovascular and cardiothoracic surgeon, Dr Naresh Trehan (b. 12 August 1946), performed the first successful heart-shrink surgery in India, which was also the first in Asia, with his team of cardiac surgeons. The surgery was performed on a 50-year-old patient, Mani Ram Gurera, on 21 May 1996 at the Escorts Heart Institute and Research Centre, New Delhi.

Dr Naresh Trehan

The Serum Institute of India, Pune, Maharashtra, is the world's largest vaccine-making company by number of doses produced and sold globally. It supplies around 1.2 billion doses to 147 countries annually.

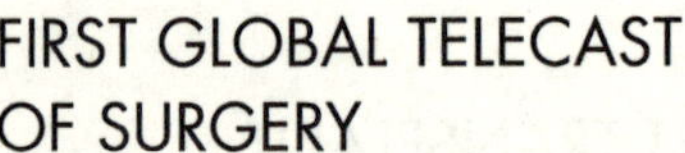

FIRST GLOBAL TELECAST OF SURGERY

On 11 June 1998, a team of doctors, led by Dr Naresh Trehan, operated upon six patients with heart ailments at the Escorts Heart Institute and Research Centre, New Delhi. The procedure was beamed live to 200 cardiac specialists and 1,000 delegates in San Francisco, US. The back-end support was provided by the Medical Products Group at Hewlett-Packard.

CINEMA AND PHOTOGRAPHY

TIMELINE

20TH CENTURY

- 1913 – First indigenous feature film, *Raja Harishchandra* is released
- 1918 – Indian Cinematograph Act 1918
- 1931 – The sound era begins with *Alam Ara*, the first talkie
- 1950s–60s – Touted as the 'Golden Era' of Indian Cinema, it saw the rise of actors such as Guru Dutt, Meena Kumari and Dilip Kumar
- 1955 – *Pather Panchali*, part of the first film trilogy, releases
- 1961 – The Film Institute of India is established along with the Film Finance Commission
- 1964 – National Film Archives are formed
- 1970s – The era of the Bollywood 'Masala' movies which saw actors like Hema Malini, Dharmendra and Rajesh Khanna among others; This also saw the rise of Amitabh Bachchan and the 'angry young man' persona; Yash Raj Films is incorporated
- 1970 – The term 'Bollywood' is coined for the Hindi-language cinema

- 1975 – *Sholay*, regarded as one of the most iconic films, releases
- 1979 – Dharma Productions is established by Yash Johar
- 1982 – Bhanu Athiya wins India's first oscar
- 1983 – *Jaane Bhi Do Yaaro*, a cult classic, directed by Kundan Shah is released
- 1986 – India becomes the largest producer of films
- 1987 – *Mr India*, a breakthrough sci-fi superhero film, releases
- 1990s – This era saw the rise of the three Khans – Shah Rukh, Aamir and Salman.
- 1995 – *Dilwale Dulhaniya Le Jayenge* releases and eventually becomes the longest-running film in Indian history

21ST CENTURY

- 2001 – *Dil Chahta Hai*, a modern classic, releases
- 2008 – *Ghajini* becomes the first Indian movie to gross ₹100 crore
- 2009 – *3 Idiots* becomes the first film to gross ₹200 crore
- 2014 – *PK* grosses ₹300 crore
- 2015 – *Bahubali* becomes the first film to gross ₹500 crore
- 2016 – *Dangal* crosses the ₹1,000 and eventually the ₹2,000 crore mark
- 2020 – Films begin to release on OTT platforms amid the COVID-19 Pandemic
- 2023 – *Adipurush* with an estimated budget of ₹700 crore becomes the most expensive film produced

CINEMA

FIRST FILMS EXHIBITED

France's famed Lumière Brothers, Louis and Auguste held the screening of six short films on 7 July 1896. They were *Entry of Cinematographe*, *Arrival of a Train at la Ciotat Station*, *Sea Bath*, *Workers Leaving the Factory*, *A Demolition* and *Ladies and Soldiers on Wheels*.

An advertisement for a Lumière film

FIRST ADVERTISEMENT FOR A FILM

The first advertisement for a film appeared in *The Times of India*, Bombay (now Mumbai), on 7 July 1896. It gave the night's programme for the screening of the six short films by the Lumière Brothers and called it, 'The marvel of the century' and 'The wonder of the world'.

FIRST FILM SHOT IN INDIA

Believed to be the first film shot in India, *Coconut Fair* was made by an unknown foreign photographer in 1897. Shortly after, a short dancing scene from the Bengali opera, *The Flower of Persia*, was made in India and exhibited at the Star Theatre, Calcutta (now Kolkata), West Bengal on 9 February 1898.

FIRST FILM CONCERN

Started by Hiralal Sen and his brother Motilal, Royal Bioscope Company was the first film concern in the country. It was started in 1898 and initially they bought films that were made in England and showcased them in India.

FIRST FILM REVIEW

The first coverage of films in printed medium with comments on the programmes started in 1899 with a local and provincial column in *The Times of India*.

FIRST FILM SHOT BY AN INDIAN

The first Riley camera was imported from the UK by H.S. Bhatavadekar (1868–1958), who shot two short films: *The Wrestlers*, which featured a wrestling match, and *Man and Monkey*, which was about a juggler training his monkeys. Both the films were released in November 1899.

FIRST NEWSREEL DOCUMENTARY FOOTAGE

B.S. Bhatavadekar filmed a reception given to Dr R.P. Paranjpye in Bombay, when he returned from the UK in 1901. Soon after, Bhatavadekar also made a short film on the landing of Sir M.M. Bhownugre at Gateway of India, Bombay, and the reception given to him by the Khoja community.

> The Indian Film Industry produces 1,500 to 2,000 films each year in about 20 languages.

FIRST CINEMA HALL

Started by J.F. Madan (1857–1923) in Calcutta (now Kolkata), the Elphinstone Picture Palace was opened in 1905. It was renamed Minerva and then renamed again to Chaplin Cinema. The Kolkata Municipal Corporation demolished the cinema hall in 2013.

FIRST FOOTAGE ON A POLITICAL EVENT

Great Bengal Partition Movement: Meeting & Procession shot by Jyotish Sarkar in Calcutta, in 1905 was the first political documentary footage.

FIRST 'TRICK' EFFECTS

Ankurachi Wadh (1912) by Dadasaheb Phalke used the single-frame exposing technique to show a bud bursting into a flower.

FIRST INDIGENOUS FEATURE FILM

Raja Harishchandra released at the Coronation Theatre in Bombay on 3 May 1913. Made by Dadasaheb Phalke (1870–1944), the silent film was a fully Indian venture and it was shown as part of a 90-minute show with four imported short films. Running for 23 days, it was screened again at multiple venues later. Dadasaheb Phalke, the director of the film, was a pioneer for the Indian film industry, fittingly called the 'father of Indian cinema'. He is credited with many firsts in the film industry and is believed to have directed over 90 feature films and 25 short films in his career. The engagement of his films with mythological themes and trick effects highly delighted his audience. His films include *Satyavan Savitri* (1914), *Lanka Dahan* (1917), *Setu Bandhan* (1932). The government of India felicitates the Dadasaheb Phalke Award each year in his honour, beginning in 1969.

Dadasaheb Phalke

FIRST CHILD ARTISTE

Dadasaheb Phalke's son, Bhalchandra, was the first child actor in Indian cinema. He played the role of the king's son Rohitashva in *Raja Harishchandra*. His daughter Mandakini was the first female child artiste and became popular for her role as Krishna. Her first film was *Krishna Janam* in 1918.

FIRST LEAD ACTORS WITH SCREEN CREDITS

D.D. Dabke as King Harishchandra and A. Salunke as Queen Taramati were the first to get screen credits for *Raja Harishchandra*.

FIRST FILMS IN DIFFERENT LANGUAGES/DIALECTS

Language/Dialects	Film	Year of Release
Assamese	*Joymoti*	1935
Bengali	*Dena Paona*	1931
Bruj	*Brij Bhumi*	1982
Garhwali	*Jagwal*	1983
Haryanvi	*Bahurani*	1983
Hindi	*Raja Harishchandra*	1913
Kashmiri	*Naizraat*	1964
Konkani	*Suzanne*	1982
Maithili	*Mamta Gawae Geet*	1982
Odia	*Sita Bibaha*	1934
Rajasthani	*Jeevi Rabaran*	1981

FIRST WOMEN ON SCREEN

Durgabai Gokhale and her daughter Kamalabai Gokhale were the first women to feature as actors as part of Dadasaheb Phalke's film, *Mohini Bhasmasur* (1913). Prior to this, male actors played female roles as well, such as A. Salunke in *Raja Harishchandra*.

FIRST BOX-OFFICE HIT

Lanka Dahan by Dadasaheb Phalke was released in 1917 and ran for 23 weeks. It became the country's first box-office hit. It has been reported that the money collected at the ticket counters had to be transported in bullock carts that were protected by armed guards!

FIRST DOUBLE ROLE

A. Salunke as Sita in *Lanka Dahan*

A. Salunke is the only artiste to have played both hero and heroine in the same film. He played Rama and Sita in Phalke's *Lanka Dahan* in 1917. This was the first instance of a double role in Indian cinema. Later in the era of talkies, Sahu Modak played the double role of a prince and a pauper in *Awara Shahzada* (Vagabond Prince) directed by Master Vithal in 1933. Among women, Neetu Singh, then known as Baby Sonia, was the first child artiste to have played a full-length double role of twin sisters in *Do Kaliyan* (1968).

The most roles played by an actor in a single film was done by Harish Raj in *Shri Sathyanarayana* (2016), where he essayed 16 roles.

FIRST FILM SERIAL

Patankar Friends and Company's film, *Rama Banvas* (The Exile of Rama) was released on 14 September 1918. It was shown in four parts and each part ran for a few weeks.

FIRST FILM STUDIO

Star Films was the first film studio in the country. It was owned by Khan Bahadur Ardeshir Irani (1886–1969) and started in 1920.

FIRST CENSOR BOARDS

The first film censor boards were set up in Bombay, Calcutta and Madras (now Chennai) in 1920. However, film censorship was centralized under one central certification board with the setting up of the Central Board of Film Certification (CBFC) in Bombay, Maharashtra, in 1951.

FIRST CERTIFIED FILM

Orphans of the Storm released in 1920 starring the Gish sisters was the first to undergo censor cuts after the Indian Cinematograph Act of 1918.

FIRST FOREIGN ACTRESS IN INDIAN CINEMA

Dorothy Kingdom of UK was the heroine in the Indian film *Shakuntala* by Suchet Singh in 1920. Suchet Singh was the first technician to be trained abroad.

FIRST HAND-PAINTED FILM POSTER

The first hand-painted poster was reportedly used for publicity in 1923 for the film *Maya Bazaar*, also known as *Vatsala Haran*. Baburao Painter, film-maker and artist, is believed to have painted the poster himself. The oldest known surviving poster is for the film *Kalyan Khajina* (1924) which was also directed by Baburao Painter.

FIRST WOMAN FILM–MAKER

The first woman to produce, direct and script a film in the silent era was Fatma Begum. She formed the Fatma Film Corporation and made *Bulbule Paristan* in 1926.

FIRST ADULT FILM

The Social Purity League of Bombay made *Social Evil*, a docudrama, in 1929 to provide information about sex problems. The first sex educational film, it was shown free of cost and was the first film given the label 'For Adults Only'.

FIRST 'SILVER JUBILEE' FILM

Madan Theatre's *Kapala Kundala* (1929) ran for 25 weeks in Calcutta . It was a silent film and was based on Bankim Chandra Chattopadhyay's novel by the same name. Amrit Manthan (1934) was the first Hindi talkie silver jubilee.

FIRST INDIAN FILM IN ENGLISH

Directed by Ezra Mir (1903–93) in 1931, Ardeshir Irani's *Noor Jahan*, starring Mazhar Khan, Nayampally, Mubarak and Vimala was given an English version a year later for foreign markets.

FIRST TALKIE

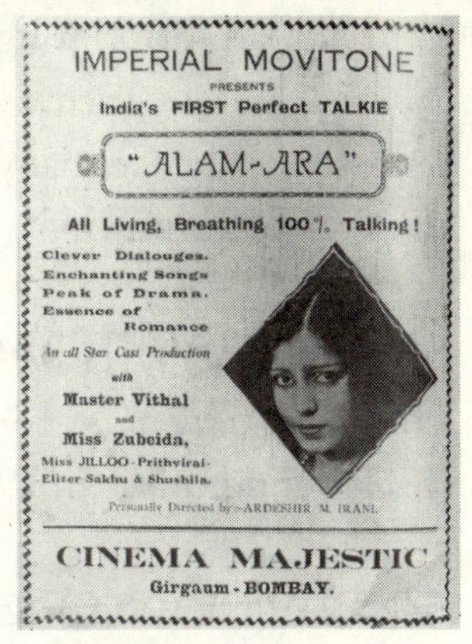

An advertisement for *Alam Ara*

Alam Ara, made by Ardeshir Irani (1886–1969), in Hindustani and released on 14 March 1931 in Bombay, became India's first talkie feature. It starred Master Vithal as hero, Zubeida as heroine, Prithviraj Kapoor in a supporting role and W.M. Khan as a singing fakir. Pirojshah Mistry and B. Irani were the first music directors.

FIRST ACTOR OF THE TALKIES – WOMAN

Zubeida Begum was part of the first talkie in India, *Alam Ara* (1931). Prior to this she had featured in 36 silent movies.

FIRST RECORDED FILM SONG

Featured in *Alam Ara*, the song, 'De de Khuda ke naam peh pyare, taaqat ho gar dene ki' was the first song recorded for film. It was sung by W.M. Khan.

> There are no prints or records of the film, *Alam Ara*, thereby making it a 'lost' film.

FIRST EXPERIMENT OF COLOUR FILMS

Madan Theatres of Calcutta made the very first attempt at colour films in 1932. *Bilwamangal*, a talkie feature was sent abroad for printing. The Prabhat Company under V. Shantaram also tried a colour processed film, *Sairandhri*, and sent it to Germany for printing. The results of both were unfit for viewing.

FIRST FILM WITH BACKGROUND MUSIC

The film *Chandidas* (Bengali) introduced the concept of background music in 1932.

FIRST AIR-CONDITIONED THEATRE

Regal Theatre in Bombay, is the country's oldest air-conditioned theatre. Opened in 1933, the theatre was constructed at a cost of ₹12 lakhs on the site from where the viceroy was given the 21-gun salute. It is believed that the Dalai Lama saw his first Western film here as did Dr Rajendra Prasad. A multi shop complex now with a cinema and shops at street level, it was also the lead theatre that hosted the Mumbai Academy of Moving Images (MAMI) in 2015 and 2016.

FIRST ANIMATED FILM

On a Moonlit Night (1934), directed by R.C. Boral was the first Indian animated film with a soundtrack.

FIRST WOMAN STUNT ACTOR

Described as 'Zorro, Tarzan and John Wayne rolled into one', Nadia (1908–96), was India's legendary woman stunt actor. Born Mary Evans, she performed incredible stunts and was more commonly known as 'Fearless Nadia'. She is known for her work in *Hunterwali* (1935).

Poster of *Hunterwali* featuring Nadia

FIRST FOREIGN FILM AWARD

The film *Seeta* (1934) by East India Films Co., Calcutta, West Bengal, which was directed by Debaki Bose, was the first film from India to win the gold medal at the Third International Exhibition of Cinematographic Art in Venice, Italy, in 1935.

FIRST FILMS WITH PLAYBACK SINGING

Playback singing was introduced in 1935 by New Theatres with a chorus song in their film, *Dhoop Chhaon* (Hindi) and *Bhagya Chakra* (Bengali). Nitin Bose directed the films and the composer was R.C. Boral.

FIRST WOMEN MUSIC DIRECTORS

Jaddan Bai, mother of the famous actress Nargis, made the film *Talashe Haq* (1935) and composed music for it herself. In the same year, Saraswati Devi scored the music for Bombay Talkies' film *Jawani ki Hawa*.

FIRST 'GOLDEN JUBILEE' FILM

Directed by Damle and Fatehlal, *Sant Tukaram* (Marathi, 1936) ran for over a year. A golden jubilee film is one that has completed a run of 50 weeks.

FIRST TO ACT IN A HOLLYWOOD FILM

Dastagir (1924–63), also popularly known as 'Sabu' in film circles, was the first to have a credited role in a Hollywood film. Hailing from the princely state of Mysore (now Mysuru), Karnataka, he was part of many such projects. He acted in Robert Flaherty's film *Elephant Boy* (1937) and his other films included *The Thief of Baghdad* (1940) and *Jungle Book* (1942).

Dastagir

FIRST USE OF NATURAL SOUNDS

Duniya Na Mane (also known as 'The Unexpected'), a 1937 film by V. Shantaram was the first film to completely dispense with background music and use only natural sounds needed to accompany the songs. There was no recorded music used for the film. In the film they established the source of the sound for songs and scenes, for example, accompaniment to a song was given by a character ringing bells or beating a stick on kitchen vessels.

FIRST SONGLESS FILM

J.B.H. Wadia's *Naujawan* released in 1937 was meant to be a fast-paced thriller and hence, it did not have any song. The makers released a special long trailer to explain this to the audience.

FIRST FILM WITH WILDLIFE

Toofani Tarzan by Wadia Brothers was released in 1937. The film made abundant use of jungle scenes and was shot with animals on locations.

FIRST FILM IN MULTILINGUAL VERSIONS

J.B.H. Wadia's *Court Dancer* (*Raj Nartaki*), featuring Sadhana Bose and Prithviraj Kapoor was directed by Madhu Bose. It was shot in Hindi, Bengali and English in 1941.

FIRST UNDERWATER STUDIO–EFFECT SCENES

Chenchu Lakshmi (1943), a Telugu language film by S. Saundara Rajan featured the lead actress, Kamala Kotnis in a few underwater scenes.

Poster of *Chenchu Lakshmi*

FIRST FAN CLUB

The Errol Flynn Fan Club established in 1949 by two boys in

Madras was India's first official fan club. After watching a film, they decided to start a fan club. The membership fee was set at ₹5 and was charged monthly and small printed pink cards with the legend 'The Flynn Fans Club' were issued to members. The members met thrice a month and screened films together.

FIRST COMPILATION FILM

J.S. Cashyap with Anyaya experimented to create a new film by cleverly editing 14 films of the Bombay Talkies studio starring Devika Rani in 1949. The credits read, re-produced, re-edited and re-directed.

FIRST ACTORS TO ACT IN 1,000 FILMS

Popular Tamil heroine of the 1950s and '60s, Manorama has acted in over 1,000 films. Her first film was *Malayitta Mangai* (1958). Her real name was Gopishantha and she received the Padma Shri in 2002. Among men, Brahmanandam Kanneganti, a well-known comedian of Telugu cinema, has received credits for acting in 1,178 films. He achieved this feat over an acting career of more than 30 years.

FIRST INTERNATIONAL FILM FESTIVAL

The International film festival was inagurated in Bombay, and also held in New Delhi, Madras and Calcutta in 1952. It was organized by the government's Films Division.

FIRST NATIONAL FILM AWARD

Established in 1954, the first National awards were given for the films of the year 1953. They were initially called 'State Awards' and two President's gold medals, 12 silver medals for regional cinema and two certificates of merit were awarded in the early years. The best actress award was called 'Urvashi' and the best actor award was called 'Bharat' in initial years. *Shyamchi Aai* (Marathi) was given the President's gold medal for All India best feature film. *Do Bigha Zameen* (Hindi) and *Bhagavan Sri Krishna Chaitanya* (Bengali) won the All India certificate of merit, *Khela Ghar* (Bengali) won the certificate of merit for Best Children's film. Jagat Murari's *Mahabalipuram* won the President's Medal for Best Documentary Film and the certificate of merit was presented to *Holy Himalayas* and *Tree of Wealth*. All three documentaries were in English.

FIRST FILMFARE AWARDS

The Filmfare awards are given annually to honour artistic and technical excellence in Hindi-language films. The awards were instituted by the Times Group in 1954. Dilip Kumar received the best actor award for his film, *Daag* and Meena Kumari bagged the best actress award for her film, *Baiju Bawra*. *Do Bigha Zameen* won the best film award and its director, Bimal Roy won the best director award for the same. Best music director was awarded to Naushad for *Baiju Bawra*.

From left to right: Bimal Roy, Meena Kumari and Naushad

FIRST LEAD ACTOR TO ACT IN 500 FILMS

Prem Nazir (1926–89), born as Abdul Kadar in Chirayinkeezhu, Kerala, played the lead role in as many as 600 films. He starred in Malayalam, Tamil, Kannada, and Telugu films, and co-starred in films with at least 85 female actors.

Prem Nazir and Shiela were paired together in 107 films – the most for any on-screen pair!

FIRST ACADEMY AWARD NOMINATION

The 1957 film, *Mother India* was the first Indian Film to be nominated for an Academy Award. The Sunil Dutt,

Poster of *Mother India*

Nargis and Rajendra Kumar starrer was nominated for the Best Foreign Film category but did not win the Oscar.

FIRST TO SCORE MUSIC FOR FOREIGN FILMS

Sitar maestro Pandit Ravi Shankar (1920–2012) was the music director for foreign films such as *The Flute and The Arrow* (Swedish, 1957), *A Chairy Tale* (French, 1957), *Alice in Wonderland* (English, 1966), and the co-production *Gandhi* (English, 1982) for which he received an Oscar nomination. Ravi Shankar, who was thc first dircctor of the National Orchestra of All India Radio (1949–55), was also the recipient of numerous international and national awards, including the Padma Bhushan.

Ravi Shankar

FIRST CINEMASCOPE FILMS

Guru Dutt's *Kaagaz Ke Phool* was released in 1959 in black-and-white Cinemascope. Later, Mahesh Kaul's *Pyar Ki Pyaas* was made in Cinemascope and colour in 1961.

S.S. Rajamouli's *RRR* was released on 10,200 screens worldwide – highest ever!

FIRST ONE–ACTOR, ONE–SET FILM

Sunil Dutt made *Yaadein* in 1964, the first experiment of its kind in the world with only one actor (himself) emoting on only one set. In 2005, Kannada film *Shanthi* became the second Indian movie with a single actor to be released.

Poster of *Yaadein*

FIRST FILM TO HAVE TWO INTERVALS

Produced by RK Films, *Sangam* (1964), starring Raj Kapoor, Vyajanthimala and Rajendra Kumar was the first film to have two intervals. Another film from R.K. Studios that had two intervals was *Mera Naam Joker* (1970).

Poster of *Sangam*

FIRST FILM SHOT WITHOUT STUDIO SETS

K.A. Abbas' *Aasman Mahal* (1965) with Prithviraj in the central role was shot on locations or interiors of palaces and houses without using any artificially constructed set.

FIRST FILM IN 70 MM

Pachchi's *Around the World*, starring Raj Kapoor and Rajshri was the first Indian film in 70 mm (using the blowing-up method) and was released in 1967. It was in Technicolor and had stereophonic sound. Around eight years later, in 1975, *Sholay* was shot on the 70 mm format in India. G.P. Sippy's blockbuster had a stereophonic soundtrack, the four channels of which could be connected to amplifiers in cinema theatres. Many theatres that were not equipped for it were provided flat (35 mm) singletrack prints.

FIRST DADASAHEB PHALKE AWARD

India's highest award in the field of cinema, the Dadasaheb Phalke Award was instituted in 1969. The first award was presented to Devika Rani for her contribution to Indian cinema. Popularly known as the 'first lady of Indian cinema', she made her debut with the film *Karma* in 1933. She started the first public limited film company, Bombay Talkies in 1934.

Devika Rani

FIRST HORROR FILM

Do Gaz Zameen Ke Neechay by the Ramsay Brothers established the horror genre in Hindi films in 1972.

Poster of *Do Gaz Zameen Ke Neechay*

FIRST WOMAN CINEMATOGRAPHER

B.R. Vijayalakshmi qualified as a cinematographer in 1981. Her first film was Bhagyaraj's *Chinna Veedu* (1985) in Tamil.

FIRST ACADEMY AWARD

Women: Bhanu Athaiya (1929–2020) won the first academy award in 1983 for Costume Design for the iconic film, *Gandhi*.

The seven Ramsay Brothers made over 30 films in the horror genre – the most produced by anyone in the country.

Men: Satyajit Ray (1921–92) won an honorary award in 1992.

FIRST 3D FILM

Produced by M.C. Punoos, *My Dear Kuttichathan* (1984), was the first Indian 3D film.

FIRST INDIAN WINNER OF THE LEGION D'HONNEUR

The only Indian film personality to be awarded the Commandeur level of France's highest civilian award, the Legion d'honneur was Satyajit Ray (1921–92). He was felicitated on 2 February 1989, one of only two film-makers in the world to have received it. He is also the only Indian film-maker to receive the Magsaysay Award.

Satyajit Ray

FIRST FILM SEQUENCE SHOT IN PAKISTAN (POST–1947)

Henna (1991) directed by Randhir Kapoor under the R.K. Film's banner was the first Hindi film shot in Pakistan since partition in 1947. Special permission was sought for it and granted by the Nawaz Sharif

Poster of *Henna*

government. Once complete, the film was also the first to be premiered in Pakistan and issued for general release.

FIRST USE OF SURROUND SOUND

When screened in big cities, *Khuda Gawah* (1992) used stereophonic four-track sound with special gadgets fitted into theatre walls and ceilings. This gave an impression that the sound was surrounding the audience, making the fight scenes, horse-riding scenes and the scenes involving the Afghan game of *buzkashi*, a heightened effect.

FIRST NUDE SEQUENCE

The Danish version of *Pyaar Ka Tarana* (1993) directed by Dev Anand and starring Akshay Anand, Mink Brar and Anita Ayoob was the first Indian film with a nude scene featuring three characters.

FIRST CHEVALIER OF THE *ORDRE DES ARTS ET DES LETTRES*

Sivaji Ganesan (1928–2001) was honoured as the Chevalier of the *Ordre des Arts et des Lettres* (Order of Arts and Letters) by the French Government for his lifelong contribution to the Indian cinema in 1995.

As many as 18,070 certifications were issued by the Central Board for Film certification (CBFC) in 2022–23.

FIRST FILM SHOWCASED AT THE UNITED NATIONS (UN)

Rajkumar Hirani's *Lage Raho Munna Bhai* was the first Indian full-length feature film to be showcased at the UN head office.

PHOTOGRAPHY

EARLIEST COMMERCIAL STUDIO

Well-known for its studio portraits of the ruling classes, Bourne and Shepherd was one of the oldest photographic businesses in the world. Established in the 1860s, the studio was the result of a partnership between Samuel Borne and Charles Shepherd. The photographers of the studio attended royal events, imperial durbars and state visits. Post independence, the studio was bought over by Indian proprietors who operated the studio under the same name in Calcutta. The studio closed down on 20 April 2016 after 176 years of operations.

FIRST USE OF THE DAGUERREOTYPE

The daguerreotype (early photography process using an iodine-sensitized silvered plate and mercury vapour) was used in Calcutta in January 1840, within a year of its first use in England. They were brought to document India's architecture and landscape.

FIRST COMMERCIAL PHOTOGRAPHER

Lala Deen Dayal

Known as the 'photographer of kings', Lala Deen Dayal of Hyderabad, was the country's best-known photographer from the British times. Beginning his career in mid-1870s, he set up studios in three cities: Indore, Bombay and Hyderabad (now in Telangana). He was appointed as the photographer to the viceroy of India in 1885.

FIRST PERSONAL STUDIO

An amateur photographer, Maharaja Sawai Man Singh of Jaipur, Rajasthan, was the first to have a personal studio. Photographic plates of his work, thousands in number, were discovered in the 1980s, in storerooms of the City Palace in Jaipur.

FIRST PHOTOGRAPHIC SOCIETY

Founded in October 1854, The Bombay Photographic Society had British Captain Harry J. Barr as its first president. It had more than 200 people as members, many of them Indian.

FIRST COURSE IN PHOTOGRAPHY

The first photography course began in Elphinstone College, Bombay, in 1855. Around the same time, the J.J. School of

Art, Bombay, and the Madras School of Art, Madras, Tamil Nadu, began similar courses.

FIRST PHOTO EXHIBITION

The Photographic Society of India organized the first All-India Photographic Exhibition in 1856 in Bombay. Lord Canning, the then governor general of India, inaugurated the exhibition.

The Museo Camera Centre for the Photographic Arts in Gurugram, Haryana, is the largest camera museum with around 2,500 cameras on display.

EARLIEST BOOK ON PHOTOGRAPHY

Written by R.B. Gakley in 1859, *Pagoda Hallibee* was the first book on photography published in India.

EARLIEST RECORDED COMMERCIAL ALBUM

Sold for ₹12 in Bombay, Maharashtra, in 1884, a gilded and bound album of a hundred photographs of Indian buildings, scenery, races, costumes, and bazaar incidents was the earliest recorded commercial album. It used to be a popular souvenir among the British.

FIRST INDIAN FELLOW OF THE BRITISH PHOTOGRAPHIC SOCIETY

A prominent landowner of the time, Sir Prodyot Coomar Tagore (1873–1942), from Calcutta, West Bengal, was an art collector besides being a keen photographer. He was elected a Fellow of the British Photographic Society in 1896, the first Indian to receive the honour. He had a studio in his Tagore Castle home and exhibited his works. He was also the founder and first president of the Academy of Fine Arts, Calcutta.

Sir Prodyot C. Tagore (standing)

OLDEST EXTANT PORTRAIT STUDIO

Hamilton Studios was set up in the E.D. Sassoon building by Sir Victor Sassoon, who was passionate about photography and constructed many public buildings in Bombay, in 1928. Photography sessions at these studios were held by appointment, and the rich and famous personalities of Bombay were seen coming for quick and glamorous shoots. Currently, the studios are run by Ajita Madhavji and can be found in Ballard Estate.

FIRST WOMAN PHOTOJOURNALIST

Homai Vyarawalla (1913–2012), from Navsari, Gujarat was the first Indian woman photojournalist to document Indian life. An alumnus of the Bombay University and the Sir J.J. School of Art, she got her degree in Economics from St Xavier's College. Her first photographs were published in *Bombay Chronicle* in 1936. She even covered wartime

Homai Vyarawalla

activities for *The Illustrated Weekly of India* and the *Far Eastern Bureau* of the British Information Service. *Life* and *Time* magazines also featured her photographs of the Indian independence movement. During her career she captured many historic moments as well as imminent political personalities such as Jawaharlal Nehru, Mahatma Gandhi and Indira Gandhi among others. In 2017, Google released a doodle as a tribute to her as India's 'First lady of the lens'.

FIRST PHOTO FILM MANUFACTURING COMPANY

Hindustan Photo Films Manufacturing Co. (HPF), a public sector unit, was set up in 1960 at Ooty (now Udhagamandalam), Tamil Nadu, to make photosensitive materials for the Indian film industry, still photography, and X-ray films for medical and industrial use. The Indu brand of raw film was introduced by them.

FIRST KODAK EXPRESS OUTLET

Skylab, established in 1978, was the first colour lab in suburban Bombay, Maharashtra. Initially the lab catered to advertising agencies, but gradually the focus shifted to providing a photo colour lab and studio for amateurs and ordinary people.

> Sipra Das was conferred the lifetime achievement award at the National Photography Awards ceremony held in 2023.

FIRST WINNER OF THE WILDLIFE PHOTOGRAPHER OF THE YEAR TITLE

The Natural History Museum organizes the Wildlife Photographer of the Year, an internationally famed and coveted contest in London, UK. Rajesh Bedi became the first Indian to win the grand title in 1986 for his photograph of the Asiatic black bear.

FIRST ASIAN TO WIN THE INTERNATIONAL PHOTOGRAPHY AWARDS

At the International Photography Awards 2004, Sharad Haksar from Chennai, Tamil Nadu, won one gold, one silver, two bronzes and 21 nominations. India finished fourth behind the US, the UK and Canada.

FIRST NATIONAL PHOTOGRAPHY AWARDS

The Photo Division of the Ministry of Information and Broadcasting announced the National Photography Awards in 2010 to commemorate the completion of 50 years of the photo division. The first awards were the lifetime achievement awards which were presented to Homai Vyarawalla, S. Paul, Benu Sen, and K.G. Maheshwari. The awards are now presented in five categories – Lifetime Achievement, Professional photographer of the year, Special mention in professional category, Amateur photographer of the year and Special mention in amateur category.

FIRST WINNER OF THE ACADÉMIE DES BEAUXARTS PHOTOGRAPHY AWARD – WILLIAM KLEIN

Raghu Rai

Raghu Rai (b. 1942) won the first-ever Académie des Beaux-Arts Photography Award – William Klein (Fine Arts Academy award for

Photography). Named the laureate, he was awarded the prize at the Palais de l'Institut de France on 30 October 2019 along with a 120,000 euros prize (approx. ₹10.79 crore). The award was instated in honour of William Klein who was a celebrated US-born French photographer and film-maker.

FIRST WINNERS OF THE PULITZER PRIZE FOR FEATURE PHOTOGRAPHY

Anushree Fadnavis and Adnan Abidi were part of the Reuters team that won in the 'Breaking News Photography' category of the Pulitzer Prize for photography in 2020. Their work covered the Hong Kong protests.

FIRST TO RECEIVE THE HASSELBLAD AWARD

Dayanita Singh from New Delhi became the first Indian and the first South Asian laureate to receive the Hasselblad Award. On 14 October 2022 in a ceremony held in Gothenburg, Sweden, she was handed her award along with the prize money of two million Swedish krona, becoming also the first to receive the prize since it was upgraded. Awarded annually since 1982, the Hasselblad awards are one of the most prestigious awards in photography worldwide. She received commendation for her 'mobile museums' (she uses objects that allow for the artwork to be constantly arranged and rearranged) in the official citation for the award.

National Photography Day is celebrated on 19 August.

THE ARTS

TIMELINE

EARLY PERIOD

- 9000 BCE–7000 BCE – Rock paintings at Bhimbetka capture the life of thc ancient man
- 2500 BCE – Warli artform flourishes showcasing the life of the people of the Warli Tribe
- 2350–2000 BCE – The Pashhupati seal from Mohenjo-daro depicts a possibly three-headed figure seated and surrounded by animals.
- 2300–1750 BCE – The Dancing girl bronze statue is dated back to this period
- 322–185 BCE – The Pillars of Ashoka show distinct style of craft
- 500 BCE–500 CE – The *Natyashastra* is believed to belong to this period
- 500 BCE – Panini's grammar treatise in Sanskrit, *Ashtadhyayi* is attributed to this period
- 2nd century BCE – The temple art and rock paintings of the Indus Valley Civilisation; Khadagiri Caves are one of the earliest examples of theatre architecture in India
- 1st century BCE – Bhasa, one of the earliest playwrights of India is believed to belong to this period

- 1st century CE – The sculptures and paintings brought about new artistic expressions
- 5th century CE – The Ajanta and Ellora caves showcase the rock-cut art
- 14–15th century CE - Standardisation of Carnatic music by Purandara Dasa
- 16th century – Miniature painting with heavy Persian influences flourishes; The Tanjore painting style emerges in the Thanjavur district of Tamil Nadu
- 1562 – Tansen, a famous musician and composer is believed to join Akbar's court around this time
- 1870s – Raja Ravi Varma's realistic artworks gain traction

20TH CENTURY

- 1913 – Rabindranath Tagore wins the Nobel Prize for Literature
- 1953 – Sangeet Natak Akademi established
- 1954 – Sahitya Akademi, Lalit Kala Akademi, National Gallery of Modern Art (New Delhi) established
- 1965 – The Jnanpith award instituted
- 1966 – M.S. Subbulakshmi performs at the UN General Assembly
- 1972 – First book fair conducted in New Delhi
- 1975 – Gopal Sharman's *The Ramayana* showcased on Broadway and West End
- 1995 – Contemporary Indian paintings are auctioned abroad for the first time

CREATIVE ARTS
LITERATURE

EARLIEST KNOWN GRAMMAR TEXT

Composed around 500 BCE by Panini, the Sanskrit grammar treatise *Ashtadhyayi* is believed to be the earliest formalized book on Sanskrit grammar. The book contains 4,000 precise rules of grammar in as many sutras, detailing an array of topics such as syntax, moods and root derivatives.

FIRST LITERARY ASSEMBLY

Madurai, the capital city of the Pandya dynasty was the venue of the great Tamil literary assembly between the 1st and 4th centuries. Called 'Sangam', poets and scholars gathered each year under the royal aegis for literary competitions and the codification of contemporary Tamil writing.

FIRST KNOWN 'MODERN' PRINTED BOOK

The first known printed book in India, titled *Conclusoes e Outras Coisas,* was printed in Portuguese in Goa by Joao de Bustamante, a Christian missionary in 1556.

FIRST KNOWN PRINTED BOOKS IN LOCAL LANGUAGES

Language	Name of the Book/Description	Year/ Decade	Press, Location
Konkani	*Doutrina Crista*	1556	Society of Jesus Press, Goa

Tamil	*A Book of Prayers*	1560	Society of Jesus Press, Goa
Urdu	Hallhead's Urdu translation of Kannada laws	1792	Honourable Company Press in Calcutta (now Kolkata, West Bengal)
Devanagari/ Hindi	*Grammar of Sanskrit and Grammar of the Hindustani Language*	1796	Chronicle Press, Calcutta
Odia	A translation of the New Testament by Pandit Mrityunjaya Vidyalankar	1807	Serampore Mission Press, Serampore, Bengal (now Srirampur, West Bengal)
Malayalam	*The Bible*	1811	Courier Press, Bombay, Maharashtra
Assamese	*Dharmapustak* (an early translation of the New Testament)	1813	Serampore Mission Press, Serampore, Bengal
Telugu	*A Grammar of Telugu*	1813	Serampore Mission Press, Serampore, Bengal
Gujarati	*Dabestane-Mazaheb,* the Gujarati translation of a Persian book, published by Fardoonjee Marazban	1815	Bombay (now Mumbai, Maharashtra)

Kannada	*A Grammar of the Karnatic Language* by William Meckerell	1820	Serampore Mission Press, Serampore, Bengal
Dogri	*Valmiki Ramayana*	1858	Sri Saraswati Press, Jammu in Jammu and Kashmir
Maithili	*Krishna Janma* edited by Grierson	1936	Vidyapati Press, Laheriasarai, Bihar

FIRST BOOK IN MOULDED TYPE

The first book in moulded type in an Indian language was in Tamil printed in 1713.

FIRST ENGLISH TRANSLATION FROM AN INDIAN LANGUAGE

The abridged rendering of the Vedanta into English by Raja Ram Mohan Roy was published in 1816.

Raja Ram Mohan Roy

FIRST INDEPENDENT PUBLISHER

Gangakishor Bhattacharya, set up a press in Calcutta, West Bengal, in 1821 and became the first Indian publisher to do so. A former employee of the Serampore Press, Serampore, Bengal, he published 18th century ballads in Bengali and adaptations from classics.

In India, the International Standard Book Number (ISBN) numbers are issued through the Raja Rammohun Roy National Agency for ISBN free of cost. It was set up in 1985.

FIRST POET IN ENGLISH IN INDIA

Henry Louis Vivian Derozio (1809–31) is considered to be the first Indian poet who wrote in English. Under the pseudonym 'Juvenis', the poems that he submitted to the newspaper *India Gazette* were published as a collection in 1827. 'The Fakeer of Jungheera', one of his most famous works was part of the second edition of the collection which was released in the following year.

FIRST BIOGRAPHICAL WORK

The first biographical work is considered to be the *Biographical Sketches of the Dekkan Poets* (1829) by Cavelly Venkata Ramaswami.

OLDEST BOOKSHOP

Opened in 1844, Higginbothams, the oldest bookshop in the country, was opened by Abel Joshua Higginbotham in Madras (now Chennai), Tamil Nadu.

FIRST PSEUDONYM

Author S. Rangarajan, who wrote more than 10 novels, 250 short stories, 10 stage plays, 10 books on science and a volume of poems, used the pseudonym 'Sujatha'. A regular contributor to Tamil periodicals such as *Ananda Vikatan*, *Kalki* and *Kumudam* (for which he was also editor for a brief period), he also wrote screenplays and dialogues for Tamil movies.

FIRST MODERN NOVEL IN ENGLISH

The first novel in English by an Indian, was *Rajmohan's Wife* by Bankim Chandra Chatterjee. It was written in the 1870s and examined contemporary social life in Bengal.

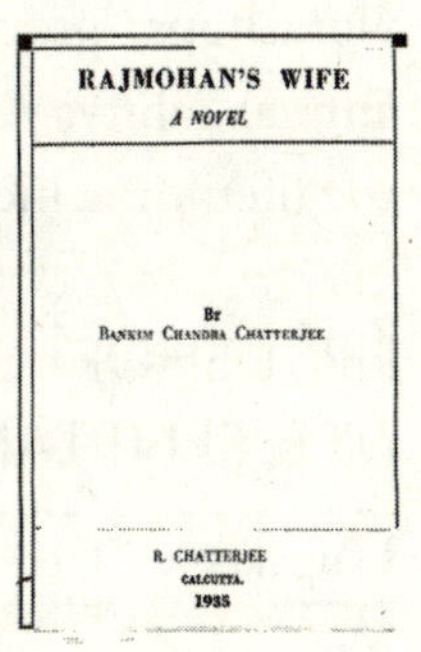
RAJMOHAN'S WIFE
A NOVEL

BY
BANKIM CHANDRA CHATTERJEE

R. CHATTERJEE
CALCUTTA.
1935

A cover of *Rajmohan's Wife*

FIRST WRITERS' COOPERATIVE

Sahitya Pravartaka Sahakarana Sangham, established in Kottayam, Kerala, on 30 April 1945 was founded by authors like Karoor Neelakanta Pillai, Prof. M.P. Paul, D.C. Kizhakemuri and others. *Thakazhiyude Kathakal* was the first book published by the cooperative.

FIRST 'NON-CLASSICAL' EPIC

The first 'non-classical' epic that forsook the classical strictures laid down by the Sanskrit epic convention was *Meghnad Badh Kavya* written by Michael Madhusudan Dutt (1824–73). He wrote the epic in blank verse in Bengali.

FIRST ACADEMY OF LETTERS

The apex body for the promotion of literature is the Sahitya Akademi and it was inagurated on 12 March 1954. Its major projects include the *Makers of Indian Literature* series and the *Histories of Indian Literature.* The Akademi organises national and regional seminars and workshops, provides grants to authors and presents the annual Sahitya Akademi award in 24 languages along with the lifetime achievement fellowship.

The present pace of publication of the Sahitya Akademi is one book every 19 hours as per their website.

FIRST SHORT STORIES AND NOVELS IN DIFFERENT LANGUAGES

Language	First Novel	First Short Story
Kannada	*Kalavati* by Yadava, 1815	'A story' by Panje Mangesh Rao, 1900
Gujarati	*Sasuvahuni ladai* (1862) by Mahpatram. Some scholars consider Nanda Shankar's *Karan Ghelo* (1886) to be the first real Gujarati novel. It is also the first historical novel in Gujarati.	'Tanakha Mandal' by Dhumketu, 1926
Tamil	*Pratapa Mudaliar Charitram* by Vedanayakam Pillai, 1879	'Mangayar Karasiyin Kadal' by V.V.S. Iyer, 1917
Hindi	*Pariksha Guru* by Lala Srinivas Das, 1882	'Indumati' by Kishorilal Goswami, 1900

Malayalam	*Kundalata* by Appu Nedungadi, 1882	'Vasana Vikriti' by Kesari Kunhiraman Nayanar, 1889
Assamese	*Bhanumati* by Pamanath Gohain Barua, 1891	'Sadhukathan Kuki' by Lawkshminath Bezbarua, 1910

FIRST ENCYCLOPAEDIA

Maharashtriya Gyana Kos, was compiled in the Marathi language by S.V. Ged. The country's first encyclopaedia, it was brought out in 28 volumes.

FIRST BOOK FAIR

On 18 March 1972, the first International Book Fair opened at New Delhi's Pragati Maidan during the International Book Year. As many as hundred Indian publishers took part, displaying about 10,000 books in English and local Indian languages. Foreign participants included those from the USSR, the US, France, New Zealand, Turkey and Sri Lanka.

FIRST KNOWN COPPER BOOK

Containing diagrams on astronomy, a 500-year-old relic, discovered in June 1987 at Attingal near Trivandrum in Kerala, had copper sheets just a little thicker than paper – 12 cm x 10 cm – bound in lead. The book was written in Vattezuthu, an early form of the Malayalam language.

FIRST LITERARY AGENCY

The first professional agency for authors, a division of Osian's Connoisseurs of Art Pvt. Ltd was set up on 9 April 2007 by Neville Tuli of Osian, Rajasthan. On 1 June 2007, Omair Ahmed was the first author they signed.

FIRST CHILDREN'S LITERARY FESTIVAL

Co-founded by Swati Roy, Jo Williams, and Venkatesh M. in 2008, Bookaroo was the first children's literary festival in India, with its first edition held in New Delhi.

Entrance to the Bookaroo festival

FIRST COMIC BOOK CONVENTION

The Annual Indian Comic Book Convention (Comic Con) was organized for the first time on 19 February 2011 by Twenty Onwards Media at Dilli Haat, New Delhi. Fifty publishers participated in it, bringing together writers, gamers, cosplayers, games and films.

FIRST VIRTUAL LITERARY FESTIVAL

LitFest X, organized between 23 October and 1 November 2015 was the country's first virtual literary festival. The event used multiple platforms like YouTube, Google Hangouts, Facebook and Twitter to present the interactive sessions to readers including book launches and book readings.

FIRST BOOK VILLAGE

On 4 May 2017, Bilhar, located in Satara District of Maharashtra, was identified as the first book village in India. Known as *Pustakanch Gaav*, the village has genre-specific libraries in 25 locations, housing more than 15,000 books, mostly in Marathi. The village is decorated with murals, paintings and artworks on the theme of books. The aim of the initiative is to share a passion for books and an appetite for knowledge.

Hind Swaraj by Mahatma Gandhi was banned by the British government in 1910. It was one of the earliest books to get banned.

PERFORMING ARTS

THEATRE

OLDEST CAVE THEATRE

The cave theatres at Sita Bengra and Jogimara in the Surguja District of Chhattisgarh are estimated to be around 3,000 years old. Sita Bengra, which predates the Lomas Rishi caves of the Mauryan period (322–187 BCE), was chiefly used for dance and drama.

OLDEST EXTANT PLAY

Palm-leaf fragments belonging to the Kushana period (around first century CE) feature a nine-act Buddhist play titles *Sariputra Prakarana*, by Ashvaghosha, the court poet of King Kanishka. It follows all the rules for drama laid down in the *Natyashastra.*

EARLIEST PLAYWRIGHT

Bhasa (third to fourth century CE) of the Chola era in south India is believed to be the earliest playwright. Well known plays by him include *Abhisheka*, *Swapnavasavadattam* and *Pratimanatakam*.

EARLIEST PLAYS

- Patanjali mentions plays such as *Kamavadha*, *Balibandhan*, and *Sariputra-Prakarana* in his text *Mahabhashya* (third century BCE).
- Bharatamuni also mentions plays such as *Devasura Sangrama*, *Amrita Manthana* and *Tripuradaha* in his *Natyashastra.*
- Uparupakas (secondary dramas) are found in the Rig Veda in the form of dialogue hymns. The most famous one tells the story of Pururava and Urvashi. Eighteen such uparupakas are mentioned in the *Sahitya Darpana*, a book on rhetoric and dramaturgy from the 14th century, authored by Pandit Vishwanath Kaviraj. These plays pre-date even the *Natyashastra.* Uparupakas were probably enacted before the public on royal occasions and temple festivals.

EARLIEST STREET PLAYS

Therukoothu, a theatre form originating during 200 BCE–200 CE in ancient Tamilakam, literally means 'street play'. It was performed on streets on an improvised stage with very few props and hardly any special costumes. Themes were taken from the epics. Therukoothu as well as other forms of street plays like Pallu, Kuravanji, and Nandi Natakam are still performed in south India.

EARLY DRAMATIC REFERENCES

There are references to drama, dancing, music, and acting in the Ramayana, the Mahabharata and the Puranas. Buddhist and Jain texts mention that monks were forbidden from watch dramatic performances. Panini (fourth century BCE) mentions dramatic works in his *Ashtadhyayi*. Patanjali (variously dated from second century BCE to the fourth century CE), describes the conditions of dramatic performers. Kautilya also refers to music, dance, and drama in the *Arthashastra*.

FIRST MODERN INDIAN PLAYS (TRANSLATIONS)

Gerasim Lebedev, a Russian adventurer, founded the first European-style proscenium drama theatre in Calcutta, West Bengal, in 1795. He was helped by the local intellectuals. Along with his Bengali tutor, Goloknath Das, he presented the plays *The Disguise* and *Love Is the Best Doctor* on

7 November 1795. These English comedies, translated into Bengali, were the first urban theatrical performances.

FIRST DRAMATIC CLUB

The first dramatic club was the Parsi Natak Mandali established in 1853 in Bombay, Maharashtra. They performed their first play *Roostum Zabooli and Sohrab* that year, followed by *King Afrasiab and Rustom Pehlvan* and *Padshah Faredun*. Other Parsi theatre clubs were the Elphinstone, established in 1860, and the Victoria, established in 1867.

FIRST 'PROTEST' PLAY

Nil Darpan, a play in Bengali about the plight of indigo farmers, was written by Dinabandhu Mitra in 1860. The play was banned by the British authorities.

FIRST COMMERCIAL THEATRE

The first commercial Parsi theatre, started by Pestonji Framji in 1870, was the first aimed at mass entertainment, while dealing with social problems. Though based in Bombay, Maharashtra, the theatre company travelled widely all over north India.

FIRST PUBLIC THEATRE HALL

The Star Theatre in Calcutta, West Bengal, was inaugurated on 21 July 1883 with the play *Daksha Yajna*. Among the first to produce plays here was the acclaimed playwright, novelist, theatre director, and actor Girish Chandra

Ghosh. The theatre shifted to its present site on Bidhan Sarani in 1888 and now mainly functions as a cinema hall with plays also being staged.

OLDEST CHILDREN'S THEATRE

Children's Little Theatre, the oldest children's theatre in the country, was founded in Calcutta, West Bengal, by Samar Chatterjee (1908–86) in May 1951. It included dance, drama, music, and puppetry.

FIRST ACADEMY FOR PERFORMING ARTS

Sangeet Natak Akademi, the national academy of music, dance and drama was set up in 1953 to promote performing arts in collaboration with states and voluntary organisations. It holds seminars and festivals, gives awards to outstanding artistes, gives financial assistance for theatre productions and traditional teachers and scholarships to student of performing arts.

FIRST AND ONLY PLAY ON BROADWAY AND WEST END

The Ramayana by Gopal Sharman, enacted in a one-woman tour de force by Jalabala Vaidya, was played at the Barbizon Plaza Theatre, Manhattan, New York, in February 1975. The play was also performed at other venues, such as the Smithsonian Institution, Washington DC, the United Nations headquarters, New York, US, and Sedler's Wells Theatre, London, UK.

FIRST OPERA IN ENGLISH BY AN INDIAN

Well-known author Vikram Seth's *Arion and the Dolphin*, which premiered in the UK in June 1994, was the first opera written in English by an Indian. Commissioned by the English National Opera, it was performed at the 964-seat drill shed of HMS *Drake*, a high-security naval base. The opera was directed by Rebecca Meitlis.

FIRST FULL–FLEDGED OPERA

The Fakir of Benares, an Indo-French opera, was staged at the Siri Fort Auditorium, New Delhi, on 27 February 2002. The opera was directed by Muzaffar Ali while his wife Meera Ali designed the costumes.

FIRST RECIPIENT OF THE KALIDAS SAMMAN

Shambhu Mitra (1915–97) from Kolkata, West Bengal, was the first recipient of the Kalidas Samman for his contribution to Bengali theatre.

DANCE

EARLIEST SCRIPTURAL MENTION OF DANCERS

The Rig Veda has the first known textual mention of dancers. Composed between c. 1500 and 1200 BCE, the Rig Veda has references to mythical apsaras (divine dancers) in the story of the celestial dancer Urvashi and the mortal king Pururava.

EARLIEST KNOWN TREATISE ON THE PERFORMING ARTS

Believed to be the work of Bharata Muni, the *Natyashastra*, is dated variously between the second and third centuries BCE and the fourth and fifth centuries CE. It is the earliest known treatise on the performing arts. The *Natyashastra* has 37 chapters with 5,569 slokas. It is the basis of classical Indian dance, music and drama, and is often referred to as the fifth Veda.

EARLIEST EVIDENCE OF FORMALIZED DANCING

The earliest evidence of formal dance is the statuette of a dancing girl from Mohenjo-daro in the Indus Valley that dates back to 2500 BCE.

Statuette of a dancing girl

FIRST KNOWN DANCE DRAMA FORM

Inspired by Jayadeva's *Gita Govinda*, in the early 17th century, Manaveda Raja, Zamorin of Calicut (now Kozhikode), Kerala, composed the *Krishna Geeti* in Sanskrit. He then went on to set it to a new dance drama form known as Krishnanattam, 'the dance of Krishna', which combined ancient theatre traditions such as Kutiyattam, ritual performances like Theyyam and folk dances like Kaikottikali.

Illustration from *Gita Govinda*

FIRST DANCE SCHOOL

Santiniketan, which was founded in 1901 in Bolpur, Birbhum District, Bengal by Rabindranath Tagore (1861–1941), had a department of dance where gurus from far reaches such as Manipur and Kerala were invited to stay and teach on campus. Santiniketan, which later evolved into the Visva-Bharati University, now has an institute of dance, drama and music, called the Sangit Bhavan.

Rabindranath Tagore: founder of the first dance school

FIRST INDIAN–EUROPEAN FUSION

Known as the 'father of modern dance' in India, Uday Shankar (1900–77), who was born in Udaipur, Rajasthan, combined European theatrical dance techniques with the classical and folk dance forms of India. He danced with Anna Pavlova, the Russian ballerina, during the 1920s and created *Hindu Wedding* as well as the duet *Radha and Krishna*, which was included in Pavlova's performance *Oriental Impressions*.

FIRST REVIVALIST DANCE SCHOOL

Founded in 1930 by the poet Vallathol Narayana Menon (1878–1958), the Kerala Kalamandalam in

The first woman dancer to win a Padma Vibhushan was Thanjavur Balasaraswati.

Trichur (now Thrissur), Kerala, was set up to re-establish Kathakali and Mohiniattam. These art forms flourished briefly under Maharaja Swathi Thirunal in the 19th century and then languished, until this revival.

FIRST TO WIN AN INTERNATIONAL DANCE COMPETITION

In July 1936, Madame Menaka (1899–1947), became the first Indian to win an international dance competition, at the Berlin Dance Olympiad. She set up her dance company in Bombay, to produce dance dramas on Indian themes. Her troupe, performed her original ballet, *Deva Vijaya Nritya*, which featured on two days and won the first three individual prizes, along with the first prize in the competition.

Madame Menaka

FIRST CLASSICAL DANCE TO BE REVIVED

Indrani Rehman (1930–99) a professional dancer, rediscovered and popularized Odissi abroad in the early 1940s. It was recognized as a classical dance form only from the 1960s.

FIRST BALLET FILM

Kalpana, released in 1948 by Uday Shankar (1900–77) used the ballet form as a major part of its narration, becoming India's first ballet film.

FIRST MODERN TRANSLATION OF THE *NATYASHASTRA*

Manmohan Ghosh translated the *Natyashastra* into English for the Asiatic Society in 1950. This was the first successful attempt at translating the definitive text on Indian performing arts.

FIRST SANGEET NATAK AKADEMI AWARD WINNERS FOR DANCE

In 1955, T. Balasaraswati (1918–84) and Shambhu Maharaj (1910–70) won the first Sangeet Natak Akademi awards for dance for contributions to Bharatanatyam and Kathak respectively.

FIRST NATIONAL DANCE SEMINAR

The first national seminar on dance was organized by the Sangeet Natak Akademi from 30 March to 7 April 1958. With Dr P.V. Rajammar as the chairman at that time, the seminar's inaugural dance was performed by leading Kathak dancer Pandit Shambhu Maharaj.

A stamp commemorating Uday Shankar

FIRST SANGEET NATAK AKADEMI AWARD FOR CREATIVE DANCE

Uday Shankar, a pioneer in the field of dance was the first to be honoured by the Sangeet Natak Akademi with an award for creative dance in 1960. In 1962, he was awarded the Sangeet Natak Akademi fellowship and in 1971, he became the first modern dancer to receive the Padma Vibhushan.

FIRST MODERN WORK ON DANCE

Published in 1968 by the Sangeet Natak Akademi, *Classical Indian Dance in Literature and the Arts* by scholar Dr Kapila Vatsyayan, was the first definitive modern work on dance, written in English.

FIRST CELEBRITY DANCE COMPETITION

Nach Baliye was the first celebrity dance competition in the country. It started with 10 couples from the television industry and aired on Star One. It premiered on 11 October 2005, with Saroj Khan, Farhan Akhtar and Malaika Arora Khan on the judging panel. The first winning couple was Sachin and Supriya Pilgaonkar.

FIRST DANCE THEATRE FORM RECOGNIZED BY UNESCO

Originating in Kerala, Kutiyattam is a traditional Sanskrit performing art form and was recognized by United Nations Educational, Scientific and Cultural Organisation (UNESCO) as a 'Masterpiece of the Oral and Intangible Heritage of Humanity' in 2008. It is believed

The thickest make-up used in any dance form in the world is the *chutti*, used in Kathakali. It is a three dimensional mask-like attachment made of rice paste and paper, which may extend to 15 cm (6 in.) from the face.

to be at least 2,000 years old and the oldest living theatre tradition globally.

MUSIC

EARLIEST BALLAD SINGING

Mentions of minstrels singing *akhyana*s (texts narrated by professional storytellers), sung to the veena, in the *marga* style of singing can be found in both Vedic and epic literature. While the Vedas mention both instrumental music and *akhyana* recitation in yagnas, the Ramayana also has several references to the singing of ballads.

EARLIEST FORM OF MUSIC

The Rig Veda has references to saman hymns, the earliest form of music in India. Saman singing is also mentioned in the *Brahmana*s as well as the Upanishads, and features as a part of spiritual observances and exercises.

EARLIEST MUSICAL NOTES

The Sama Veda, which is believed to date to c. 1200–1000 BCE, mentions seven musical notes in saman singing, viz., Krushta, Prathama, Dvitiya, Tritiya, Chaturtha, Mandra/Panchama and Antya/Atisvara.

EARLIEST REFERENCE TO MUSICAL PERFORMANCES

The grammarian Panini (fourth century BCE) in his comments on *nritya* (dancing) mentions composers of sutras on dancing. The *Pali Pitaka* (c. 300 BCE) mentions two disciples of Gautama Buddha attending one such recital.

EARLIEST MUSICAL INSTRUMENTS

Drums came into being during the Vedic period. The earliest drums included the *dundubhi* and *adambara*, ordinary drums; *bhumi dundubhi*, an earth drum made by digging a hole in the ground and covering it with hide; and *vanaspati*, a wooden drum. Early stringed instruments included the *skanda veena* and *karkari*, ordinary lutes; *vana*, a lute with a hundred strings; and the veena (similar to the present-day one). Wind instruments included the *tunava*, a wooden flute; the *nadi*, a reed flute; and *bakura*, whose shape is unknown.

FIRST MENTION OF THE DRUM

Drums were first mentioned in the *Mahajanaka Jataka* (second century BCE) that mentions them along with horns, gongs and cymbals. Two ancient Tamil books, *Purananuru* and *Pattupattu* (c. 100–200 CE) also mention the drum as an instrument that occupies a position of great honour in the musical tradition of India.

FIRST MEDIEVAL TREATISE ON MUSIC

Someshvara III, the Chalukyan king who ruled in the Karnataka region in the 12th century CE, wrote the *Manasollasa,* which is an encyclopaedic work in Sanskrit on a variety of topics, including music. The music section, one of the largest sections in the book, with 2,500 verses dedicated to it is considered the earliest treatise on music.

The piano may be classified as both a string instrument and a percussion instrument.

EARLIEST FORM OF CLASSICAL SONG

Until medieval times, the Dhrupad, originally called Dhruvapada, was the prevailing mode of music. While this form traces its roots to the *Natyashastra,* it was developed by Swami Haridas and the legendary singer Tansen in the 15th century.

FIRST FUSION MELODY

Amir Khusrau (1253–1325), a renowned singer from the court of Alauddin Khilji (r. 1296–1316) is credited for the introduction of the qawwali mode of singing which is a mixture of Persian and Indian music. The sitar, a modification of the veena was also introduced by him.

FIRST TO STANDARDIZE CARNATIC MUSIC

Purandara Dasa (1484–1564) is revered as Sangeet Pitamaha (grandfather of music). He standardized Carnatic music for teaching, besides classifying 35 types of *tala*. He pioneered a musical notation system that is still being used.

FIRST RAGA

The Carnatic Mayamalavagowla (equivalent to the raga Bhairavi in Hindustani music) is believed to be the first raga that was used by Purandara Dasa (c. 1484–1565) as a teaching scale. Also called Adi Raga, it is said to have emanated from Lord Shiva.

OLDEST GHARANA

The Gwalior gharana was founded in the 16th century by Nathan Khan Pir Bakhsh.

OLDEST MUSICAL INSTRUMENT

A lithophone (stone chimes comparable to a xylophone), around 3,000–4,000 years old, was identified by German archaeologists in Sankarjang Village in Angul District, Odisha. All the 20 similar-shaped polished basalt stones found possibly formed fragments of a lithophone, with excellent acoustic quality, as the edges were ground thin to achieve a specific pitch.

FIRST VOICES RECORDED ON GRAMOPHONE

The voices of Dr Harnamdas and Ahmed singing songs based on the Ramayana and the *aayats* of the Quran were recorded by the Gramophone Company in 1899 in London, UK.

Tyagaraja, Muthuswamy Dikshitar and Syama Sastri are together known as the trinity of Carnatic music.

FIRST GRAMOPHONE RECORD

In 1898, at the Beliaghata factory of the Gramophone and Typewriter Ltd, the historic moment of Indian music being produced on a gramophone record took place. The production of disc records was started at the Sealdah factory, Calcutta in July 1908. The factory was closed after two decades and a new factory was set up on Jessore road.

FIRST MUSIC SCHOOL

Gandharva Mahavidyalaya set up by Pandit Vishnu Digambar Paluskar (1872–1931) was India's first known music school. It was set up in Lahore (now in Pakistan) on 5 May 1901 and ran on public donations and fundraising concerts performed by him. Another branch was opened in Bombay, Maharashtra, in September 1908, and Pandit Vinayakrao Patwardhan started a branch in Poona (now Pune), Maharashtra, on 8 May 1932. The original school was also shifted from Lahore to Bombay in 1947.

FIRST GRAMOPHONE COMPANY

J. Watson Harrod, opened a branch of the Gramophone Company Ltd on 7 July 1901 in Calcutta. The first factory to process and press records was set up in 1908.

FIRST SINGER TO BE RECORDED ON GRAMOPHONE

Fred Ginsberg introduced the gramophone in India by cutting the first disk in 1902 in Calcutta. Gauhar Jaan (1873–1930) was selected to be the first singer to be recorded on gramophone. This historic assignment fetched her a payment of ₹3,000 for the session.

FIRST RECORDED SONG

'Kanha Jeevan Dhan' was recorded in 1902 for the play *Srikrishna* on a 22.86 cm, one-sided disc made by Gramophone and Typewriter Ltd. The song was recorded by Sashi Mukhi of Classic Theatre in Calcutta.

FIRST SET OF RECORDS

On 19 March 1906, H. Bose's Talking Machine Hall, a recording shop in Calcutta, released the first set of phonograph records. The set featured four songs by D.L. Roy and eight songs by Rabindranath Tagore.

FIRST FOREIGN CONCERT TOUR BY A WOMAN INSTRUMENTALIST

The *Amrita Bazar Patrika,* on 11 September 1912 reported that Satyabala Devi, a Bengali teenager, had gone to America in the summer of 1911 to play the veena. The article stated that she was the first Indian woman to successfully perform an instrumental music concert abroad.

The Gramophone Company of India Ltd was renamed Saregama India Ltd on 3 November 2000.

FIRST RECORDED MUSIC

The Shining Star Society, recorded sets of discs in the 1930s with mythological themes. The popular sets included the 10-disc *Ramayana* by Saraswati Stores, followed by sets like, *Tukaram* (four discs), *Purandara Dasa* (five discs), and *Siruthondar* (three discs).

FIRST WOMAN INSTRUMENTALISTS

Name	Instrument	Year/Decade
M.S. Lavanya and M.S. Subbulakshmi (Sisters)	Saxophone	1920s
Sharan Rani Backliwal	Hindustani Instrumental music; Sarod	1930s
Madurai M.S. Ponnuthayi	Nadaswaram	1940s
Bageswari Gamar	Shehnai	1983
Meagan Pandian	Harp	2000s

FIRST DUO TO INTRODUCE *JUGALBANDI*

Instrumental duets or *jugalbandi* was introduced by Pandit Ravi Shankar (1920–2012) and Ustad Ali Akbar Khan (1922–2009). They performed the *jugalbandi* for the first time at the debut performance of the Pandit Ravi Shankar in 1939, with him playing the sitar and Khan playing the sarod.

FIRST TO PERFORM AT THE UNITED NATIONS (UN)

M.S. Subbulakshmi (1916–2004) performed in a concert at the UN General Assembly on UN Day, 23 October 1966. This was the first time an Indian performed at the UN. She was awarded the Padma Bhushan in 1954, the Padma Vibhushan in 1975, and became the first musician to be awarded the Bharat Ratna in 1998. Subbulakshmi was also the first Indian musician to receive the Ramon Magsaysay Award for Public Service in 1974.

FIRST INDIAN PERFORMER AT THE ROYAL ALBERT HALL

The Royal Albert Hall, an iconic venue in London, UK, became the venue for Lata Mangeshkar's (1929–2022) performance in 1974. Prior to this, no Indian had performed at the venue. However, after this debut, many Indians have now performed here. These include, sitar players Pandit Ravi Shankar and Anoushka Shankar, flautist Hariprasad Chaurasia and singer Shreya Ghoshal, among others.

FIRST ELECTRONIC INSTRUMENTS

M.G. Raj Narayan invented the talometer, an electronic tala aid in June 1978. It helps musicians to get a precise, unerring and continuous course of cycles in all the talas. The first electronic tanpura was also developed by him in December 1979. This innovative box-like device had knobs for fine tuning. In 1988, he developed the first electronic tabla, designed to produce the actual sounds of a tabla as played in a live performance.

FIRST WHISTLING LP

An album of Carnatic and Hindustani ragas entirely whistled by Siva Prasad from Hyderabad (now in Telangana) was released on 15 June 1985.

LP stands for Long – playing record.

FIRST COMPACT DISC

Shagufta, an album by Pankaj Udhas (b. 17 May 1951) was the first to be formally released in a compact disc (CD) format. It was released by Music India in December 1987.

FIRST GRAMMY AWARD–WINNING INDIAN PERCUSSIONIST

T.H. 'Vikku' Vinayakram (b. 11 August 1942) won the Grammy Award in 1991, becoming the first Indian percussionist to win the accolade. He won it for his participation in *Planet Drum* by Mickey Hart. A renowned *ghatam* player, Vinayakram was also credited for popularizing Carnatic music and was honoured with the Padma Shri in 2002, followed by the Padma Bhushan in 2014.

FIRST INDIAN BAND ON MTV

In September 1993, Rana Banerjee and Sanjoy Sengupta's band, Extinct, became the first Indian group to be featured on MTV Asia.

FIRST ALL-WOMAN HINDUSTANI–CARNATIC MUSIC BAND

Anuradha Pal from Mumbai, Maharashtra, founded Stree Shakti, the first all-woman Hindustani-Carnatic music band, in 1996. They performed in India and internationally as well including at festivals such as the BBC Music Live and Rhythm Sticks.

FIRST ALL-GIRL POP MUSIC BAND

After a nationwide hunt from 12 January 2001 across 10 cities, Channel [V] handpicked five girls – Pratichi Mohapatra, Mahua Kamat, Neha Bhasin, Anoushka Manchanda and Seema Ramchandani – to constitute India's first customized all-girl band, Viva. It disbanded in 2003.

FIRST WOMAN RAPPER

Taran Kaur Dhillon (b. 29 July 1979) aka Hard Kaur was the first woman rapper of Indian origin. She topped the UK charts with her song 'Ek Glassy' in 2007, and her first solo album *Supawoman* released the same year with 11 tracks. She co-wrote and performed the title track of the film *Johnny Gaddaar* (2007).

FIRST ACADEMY AWARD FOR INDIAN MUSIC

In 2009, the movie *Slumdog Millionaire* set many firsts for the Indian film music industry at the Academy awards. Resul Pookutty won the Oscar for Best sound mixing and the song 'Jai Ho' won Gulzar (lyricist) and A.R. Rahman (music) an Oscar in the Best Original Song category. The film also won the award in the Best Score category. More recently, at the 95th Academy awards (2023), the song 'Naatu Naatu' from *RRR*, won the award for the Best original song. It became the first Indian song in a regional language to win an Oscar.

FIRST AND ONLY INDIAN TO WIN BOTH AN OSCAR AND A GRAMMY AWARD

Composer and Singer A.R. Rahman (b. 1967), won two Grammy awards following his win at the academy awards for the soundtrack of Danny Boyle's *Slumdog Millionaire,* becoming the first Indian to win an individual Grammy. He won the first Grammy in the Best Compilation Soundtrack for a Motion Picture category. The second was for the song 'Jai Ho' in the Best Motion Picture Song category for the same in 2009. He won the Academy awards for Best Original Score and shared the Best Original Song Oscar with Gulzar for the song 'Jai Ho'. Hailing from Tamil Nadu, Rahman was inducted into the musical world from an early age. He began his career in films in 1992 with Mani Ratnam's *Roja*. Since then Rahman has traversed boundaries by working

A.R. Rahman (right)

in multiple language films across the globe. In addition to the awards listed above he has won six national awards, a Golden Globe award, a BAFTA award and was also felicitated with the Padma Bhushan.

Berklee College of Music, US, awarded A.R. Rahman an honorary doctorate in 2014.

FIRST GRAMOPHONE MUSEUM

Discs and Machines – Sunny's Gramophone Museum and Records' Archive in Kottayam, Kerala, is a unique repository of around 110,000 records and more than 260 gramophones. A collection curated over 32 years, the museum was opened to public on 25 January 2015. A copy of the first recorded song in India is also on display here. The museum may be visited by appointment.

Gramophone*

FIRST ASIAN TO WIN THE GOLDEN REEL AWARD

Resul Pookutty (b. 30 May 1971) was the first Asian to win the 63rd American Motion Picture Sound Editor's Golden Reel Award in 2016 for Best Sound for the documentary

*Representative image

India's Daughter. He was awarded the National Film Award for Best Audiography and the Padma Shri in 2010.

Resul Pookutty (left)

FIRST VIRTUAL MUSIC FESTIVAL

A two-day virtual music festival, Sunburn Home Festival, was organized from 11 to 12 July 2020. Featuring a lineup of international stars such as Bassjackers, Vini Vici and Ummet Ozcan, among others. The highlight of the event was the application of extended reality (XR) technology offering a mixed reality and holistic environment, also used for the first time.

The Pratibha Sangam competition, a global competition for performers around the world in Indian classical music and dance, was started by the Indian Council of Cultural Relations (ICCR) on 16 April 2022.

VISUAL ARTS
PAINTING AND SCULPTURES

EARLIEST PAINTINGS DISCOVERED

Painted pottery, mostly in fragments, excavated at Mohenjo-Daro, Chanhudaro, Harappa, and other places in the Indus Valley, are dated to 3000–2250 BCE.

EARLIEST ROCK PAINTINGS

The oldest and largest collection of rock paintings in India is at Bhimbetka, about 46 km from Bhopal, Madhya Pradesh. Found in more than 700 rock shelters, the paintings dated to around 30,000 years ago and depict people's everyday lives such as hunting, dancing, and decoration of bodies.

Rock paintings at Bhimbetka

EARLIEST DATED FREE–STANDING SCULPTURES

The Parkham Yaksha and Yakshi statues, are considered the oldest dated free-standing Indian sculptures. They were found in Parkham, a village in Uttar Pradesh, almost 20 km from the south of Mathura. They are believed to be dating between 200–50 BCE.

EARLIEST EXAMPLE OF SCULPTURES CARRYING THE ARTIST'S NAME

The Dwarf Yaksha by the artist Kanhadasa (second century BCE) shows a happy smile on the yaksha's face. It is probably the first attempt in Indian art to endow an image with vivid emotional expression. It carries the inscription, 'kanhadaasena hiramkaarena kataa', meaning 'made by Kanhadasa, a goldsmith' it is also believed to be one of the earliest sculptures carrying the artist's name.

EARLIEST EXAMPLES OF PORTRAIT SCULPTURE

Portrait sculptures, the only example of the kind in ancient India is considered one of the greatest contributions of Kushana sculpture (c. 2 BCE to 6 CE) comprising the Mathura school of art. They include portraits of King Kanishka, Vima Kadphises and Chastana, among others. A distinctive feature that makes it easy to identify statues belonging to this school because they are all carved in spotted red sandstone taken from the quarries of Sikri close to Mathura.

EARLIEST EXAMPLES OF CONTINUOUS NARRATION IN A SINGLE PIECE OF ART

The Sunga and Satavahana sculptures (c. 2 BCE to 5 CE) are the earliest examples of continuous narration in a single piece of art. Various episodes of a story which occurred at the same place but at different periods are represented on a single carving. For example, in the panel Mriga which depicts the story of the golden stag, the three successive episodes of the story are represented in the same panel.

EARLIEST USE OF TEMPERA METHOD

The Ajanta Caves are rock-cut Buddhist cave monuments in Aurangabad, Maharashtra, dating back from the second century BCE to about 650 CE.

Ajanta caves were declared a UNESCO World Heritage Site in 1983.

The paintings in these caves used the tempera method. Tempera method is the technique of first pressing the rough mud plaster containing some organic matter like cow dung and animal hair on the surface of the rocks and then a coat of fine lime plaster is laid all over it. This layer is allowed to dry thoroughly before applying colour on it. The scenes represented in these caves are mostly from Buddhist texts and events from the Buddha's life.

OLDEST EXTANT MURALS

Two 1,000-year-old Chola paintings, which were found at the Brihadeeswarar Temple in Thanjavur, Tamil Nadu, are believed to be the oldest existing mural paintings. They depict two women who are watching a procession from a balcony.

FIRST MUGHAL ILLUMINATED MANUSCRIPT

Emperor Humayun engaged Mir Sayyid Ali and a group of painters to paint the '*Dastan-i-Amir*' (the story of Amir Hamza), which featured as many as 1,375 miniatures painted on cotton cloth in the Persian Safavid style. The work on the manuscript was underway in the 1560s.

FIRST FINE ARTS EXHIBITION

On 1 February 1831, the first fine arts exhibition was held in the Public Library, Calcutta, by the Brush Club, with paintings drawn by foreign artists in India.

FIRST MODERN ART SCHOOL

The Mechanical Institute was founded by Frederik Corbyn and Tarapada Chakrabarty in Calcutta, West Bengal, on 2 February 1839. Initially named 'Society for the Promotion of Industrial Art', it was finally renamed the School of Industrial Art on 16 August 1854. It held its first exhibition from 22 January to 3 February 1855.

FIRST PAINTING GALLERY

Maharaja Ram Singh, a 19th century king of Jaipur built a unique hall in the garden of the Ram Niwas Bagh Palace. It was fully displayed with paintings and called the Ram Vilas. The walls of this hall were covered with imitations of several Greek, Roman, Persian, and Chinese paintings.

Raja Ravi Varma's painting, *Damayanthi*

FIRST REALIST PAINTER

Raja Ravi Varma (1848–1906) from the princely state of Travancore (now in Kerala) painted themes mainly from Indian mythology and legends in the realistic style of the West, making him the first realist painter in the country and the pioneer of a new movement in Indian art. Lord Curzon, the then viceroy bestowed the Kaisar-i-Hind Gold Medal on him in 1904.

FIRST ACADEMY OF VISUAL ARTS

The Lalit Kala Akademi was set up at Delhi in 1954 as a national academy of fine arts. It has regional centres known as Rashtriya Lalit Kala Kendra at Lucknow, Kolkata, Chennai, Mumbai, Bhubaneswar, Garhi NERC Agartala and Ahmedabad. The Akademi organises national exhibitions of contemporary Indian art, gives awards, organizes Triennale-India once every three years and also organizes a Rashtriya Kala Mela (national art fair) where artists from all over the country present their work.

The Lalit Kala Akademi awards up to 40 scholarships in a year.

FIRST AUCTION OF CONTEMPORARY INDIAN PAINTINGS ABROAD

On 12 June 1995, Sotheby's hosted the first-ever auction of contemporary Indian paintings in New York, US. The 38 artists whose works were displayed included Jogen Chowdhury, M.F. Husain, Arpita Singh, Ganesh Pyne, S.H. Raza, and Jamini Roy.

FIRST ART BANK

Set up in 2007 by curator Adishwar Puri, the Art Bank, primarily for novice collectors apprehensive of making bad choices, now has corporations, government institutions, banks, and hospitals as clients. The artists who register benefit by receiving 50 per cent of the rental value of the work.

FIRST ART SUMMIT

Held between 22–24 August 2008 at Pragati Maidan, New Delhi, the first India Art Summit had 34 exhibition galleries that exhibited over 550 artworks and sold more than half of them. The summit was brought to India by Hanmer MS&L Communications Pvt. Ltd.

FIRST WINNER OF THE USF WORLD CHAMPIONSHIP

Sand artist Sudarsan Pattnaik won the first prize at the USF World Championship on 12 June 2008 at Berlin, Germany. With sand artists participating from countries like Denmark, Spain, Morocco, Italy, France, etc. the championship started on 5 June. Pattnaik created a 25 ft sculpture with the plea 'Save my family' held up by a polar bear image at the top. Pattnaik and his student Jitendra Kishore Jagadev were the only representatives from India at the competition. The sculpture showed the horrors of climate change and global warming.

FIRST TO BE INVITED AT MONUMENTA

Monumenta is an artistic project where each year an internationally-renowned artist is invited to turn their vision to the vast Nave of Paris' Grand Palais, Paris, and to create a new artwork especially for this space. For its fourth year, the French Ministry for Culture and Communication invited Anish Kapoor to produce a new work between 11 May to 23 June 2011. Anish Kapoor's gigantic sculpture, 'Leviathan' consisted of three linked spheres that stretched 35 yards into the air. Over two years it was engineered in Britain and designed in Italy, while Kapoor turned to French textile manufacturers Serge Ferrari to create the uniquely tinted and light-sensitive fabric that was inflated to fill more than half of the Grand Palais. The exhibition, which the artist dedicated to Chinese artist Ai Weiwei, received more than 250,000 visitors.

A poster for Anish Kapoor's exhibition at Monumenta 2011

FIRST PUBLIC ART DISTRICT

The Lodhi Art District in New Delhi, inaugurated by the Central Public Works Department on 1 March 2019, is the first public art district in the country. Conceptualized and realized by the St+Art India Foundation, a not-for-profit that works on art projects in open spaces, the artistic transformation of the district began in 2015.

With the support of the local community and civic and cultural bodies, more than 50 artists of 23 nationalities have reimagined the area's facades by creating murals that bring the viewer into a contemporary urban art museum. A total of 56 walls with an area of approximately 16,310 sq. m have been painted by the artists. This was followed by the Mahim (East) art district in Mumbai, Maharashtra; the Maqta art district in Hyderabad, Telangana; and the Panjim (Panaji) art district in Goa.

FIRST OFFICIALLY RECOGNIZED FEMALE GRAFFITI ARTIST

Kajal Singh from New Delhi is the first recognized female graffiti artist from India. Her art form includes the use of bright colours and different font styles that instantly pop out. Besides India, she has left her signature in countries like Germany, China, US, Russia, and Indonesia. She was part of the Indo-German Hip-Hop Urban Art Project (2012), Each One Teach One (2013), 25 Years of the Berlin Wall (2014), Hip-Hop Cultural Exchange (2015), and On The Run Exhibition (2016). She was honoured as the 'First Lady' of graffiti in India by the Ministry of Women and Child Development, Government of India on 20 January 2018.

LIBRARIES AND MUSEUMS

FIRST LIBRARY

A library was set up by Christian missionaries at Serampore, Bengal (now Srirampur, West Bengal) in 1800 (later the William Carey Library), which became the central hub of their educational activities. Reverend John Fountain, who was sent to India in 1796 to assist William Carey, a missionary, took charge as the first librarian.

FIRST MOBILE LIBRARY

On 21 October 1931, a bullock cart (shaped like a small stall), laden with books at Melavasal, a village near Mannargudi in Tamil Nadu is reportedly the first mobile library in the country. Initiated by Rao Bahadur S.V. Kanagasabai Pillai, an engineer, the library was inaugurated by S.R. Ranganathan, better known as the 'father of library science' in India. The mobile library carried books on topics such as beekeeping and other cottage industries, aiming to equip farmers with vocational training. A replica of the cart is displayed at the Tamil University in Thanjavur, Tamil Nadu.

FIRST SCIENCE MUSEUM

Industrialist Ghanshyam Das Birla (1894–1983) set up the first science museum at Birla Institute of Technology and Science (BITS), Pilani, Rajasthan, in 1954. The museum displays exhibits on science and technology that are interactive so as to ease the understanding and accessibility of science and technology. It was shifted to a building specially designed for it in 1965.

FIRST RAILWAY MUSEUM

The Rail Transport Museum was inaugurated by Kamlapati Tripathi, the then minister of railways, on 1 February 1977, at Chanakyapuri, New Delhi. It was the first rail museum in India. In 1955, it was renamed the National Rail Museum and it features historical exhibits and artefacts related to the history of rail transport in India.

Locomotive number plates at the National Rail Museum

FIRST MUSEUM OF UTENSILS

Vishalla Environmental Centre for Heritage of Art, Architecture and Research (VECHAAR), houses heritage utensils, including 5,400 pans, pots, serving vessels and other kitchen equipment in a village-like complex in Ahmedabad, Gujarat. The museum was set up by its collector and owner, Surendra C. Patel and anthropologist Jyotindra Jain in April 1981.

FIRST KITE MUSEUM

The rarest kites in the world are housed in a museum in Ahmedabad, Gujarat. Established in 1985 by Bhanubhai Shah, whose generous donation of over 50 years to the Ahmedabad Municipal Corporation kickstarted the project. Kites in various shapes and sizes are housed in the basement of Sanskar Kendra.

FIRST OPERATIONAL DIGITAL LIBRARY NETWORK

Started as a project of the India International Centre, New Delhi, in 1988, DELNET was the first operational digital library network. It was registered as a society in 1992.

The National Library, Kolkata, has more than 2.6 million books and 500,000 manuscripts and is the largest in the country in terms of books.

FIRST MUSEUM OF TOILETS

The Sulabh International Museum of Toilets at Mahavir Enclave in New Delhi was established in 1992 and is the first of its kind in the world. A museum dedicated to toilets, it has 300 exhibits with a mix of originals, models and photographs. Tracing a history of over 4,500 years, the museum charts a chronological journey in terms of developments in technology, social etiquettes and customs and legislative efforts through its exhibits.

FIRST ONLINE BRAILLE LIBRARY

The National Institute for the Visually Handicapped (NIVH), Dehradun, Uttarakhand, launched the online Braille library in 2012 to commemorate the birth anniversary of Louis Braille on 4 January. The library has made accessible 12,000 books in over 10 languages in a user-friendly format.

FIRST TRANSPORT MUSEUM

The Heritage Transport Museum in Haryana opened on 7 December 2013. It has an elaborate collection of 2,500 objects, including bullock carts, palanquins, vintage scooters, a 1946 Piper aircraft, transport toys from the 1920s to now, and other related artefacts.

FIRST CLASSICAL LIBRARY

The Murty Classical Library of India was set up with the mission to present pre-modern classics of Indian literature from the past two millenniums to a new generation. The classics were published first in January 2015. The classics are printed in a way that the original text is accompanied by a modern English translation on the opposite page.

FIRST TRANSGENDER RESOURCES LIBRARY

As part of the transgender resource centre in Viswanathapuram, Tamil Nadu, India's first transgender library was opened in 2016. The primary focus of the centre is to make accessible materials that would help educate people about non-binary gender and ambisexual people.

FIRST ELECTION MUSEUM

Located in the office premises of the chief electoral officer at Kashmiri Gate, Delhi, the Election Museum was inaugurated in 2016. It depicts the journey of the elections in India that began in 1952, through four sections: library, audio-visuals, photo gallery and electoral management. The display constitutes over 200 archived photographs, maps, references and artefacts.

FIRST UNDERGROUND MUSEUM

The Rashtrapati Bhavan houses India's first underground museum that was opened on 2 October 2016. It showcases a collection of artefacts associated with all the past presidents of the country, including items such as their personal belongings and vehicles along with exhibits that showcase the history of India's struggle for freedom. More than 2,000 artefacts are on display in the 12,077.39 sq. m space.

FIRST PARTITION MUSEUM

Amritsar, Punjab is home to the world's first museum on the Partition of India. Set up on 24 October 2016, the museum is housed in a restored portion of the Town Hall and commemorates the victims of the partition, its survivors and the legacy it carries. Photographs, clothes, utensils and memorabilia of the time are showcased at the museum.

FIRST SPORTS MUSEUM – PERSONAL COLLECTION

Fanattic Sports Museum, located at Ecospace in New Town, Kolkata, over an area of 622.45 sq. m was opened in 2017. The multi-sports museum displays memorabilia from cricket, hockey, football, the Olympics and Paralympics. Boria Majumdar's (a renowned cricket historian) collection of over 25 years is also on display. Highlights of the museum include Sachin Tendulkar's glove, Lionel Messi's shoe, artefacts donated by Olympic gold medallist Abhinav Bindra and Paralympics silver medallist Deepa Malik, among others.

FIRST WAX MUSEUM

In December 2017, the Madame Tussauds Delhi, a part of the famous international chain of wax museums was opened in New Delhi. Over 40 life-size wax sculptures of political leaders, and celebrities from sports and music, to cinema and politics were on display. It was shifted to DLF Mall of India, Noida, Uttar Pradesh, in 2022.

FIRST INTERACTIVE MUSEUM OF MUSIC

The Indian Music Experience (IME), in Bengaluru, Karnataka provides a unique experience. An interactive museum, set up in 2018, it showcases the musical journey and the visitors can interact with the instruments to create their own music. It has a sound garden with at least 10 musical sculptures that can be played. Small theatres, audio-video kiosks, a learning centre that offers music classes and workshops regularly.

FIRST NATIONAL MUSEUM OF INDIAN CINEMA

The National Museum of Indian Cinema (NMIC) in Mumbai, Maharashtra, was inaugurated in January 2019. It was conceived in 1997 and has been designed by the National Council of Science Museums, implemented by the Films Division, under the Ministry of Information and Broadcasting, Government of India. Placed in a 19th century heritage bungalow, Gulshan Mahal, it extends to a newer high-tech building with five floors. Projectors, recording equipment, archived posters, cameras and biographies of cinema personalities are on display in the museum.

Prime Minister Narendra Modi at the National Museum of Indian Cinema, Mumbai

FIRST DINOSAUR MUSEUM

The Dinosaur Museum at the Balasinor Dinosaur Park in Gujarat was inaugurated in June 2019. The museum is equipped with modern technology like 3D projection, virtual reality (VR) presentations, life-size dinosaur replicas and interactive kiosks. The displays including fossil records from the area depict the history of dinosaurs such as the *Rajasaurus narmadensis* from origin to extinction.

THE PRIME MINISTERS' MUSEUM

Located in the Teen Murti Estate in New Delhi, the Pradhanmantri Sangrahalaya, is a museum to celebrate all former Prime Ministers of India. Inaugurated on 14 April 2022, the museum consists of 43 galleries showcasing the lives and tenures of former Prime Ministers.

> The Pradhanmantri Sangrahalaya received 115,161 visitors in the first six months.

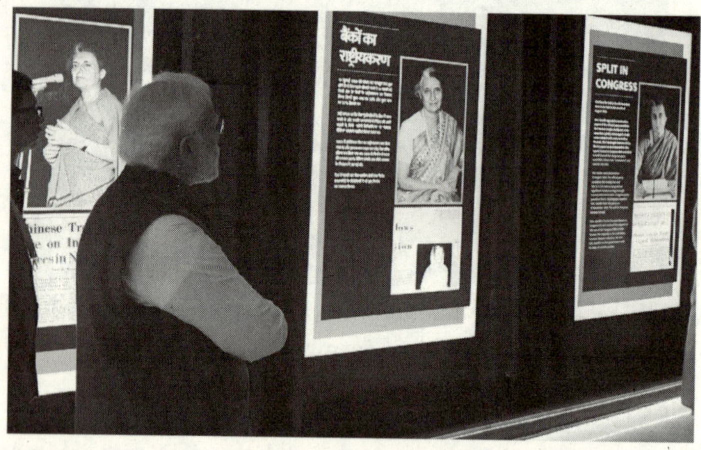

Prime Minister Narendra Modi at the inauguration of the Pradhanmantri Sangrahalaya

MEDIA AND COMMUNICATIONS

TIMELINE

EARLY PERIOD

- 321–297 BCE – Earliest evidence of a formalised postal service was evidenced in the reign of Chandragupta Maurya
- 1556 – First printing press comes to India
- 1780s – Print media begins in India
- 1846–1904 – Evidences of a regular postal system using Bullocks
- 1852 – First stamp called the Scinde Dawk is released

20TH CENTURY

- 1921 – First amateur Radio is licensed
- 1927 – Beginning of Radio broadcasting
- 1931 – First Pigeongram
- 1936 – All India Radio is established
- 1959 – Doordarshan is launched
- 1966 – Press Council of India is formed
- 1982 – Colour TVs are introduced

- 1986 – Mahanagar Telephone Nigam Limited (MTNL) is established
- 1987 – Ramanand Sagar's *Ramayan* launched on Television
- 1990s – Emergence of Satellite Television
- 1993 – Experiments with privatising radio broadcasting
- 1995 – First mobile call made between Jyoti Basu and Sukh Ram; Videsh Sanchar Nigam Limited (VSNL) becomes the first provider of Internet services
- 1997 – Telecom Regulatory Authority of India (TRAI) is established

21ST CENTURY

- 2000 – Bharat Sanchar Nigam Limited (BSNL) is formed; arrival of cable internet; first net fax service begins
- 2003 – Private and Direct-to-Home (DTH) services begin in India
- 2005 – Orkut, a social media site launched in India
- 2010 – 3G spectrum is auctioned by the Government
- 2012 – 4G services are offered
- 2013 – The last telegram is sent
- 2015 – Over-the-top (OTT) services gain popularity
- 2019 – Merger of MTNL and BSNL announced
- 2020 – India crosses 500 million internet users
- 2022 – 5G services launched

FIRST EVIDENCE OF POSTAL COMMUNICATION

The earliest evidence of a systematic mail service in India can be found during the reign of Chandragupta Maurya (r. 321–297 BCE), when confidential reports were dispatched from the emperor to the outlying provinces, and from the provinces back to the ruler. Alauddin Khilji (r. 1296–1316) was known to organize a regular foot-runner service as early as 1296. Sikandar Lodi (r. 1488–1518), set up small posts across his kingdom to send firmans daily to his armies and Babur (r. 1483–1530), the founder of the Mughal Empire, set up horse couriers from his capital at Agra up to Kabul, maintaining a regular 'postal' system.

FIRST PRINTING PRESS

In 1556, the first printing press came to India, when the patriarch designate of Abyssnia (now Ethiopia, Africa) broke his journey at Goa. Upon his passing the printing press was left behind. A Spaniard called João de Bustamante and his Indian assistant were the printers.

FIRST POST OFFICE

The first post office in the country was set up in 1727 by the East India Company in Calcutta, Bengal (now Kolkata, West Bengal). It was later merged with the General Post Office, Kolkata. Designed by Walter B. Grenville in 1864, the building has the Philatelic Bureau at one end. Here is a table about the firsts in many different types of post-offices in the country:

Type	Location	Date/Year of Establishment
First all-woman post office	Coimbatore, Tamil Nadu	January 1966
First drive-in post office	Pune, Maharashtra	11 November 1975
First post office outside India	Dakshin Gangotri, Antarctica	24 February 1984
First floating post office	Srinagar, Jammu and Kashmir	2011
First mobile post office	Started in Pune, Maharashtra	1 November 2011

FIRST NEWSPAPER

India's first and also Asia's first newspaper, *Hicky's Bengal Gazette* or the *Original Calcutta General Advertiser,* was launched on 29 June 1780 by James Augustus Hicky.

HICKY's
BENGAL GAZETTE;
OR THE ORIGINAL
Calcutta General Advertiser.

Hicky's Bengal Gazette

FIRST PRESS REGULATION

The first regulation introducing an element of censorship to enforce restrictions related to wartime press was part of the Censorship of Press Act of 1799. This was enacted by Lord Wellesley, the then governor general who anticipated a French invasion in India. A special administration unit scrutinized each publication to prevent information leaks.

FIRST MULTILINGUAL PRESS

Christian missionaries set up a multilingual press for all the main local Indian languages in 1800 in Serampore, Bengal (now Srirampur, West Bengal).

FIRST MAIL BY STEAMBOAT

The earliest recorded mail delivery in Asia, was in 1828 when a mail was sent by a steamboat service between Calcutta and Allahabad (now Prayagraj), along 1,266 km of the River Ganga.

Chandamama is the oldest known children's magazine and was launched in July 1947 in Telugu.

FIRST DEAD LETTER OFFICE

A dead letter office or a returned letter office, is a post office for undelivered and unclaimed letters. The first such post office in India was set up during 1834–37 in Benson Town in Bangalore (now Bengaluru), Karnataka.

FIRST POSTMEN

Postmen were first engaged on a security bond as part of the postal reforms carried out in 1840 in Bengal. They were dressed in uniform and wore badges supplied by the post office. They were allowed to earn baksheesh of

2 pies (1 pie=1/192 of a rupee) on each letter delivered, in addition to the collection of postage due to the post office.

FIRST USE OF BIRDS AND ANIMALS FOR MAIL

- **Bullock mail:** Between 1846 and 1904, bullock carts were used along the Grand Trunk Road between Allahabad, and Delhi to deliver mail. As many as 41 government employed bullock 'trains' operated in the north-west regions and Punjab by 1875.
- **Camel post office:** On 27 October 1977, a mobile post office on camelback was started at Mithariya, Bikaner District, Rajasthan. The postmaster was given a special allowance for maintaining the camel.
- **Pigeon post:** The first pigeongram was carried from Asansol to Calcutta on 18 February 1931 in Bengal with 42 homing pigeons (21 military and 21 civilian). Till 2004, the Odisha Police used pigeons as messengers and had around 900 homing pigeons.

FIRST STAMP

India's first stamp was the half-anna, Scinde Dawk (Provincial) and was issued with the help of Edward Lees Coffey, the postmaster of Karachi, on 1 July 1852 in Scinde District, Karachi (now in Pakistan). It was embossed on circular red wafers used as seals on letters, with the East India Company emblem and the legend Scinde District Dawk around the circumference. Withdrawn in 1854, it was Asia's first ever adhesive stamp. Here's a look at the different kinds of stamps issued in the country:

Type of stamp	Date/Year of Issue	Details
First Commemorative	9 February 1931	To celebrate the laying of the foundation of Delhi as the capital, these stamps featured six important landmarks of the city
First of Independent India	21 November 1947	It featured the inscription 'Jai Hind'
First charity stamps	26 January 1950	Three 'Healthy India' stamps were brought out in denominations of one anna, four annas and one rupee
First featuring a woman	1 October 1952	The stamp featured Mirabai, a 16th century Bhakti poet
First autograph inscribed	7 May 1961	To commemorate the birth centenary of Rabindranath Tagore, the stamp had his signature inscribed on it
First featuring wildlife	1962	It was a 15-paisa stamp featuring the Indian Rhinoceros

First featuring a foreigner	8 May 1963	Henri Durant, the first recipient of the Nobel Prize
First featuring a sportsperson	27 September 1973	It featured cricketer Sir Ranjitsinhji Vibhaji Jadeja
First issued jointly with another country	1987	India and erstwhile USSR issued a set of two stamps on the Festival of India in the USSR
First aromatic	2006	It had the scent of sandalwood

FIRST LETTER BOXES

In October 1854, letter boxes that were located away from the post offices were introduced, marking a new milestone in the history of Indian post.

FIRST INDIAN POSTMASTER GENERAL

Men: Rai Bahadur Saligram became the first Indian postmaster general for the North-Western Provinces in 1881.

Women: Sushila Chaurasia became the first woman to become postmaster general in the country. She assumed charge of the Madhya Pradesh circle on 24 May 1979.

The last telegram was sent on 14 July 2013 from Delhi ending a 163–year-old telegram service.

FIRST AIRMAIL

On 18 February 1911, Henri Pequet flew a Humber-Sommer

biplane from Allahabad to Naini (a distance of only 18 km) carrying 6,500 letters and postcards in India's and the world's first air mail.

FIRST RADIO BROADCAST

The Radio Club of Bombay made the first ever broadcast in the country in June 1923, from Bombay (now Mumbai, Maharashtra). Following this, the Calcutta Radio Club was set up West Bengal in about five months.

FIRST NEWSPAPER TO BE PRINTED IN COLOUR

The *Hindu,* headquartered in Madras (now Chennai, Tamil Nadu), started off as a weekly in 1878 and became a daily in 1889. In 1940, this family run newspaper, was the first to be printed in colour. It was also the first Indian newspaper to own aeroplanes to distribute newspapers (1963), and the first newspaper to digitize and be available online (1995).

FIRST NEWS AGENCY

The Press Trust of India (PTI), a non-profit sharing cooperative of Indian newspapers, was established on 27 August 1947. It provided news, photographs, features and infographics after taking over the Associated Press of India and the Indian operations of Reuters from February 1949 onwards.

A stamp commemorating the Press Trust of India

FIRST NEWSPRINT FACTORY

A factory at Nepanagar, Burhanpur District, Madhya Pradesh was the first paper mill in India to manufacture newsprint in January 1955.

The largest philatelic bureau in the country is the Mumbai General Post Office Philatelic Bureau.

FIRST POSTWOMAN

On 19 February 1959, K. Padmakshy Amma joined service in the Thiruvananthapuram postal division in Kerala as the country's first postwoman.

FIRST TV TELECAST

On 15 September 1959 the first experimental TV telecast was carried out in Delhi from a makeshift studio with the help of a single transmitter of 500W, that could carry signals up to 25 km for an operational time of one hour per day. The studio was later relocated to Rajpath for the first live telecast of the Republic Day parade in 1960.

FIRST STD SERVICE

Lucknow and Kanpur in Uttar Pradesh got the facility for subscriber trunk dialling (STD) on 26 November 1960.

FIRST NEWSREADER

Pratima Puri became the first TV newsreader when she did a five-minute news bulletin for Doordashan in 1965.

FIRST ISD SERVICE

The first operator-dialled service to international subscribers was set up using the Arvi earth station for satellite communication in Arvi near Poona (now Pune), Maharashtra in 1971. Commissioned in 1973, the first intercontinental telephone exchange and the first international subscriber dialling (ISD) telephone service was introduced between Bombay (now Mumbai), Maharashtra, and London, UK, in 1976.

FIRST FREQUENCY MODULATION (FM) SERVICE

All India Radio (AIR) inagurated an FM service from Madras on 23 July 1977. Radio City Bangalore was the first private radio station and was launched on 3 July 2001.

All India Radio is the largest media organization in the country covering 92 per cent of the country while broadcasting in 23 languages and 179 dialects.

FIRST NATIONAL TV TELECAST

Nationwide telecasts on Doordarshan began on 15 August 1982 from its TV studio in Mandi House, New Delhi.

A stamp commemorating Doordarshan

FIRST PRIVATE CHANNEL

Launched in October 1992, Zee TV, became the first private television channel in the country, in collaboration with Star TV and Zee Telefilms Ltd.

FIRST PRIVATE FM BROADCASTER

The Times Group launched Times FM in 1993 from Ahmedabad, Gujarat. It ran till June 1998 and was then relaunched as Radio Mirchi in 2000. Over the years, Radio Mirchi has seen a successful coverage and has expanded its presence across 63 cities in India and multiple stations in the UAE and the US.

FIRST CHAIRMAN OF THE WORLDTEL INITIATIVE

Satyanarayan Gangaram Pitroda (b. 1942), popularly known as Sam Pitroda is a telecommunication engineer and entrepreneur. Hailing from Odisha, he has revolutionised Indian telecommunication. As a telecommunication engineer in US, he filed many patents regarding his inventions, including the electronic diary. However, his visits to India highlighted the big gap in telecommunications and he chose to change the story. He was the principle advisor of the Centre for Development of Telematics (C-DOT), a facility for research and development, started by the Government of India on 25 August 1984. In 1995, he was appointed as the chairman of the WorldTel initiative by the

Satyanarayan Gangaram 'Sam' Pitroda (right)

International Telecommunication Union which focussed on the growth and development of telecommunication services in developing countries. He was awarded the Lal Bahadur Shastri National Award in 2000 and the prestigious World Telecommunication and Information Society Award in 2011.

FIRST PRIVATE PRODUCER OF NATIONAL NEWS

New Delhi Television Ltd (NDTV) became the first private producer of national news in February 1995 with the show titled 'The News Tonight'. The show was hosted by Prannoy Roy at 8 p.m.

FIRST CALL USING A MOBILE PHONE

Sukh Ram, the then union telecom minister and Jyoti Basu, the then chief minister of West Bengal spoke to one another over handheld mobile phones on 31 July 1995, over Modi Telstra's MobileNet service.

FIRST PROVIDER OF INTERNET SERVICES

The first provider of Internet services in India was Videsh Sanchar Nigam Limited (VSNL), under DoT, Ministry of Telecommunications, Government of India. It was launched on 15 August 1995.

On 31 January 1948, the radio commentary by Melville de Mellow on Mahatma Gandhi's last journey ran for more than seven continuous hours.

FIRST CELLULAR SERVICE

The first cellular service provider in the country was Modi Telstra, a joint-venture company of the B.K. Modi Group and the Telstra Corporation of Australia on 23 August 1995. The network was constructed by Telecommunication Engineering Centre and the Modi Telstra team.

FIRST FREE EMAIL SERVICE

Hotmail was the first free email service launched in 1996 by Sabeer Bhatia and his colleague Jack Smith. An Indian American businessman, Sabeer led Hotmail as its president and CEO until its eventual acquisition by Microsoft in 1998.

FIRST NET FAX SERVICE

On 25 April 2000, Satyam Infoway launched Satyamfax in association with Singapore Telecom, becoming the first to provide fax to fax, web to fax, email to fax, and PC desktop to fax services.

FIRST SHORT MESSAGE SERVICE (SMS) PROVIDER

The first SMS provider in India was Hutchison Max that offered a global text messaging service in 2001.

FIRST 3G OPERATORS

Mahanagar Telephone Nigam Limited (MTNL), a public sector telecom service provider was the first to provide 3G mobile service in parts of Delhi in December 2008. The first private service provider to extend this service was Tata Docomo when it launched its 3G mobile service on 5 November 2010.

FIRST DIRECT-TO-HOME (DTH) SERVICE

Dish TV was launched on 2 October 2013 and was the first DTH service in India.

FIRST HOT-AIR BALLOON CARRYING MAIL

On 3 January 2016, a special postal cover was carried in a hot-air balloon carrier of India Post from Sakthi Mills Ground, Coimbatore District, Tamil Nadu, to the postmaster of Kovipalayam, Pollachi.

FIRST TELECOM COMPANY TO LAUNCH 5G SERVICES

Bharti Airtel became the first telecom service in the country to launch 5G services on 1 October 2022. The services were launched in eight cities including, Delhi, Mumbai, Varanasi and Bengaluru. Earlier on 28 January 2021, Bharati Airtel successfully demonstrated live 5G services over a commercial network in Hyderabad, Telangana. The carrier displayed 10x speed, 10x latency (this is the time taken for data to pass from one point to another) and 100x concurrency (multiple instructions executed at the same time) in comparison to the technologies that existed before it.

An office building of Bharti Airtel

SPORTS

TIMELINE

EARLY PERIOD

- 3rd millennium BCE – Dholavira, Gujarat shows traces of a stadium with terraced stands
- 4th century BCE – Origins of Kabaddi are attributed to this period
- 13th century – Indigenous forms of wrestling exist such as Malla-Yuddha which later developed into 'Dangals' and eventually modern-day wrestling in India
- 19th century – Snooker originates in India among the British Army officers stationed here; Modern Polo evolved from existing games such as *Kanjei-bazee* or *Pulu* that was played in Assam

20TH CENTURY

- 1900 – Norman Pritchard represents India in the Paris Olympics and wins two silver medals
- 1920 – India sends an official contingent to the 1920 Antwerp Olympics
- 1924 – The National Games of India are held for the first time
- 1927 – Indian Olympic association is formed

- 1928 – India wins its first gold medal at the Olympics (Hockey); The Board of Control for Cricket in India (BCCI) is formed
- 1934 – India makes a debut at the Commonwealth Games
- 1951 – The first ever Asian Games are held in New Delhi
- 1958 – Milkha Singh, the 'Flying Sikh' (Athletics) wins three gold medals at the Asian Games
- 1968 – India makes its debut at the Olympic Paralympic games
- 1981 – India participates in the inaugural World Games
- 1983 – India wins its first Cricket World Cup under the captaincy of Kapil Dev
- 1984 – India participates in the South Asian Games
- 1986 – P.T. Usha (Athletics) wins four gold medals at the Asian Games

21ST CENTURY

- 2008 – Abhinav Bindra (Shooting) wins the first individual gold medal at the Olympics
- 2010 – India hosts the Commonwealth Games
- 2011 – India wins the Cricket World Cup under the captaincy of Mahendra Singh Dhoni
- 2019 – P.V. Sindhu becomes the first Badminton World Champion; Mary Kom becomes the first boxer in the world to win eight World Championship medals
- 2020 – Neeraj Chopra wins the first gold medal in Athletics at the Olympics; Motera stadium, the largest in the world is completed
- 2023 – India crossed the 100-medal mark at the Asian Games

ARCHERY

FIRST WINS IN THE ASIAN GAMES

Event	Medal	Athlete/Team	Games
Men			
Individual Recurve	Silver	Tarundeep Rai	2010 Guangzhou
Team Recurve	Silver	Atanu Das, Dhiraj Bommadevara and Tushar Shelke	2022 Hangzhou*
	Bronze	Mangal Singh Champia, Tarundeep Rai, Jayanta Talukdar and Vishwas	2006 Doha
Individual compound	Gold	Ojas Pravin Deotale	2022 Hangzhou
	Silver	Abhishek Verma	2014 Incheon
Team Compound	Gold	Rajat Chauhan, Sandeep Kumar and Abhishek Verma	2014 Incheon
	Silver	Rajat Chauhan, Aman Saini and Abhishek Verma	2018 Jakarta – Palembang
Women			
Team Recurve	Bronze	Dola Banerjee, Rimil Buriuly and Deepika Kumari	2010 Guangzhou
Individual Compound	Gold	Jyothi Surekha Vennam	2022 Hangzhou

* The games were held in the year 2023 due to the COVID-19 pandemic but were called 2022 Asian Games

	Bronze	Trisha Deb	2014 Incheon
Team Compound	Gold	Aditi Swami, Jyothi Surekha Vennam and Parneet Kaur	2022 Hangzhou
	Silver	Muskan Kirar, Madhumita Kumari and Jyothi Surekha Vennam	2018 Jakarta – Palembang
	Bronze	Trisha Deb, Purvasha Shende and Jyothi Surekha Vennam	2014 Incheon
Mixed			
Team Compound	Gold	Jyothi Surekha Vennam and Ojas Pravin Deotale	2022 Hangzhou

FIRST WINS AT THE COMMONWEALTH GAMES

Archery is an optional sport at the Commonwealth Games and has featured twice, once in 1982 Brisbane and then in 2010 New Delhi games. India won all its eight medals in the sport in 2010. In the men's individual recurve event, Rahul Banerjee and Jayanta Talukdar won the gold and bronze medal respectively. For the men's recurve team event, they teamed up along with Tarundeep Rai and scored the bronze medal. The men's compound team comprised of Ritul Chatterjee, Jignas Chittibomma and Chinna Raju Srither and they won the silver medal. In the Women's events, Deepika Kumari won the gold medal and Dola Banerjee won the bronze medal in the Women's recurve individual event. For the women's recurve team event, Dola Banerjee, Deepika Kumari and Bombayla Devi Laishram teamed up

Deepika Kumari (center)
and Dola Banerjee (right)

to snatch the gold medal. The women's compound team won the bronze medal and the team comprised Bheigyabati Chanu, Jhano Hansdah and Gagandeep Kaur.

FIRST OLYMPICS REPRESENTATION

Men: The Indian national archery team, with Shyam Lal, Limba Ram and Sanjeeva Singh, participated in the individual and team archery events at the Olympics in 1988 at Seoul, South Korea.

Women: The first women to represent India in archery were Dola Banerjee, Reena Kumari and Sumangala Sharma at the 2004 Olympic Games in Athens, Greece.

Archery comes from the Latin word 'arcus' which means bow.

FIRST GOLD MEDAL IN THE ASIAN PARA GAMES

India's maiden archery gold was won by Harvinder Singh in the Asian Para Games 2018 in the men's individual recurve. He outplayed China's Zhao Lixue 6–0 in the W2/ST category.

FIRST MEDAL IN PARALYMPIC GAMES

Harvinder Singh clinched India's first-ever archery medal at the 2020 Paralympics by winning the bronze medal in the men's singles recurve archery in Tokyo, Japan.

Pooja Khanna was the first to qualify for Paralympic games in 2016.

FIRST WORLD ARCHERY PARA CHAMPIONSHIPS GOLD

Sarita and Rakesh Kumar won the gold medal by beating Brazil in the final, winning India's first gold medal in World Archery Para Championships in 2023.

FIRST TO WIN TWO GOLD MEDALS IN A SINGLE EDITION OF THE ASIAN PARA GAMES

Sheetal Devi, a teenager from Jammu and Kashmir, won a total of three medals, including two gold at the Asian Para Games in 2023 in Hangzhou, China. She is also the world's first armless archer to compete internationally.

Sheetal Devi ranked world No. 1 in Para archery in November 2023.

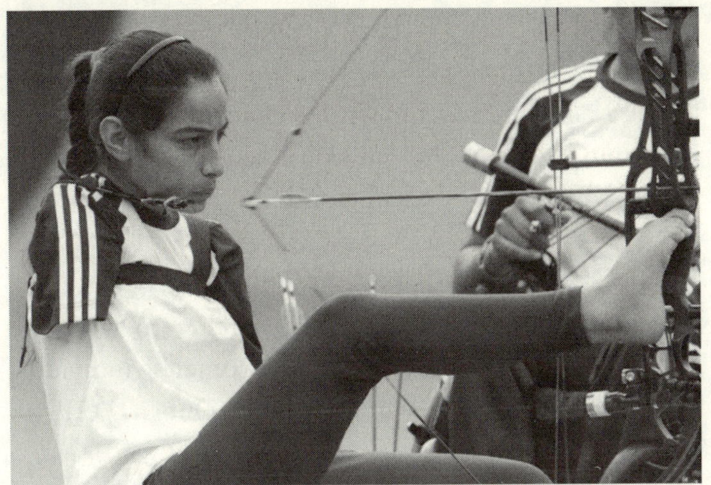

Sheetal Devi

FIRST MEDAL – WORLD CHAMPIONSHIP

In 2005, the Indian men's archery team won a silver medal, at the 43rd World Outdoor Target Archery Championship in Madrid, Spain. The recurve team comprised Tarundeep Rai, Gautam Singh Sardar, Jayanta Talukdar and Robin Hansda.

FIRST GOLD MEDAL – WOMEN'S COMPOUND TEAM – WORLD CHAMPIONSHIP

The Indian team comprising Jyothi Surekha Vennam, Aditi Swami and Parneet Kaur won the gold medal at the 2023 Berlin World Archery Championship. They beat Mexico 235–229 in the final.

FIRST INDIVIDUAL TITLE – WORLD CHAMPIONSHIP

Aditi Swami created history by clinching the women's compound gold in the individual category at the 2023 Berlin World Archery Championship.

FIRST GOLD MEDAL IN A WORLD CUP

Dola Banerjee is the only Indian archer to win gold in a World Cup final, in the women's individual recurve event at the World Cup in Dubai, UAE, in November 2007.

FIRST ARCHERY WORLD CUP TEAM GOLD – WOMEN

Rimil Buriuly, Bombayla Devi Laishram, and Deepika Kumari won the first back-to-back World Cup titles at the Archery World Cup (stage 4) at Wroclaw, Poland, on 25 August 2013, after winning the first medal at the World Cup (stage 3) in Medellin, Colombia, in July.

FIRST WORLD CUP COMPOUND TITLE – MEN

Team: The men's compound archery team of Abhishek Verma, Chinna Raju Srither, and Amarjeet Singh bagged the World Cup (stage 1) on 20 May 2017 in Shanghai, China, scoring 226–221 against Colombia.

Individual: Abhishek Verma won the World Cup (stage 3) event on 15 August 2015 at Wroclaw, Poland.

FIRST INDIAN COMPOUND ARCHERY WOMEN'S TEAM TO BE RANKED WORLD NO. 1

In 2018, the Indian compound archery women's team of Jyothi Surekha Vennam, P. Lily Chanu, Trisha Deb, Muskan Kirar, Divya Dhayal and Madhumita became the first ever team from India to be ranked world no. 1.

ATHLETICS

FIRST INDIVIDUAL MEDALS – WOMEN – ASIAN GAMES

Roshan Mistry bagged a silver in the 100 m race and Mary D'Souza won the bronze in the 200 m race in the 1951 Asian Games in Delhi.

FIRST INDIVIDUAL GOLD – ASIAN GAMES

Men: On 8 March 1951, Ranjit Singh won the gold in the 800 m marathon, clocking in at 1 hour 59 minutes 3 seconds.
Women: In 1970, Kamaljeet Sandhu won the 400 m race in 57.3 seconds.

FIRST DOUBLE GOLD AT THE ASIAN GAMES

Lavy Pinto won the first double gold at Asian Games in the 100 m and 200 m races in Delhi, 1951.

FIRST TEAM GOLD – ASIAN GAMES

Christine Brown, Violet Peters, Mary D'Souza and Stephanie D'Souza won the 4 x 100 m relay race with a timing of 49.5 seconds at the 1954 games held in Manila, Philippines in 1954.

FIRST MEDAL – COMMONWEALTH GAMES

Men: Milkha Singh won the gold medal at the 440 yards (400 m) race at the Cardiff games. This was also the first gold medal at the tournament.

Women: Anju Bobby George won the bronze medal in long jump with a best of 6.49 m at the 2002 Commonwealth Games in Manchester, UK. She was followed by Neelam J. Singh, who won a silver in the women's discus throw.

FIRST CLEAN SWEEP IN A MAJOR INTERNATIONAL MEET

Krishna Poonia, Harwant Kaur, and Seema Antil bagged the gold, silver, and bronze medals respectively in the women's discus throw in the 2010 Commonwealth Games in New Delhi.

FIRST MEDALLISTS – OLYMPICS

Event	Athlete	Medal	Games
Men's 200 m	Norman Pritchard	Silver	1900 Paris
Men's 200 m hurdles	Norman Pritchard	Silver	1900 Paris
Men's Javelin Throw	Neeraj Chopra	Gold	2020 Tokyo

Neeraj Chopra (left)

FIRST WOMEN AT THE OLYMPICS

Nilima Ghose and Mary D'Souza represented India in the 1952 Helsinki Olympics.

FIRST WOMAN CAPTAIN AT THE OLYMPICS

At the 1992 Olympic Games held in Barcelona, Spain, Shiny Wilson captained the Indian athletes' contingent.

On 24 September 2019, P.T. Usha was presented with the Veteran Pin by World Athletics.

FIRST PARTICIPATION IN THE PARALYMPICS

In 1968, India made its Paralympics debut at the Tel Aviv Games. India competed again in 1972 and then consistently from the 1984 New York Games in the US.

FIRST TRIPLE MEDAL IN THE PARALYMPICS

India's Joginder Singh Bedi had won three medals – a silver each in javelin and shot put, and a bronze in the discus throw – at the 1984 Paralympics in Stoke Mandeville and New York, US.

FIRST PARALYMPICS GOLD – WOMEN

Deepa Malik became the first Indian woman to win a medal at the Paralympics by bagging a silver medal in shot put in the 2016 Paralympic Games. She also won gold in the F-53/54 javelin event at the para athletic Grand Prix held in Dubai in 2018.

Deepa Malik

FIRST GOLD IN JAVELIN – PARALYMPICS – MEN

Sumit Antil won the gold medal in the men's javelin throw F64 category at the 2020 Summer Paralympics in Tokyo, Japan.

FIRST MEDAL – WORLD CHAMPIONSHIP

Anju Bobby George won a bronze in long jump at the 2003 World Championships in Paris, France, in August, with a leap of 6.70 m. She surpassed this at the 2004 Olympics in Athens, Greece, finishing sixth with a 6.83 m jump.

BADMINTON

FIRST WINS AT ASIAN GAMES

Category	Details
Men	
Team	Prakash Padukone, Davinder Ahuja, Dinesh Khanna, Partho Ganguli and Raman Ghosh – Bronze – 1974 Tehran
	Prannoy H.S., Lakshya Sen, Satwiksairaj Rankireddy, Chirag Shetty, Srikanth Kidambi, Mithun Manjunath, Arjun M.R., Dhruv Kapila, Rohan Kapoor and K. Sai Pratheek – Silver – 2022 Hangzhou
Singles	Syed Modi – Bronze – 1982 New Delhi
Doubles	Leroy D'Sa and Pradeep Gandhe – Bronze – 1982 New Delhi
	Satwiksairaj Rankireddy and Chirag Shetty – Gold – 2022 Hangzhou
Women	
Team	Arnita Kulkarni, Hufrish Nariman, Kanwal Thakur Singh, Ami Ghia, Madhumita Goswami and Vandana Chiplunkar – Bronze – 1982 New Delhi
Singles	Saina Nehwal – Bronze – 2018 Jakarta – Palembang
	P.V. Sindhu – Silver – 2018 Jakarta – Palembang
Mixed	
Doubles	Leroy D'Sa and Kanwal Singh Thakur – Bronze – 1982 New Delhi

Satwiksairaj (left) and Chirag Shetty (right): part of the silver medal winning team at the Asian Games

FIRST MEDALLIST – WOMEN – SINGLES – BWF WORLD TOUR FINALS

Gold: P.V. Sindhu won the title in 2018 in Guangzhou, China.

Silver: Saina Nehwal won the silver in Liuzhou, China in 2011.

Bronze: Saina Nehwal won a bronze in Kota Kinabalu, Sabah, Malaysia, in 2008.

Saina Nehwal

FIRST MEDALLIST – MEN – SINGLES – BWF WORLD TOUR FINALS

K. Srikanth bagged a bronze medal in Dubai, UAE, in 2014.

FIRST SILVER MEDALLISTS – MIXED – DOUBLES – BWF WORLD TOUR FINALS

V. Diju and Jwala Gutta finished runner-up in the mixed doubles in Johor Bahru, Malaysia, in 2009.

FIRST MEDAL – SINGLES – COMMONWEALTH GAMES

Men: In 1966, Dinesh Khanna won a bronze medal in the British Empire and Commonwealth Games.

Women: In 2002 in Manchester, UK, Aparna Popat won a bronze medal.

The game is believed to have originated in India among British expatriates.

FIRST MEDAL – TEAM – COMMONWEALTH GAMES

Men: In 1998, P. Gopichand, Abhinn Shyam Gupta, Jaseel P. Ismail, George Thomas, Marcos Bristow, Vincent Lobo and Nikhil Kanetkar won a silver in Kuala Lumpur.

Women: Manjusha Kanwar, P.V.V. Lakshmi, Aparna Popat, Madhumita Bisht, C. Deepthi, K. Neemila Chowdhary, Archana Deodhar won a bronze in Kuala Lumpur in 1998.

Mixed: Anup Sridhar, Rupesh Kumar, Chetan Anand, Aparna Popat, Jwala Gutta, Shruti Kurien, Saina Nehwal, Trupti Murgunde, V. Diju, and Sanave Thomas won the bronze in Melbourne in 2006.

FIRST MEDAL – DOUBLES – WOMEN – COMMONWEALTH GAMES

In 1978, Kanwal Thakur Singh and Ami Ghia won a bronze in Edmonton, Canada.

FIRST GOLD MEDALS AT THE COMMONWEALTH GAMES

Athlete/Team	Event	Games
Prakash Padukone	Men's singles	1978 Edmonton
Saina Nehwal	Women's singles	2010 New Delhi
Jwala Gutta and Ashwini Ponnappa	Women's doubles	2010 New Delhi
Team India	Mixed Team	2018 Gold Coast
Satwiksairaj Rankireddy and Chirag Shetty	Men's doubles	2022 Birmingham

FIRST NATIONAL CHAMPIONS

Name	Category	Year
Vijay Madgavkar	Men's – singles	1934
D. Minas and V. Minas	Men's – doubles	1934
T.P. Boland	Women's – singles	1935
T.P. Boland and Cameron	Women's – doubles	1935
N. Knight and I. Brydges	Mixed – doubles	1936

FIRST MEDAL – OLYMPICS

Saina Nehwal won the first medal, a bronze in the women's single event at the 2012 London Olympics.

FIRST SILVER MEDAL – OLYMPICS

At the 2016 Rio De Janeiro Olympic games, P.V. Sindhu bagged the silver medal in the women's singles event.

FIRST MEDALS – MEN'S SINGLES – PARALYMPICS

Gold: Promod Bhagar won the men's singles in the SL3 category in the 2020 Tokyo Paralympics.

Silver: Suhas Yathiraj won the silver medal in the SL4 category in Tokyo, Japan in 2020.

Bronze: Manoj Sarkar was the first bronze medallist winning his medal in the SL3 category in 2020 Tokyo Paralympics.

FIRST MEDALLIST – SINGLES – WORLD JUNIOR CHAMPIONSHIPS

Girls: Saina Nehwal won a silver medal in the girls' singles in Incheon, South Korea, in 2006.

Boys: R.M.V. Gurusaidutt claimed a bronze medal in the boys' singles in Pune, India, in 2008.

FIRST SILVER MEDALLIST – BOYS – SINGLES – WORLD JUNIOR CHAMPIONSHIPS

Siril Verma received a silver medal in the boys' singles in Lima, Peru, in 2015.

FIRST WINNER AT THE ALL ENGLAND CHAMPIONSHIP

Prakash Padukone won in London, UK, in 1980.

FIRST WINNER OF THE WORLD CUP – MEN – SINGLES

Prakash Padukone won in Kuala Lumpur, Malaysia, in 1981.

FIRST MEDAL IN THE UBER CUP – WOMEN'S – TEAM

India claimed its first bronze medal in New Delhi, India, in 2014.

FIRST MEDAL IN THE THOMAS CUP – MEN – TEAM CHAMPIONSHIP

India defeated Indonesia at the Thomas Cup 3-0 to win the prestigious title in 2022 for the first time ever, with World Championships medallist Lakshya Sen, K. Srikanth, Chirag Shetty and Satwiksairaj Rankireddy.

FIRST DUO TO WIN SUPER 1000 TITLE

Satwiksairaj Rankireddy and Chirag Shetty became the first Indian pair to win Super 1000 title as they won the men's doubles final at Indonesian

Prakash Padukone co-founded the Olympics Gold Quest, a non-profit to support Indian athletes and help them to work towards Olympic gold medals.

Open 2023. They are also the first Indian pair to win a BWF World Tour Title at all levels.

BOXING

FIRST WINS AT THE ASIAN GAMES

Event	Medal	Athlete	Games
Men			
Lightweight (48 Kg)	Bronze	Birju Shah	1994 Hiroshima
Lightweight (49 Kg)	Gold	Amit Panghal	2018 Jakarta – Palembang
Lightweight (60 Kg)	Bronze	Sunder Rao	1958 Tokyo
	Gold	Padam B. Mall	1962 Jakarta
Flyweight	Bronze	Chander Narayanan	1974 Tehran
	Silver	Shahuraj Birajdar	1986 Seoul
Bantamweight	Silver	Narayan More	1966 Bangkok
	Bronze	G.D. Kamble	1986 Seoul
	Gold	Dingko Singh	1998 Bangkok
Featherweight	Silver	Muniswamy Venu	1970 Bangkok
	Bronze	John Williams	1986 Seoul
Light welterweight	Bronze	C.C. Machaiah	1978 Bangkok
	Silver	Seera Jayaram	1986 Seoul
Welterweight	Bronze	C.C. Machaiah	1982 New Delhi
Light Middleweight	Bronze	Buddy D'Souza	1962 Jakarta
Middleweight	Silver	Hari Singh	1958 Tokyo
	Bronze	Surendra Sarkar	1962 Jakarta

	Gold	Vijender Singh	2010 Guangzhou
Light Heavyweight	Silver	Mehtab Singh	1974 Tehran
	Bronze	Dhan B. Gurung	1986 Seoul
Heavyweight	Gold	Hawa Singh	1966 Bangkok
	Silver	Til Bahadur	1974 Tehran
Super Heavyweight	Silver	Jaipal Singh	1986 Seoul
	Bronze	Raj K. Sangwan	1994 Hiroshima
	Bronze (+92 Kg)	Narender Berwal	2022 Hangzhou
Women			
Flyweight	Bronze	Mary Kom	2010 Guangzhou
	Gold	Mary Kom	2014 Incheon
Women's 50 Kg	Bronze	Nikhat Zareen	2022 Hangzhou
Women's 54 Kg	Bronze	Preeti Pawar	2022 Hangzhou
Women's 57 Kg	Bronze	Parveen Hooda	2022 Hangzhou
Lightweight	Bronze	Laishram S. Devi	2014 Incheon
Middleweight	Bronze	Kavita Goyat	2010 Guangzhou
Women's 75 Kg	Silver	Lovlina Borgohain	2022 Hangzhou

FIRST MEDALLISTS – MEN – COMMONWEALTH GAMES

Gold: Mohammed Ali Qamar won the gold medal in the lightweight category in Manchester, UK, in 2002.

Silver: Chandra Narayanan won the silver medal in 1974 at the Christchurch, New Zealand games.

Bronze: At the Christchurch, New Zealand games held in 1974, Muniswami Venu won the first bronze medal.

FIRST MEDALLISTS – WOMEN – COMMONWEALTH GAMES

Gold: Mary Kom at the 2018 Gold Coast games.

Silver: Laishram Sarita Devi at the 2014 Glasgow games.

Bronze: Pinki Rani at the 2014 Glasgow games.

FIRST NATIONAL CHAMPIONSHIP

The National Boxing Championship was organized for the first time by the Indian Amateur Boxing Federation in Bombay (now Mumbai) from 18–22 March 1950.

FIRST OLYMPIC MEDAL

Men: Vijender Singh won a bronze in the middleweight category in the 2008 Beijing Olympics.

Women: M.C. Mary Kom won a bronze in the 51 kg category in the 2012 London Olympics.

Mary Kom (left)

M.C. Mary Kom became the first Indian woman to receive the AIBA Legends award.

FIRST SILVER MEDAL IN THE WORLD BOXING CHAMPIONSHIPS – MEN

Amit Panghal was the first Indian male boxer to win a silver medal in the World

Boxing Championships 2019. Before this Indians have won six bronze medals.

FIRST WORLD BOXING CHAMPIONSHIPS MEDAL – WOMEN

M.C. Mary Kom from Manipur bagged a silver medal in the 48 kg category in the US in December 2001.

FIRST MEDAL IN THE WORLD CHAMPIONSHIP – SENIOR – MEN

Vijender Singh won a bronze medal in the 2009 Milan World Cup in Italy.

Vijender Singh

FIRST MEDAL AT THE WORLD CUP – MEN

Zoramthanga defeated teammate Dharmender Yadav 17–4 on points to win the light flyweight bronze on 17 November 1990 in Bombay, Maharashtra.

CHESS

FIRST GM NORM

In the 1985 Commonwealth championship in London, UK, Pravin Thipsay was the first to achieve GM norm.

FIRST GRANDMASTER (GM)

On 28 December 1987, Viswanathan Anand became India's first GM at the Sakthi Finance Grandmaster tournament in Coimbatore.

Viswanathan Anand

FIRST WINNER AT THE WORLD JUNIOR CHESS CHAMPIONSHIP

In 1987, Viswanathan Anand became the first Indian to win the World Junior Chess Championship when he was 18 years old.

Viswanathan Anand was the first player to win five titles of the Tata Steel Chess Tournament (previously called the Corus Chess Tournament).

FIRST INTERNATIONAL MASTER (IM)

Men: Manuel Aaron from Tamil Nadu became an International Master in 1961.

Women: S. Vijayalakshmi got the title of International Master in September 2000.

FIRST OLYMPIAD MEDAL

Rafiq Khan won a silver medal in the 1980 Olympiad.

FIRST WGM NORM

Bhagyashree Thipsay was the first to receive a Woman Grand Master (WGM) norm in 1986 in the Lloyds Bank Master's tournament.

FIRST WOMAN INTERNATIONAL MASTER (WIM)

Jayshree Khadilkar became a WIM in 1978.

FIRST TIME WHEN INDIA WON MEDALS IN BOTH SECTIONS OF OLYMPIAD

India won bronze medals in open and women sections of the Olympiad in Mahabalipuram, Tamil Nadu, in 2022.

D. Gukesh

FIRST OLYMPIAD GOLD ON TOP BOARD

D. Gukesh won the gold on top board in Mahabalipuram, Tamil Nadu in 2022.

FIRST MEDALS – ASIAN GAMES

Women's Individual Rapid: K. Humpy won the gold in the Doha Asian Games in 2006. Harika Dronavalli won the first bronze in 2010 at Guangzhou, China.

Mixed Team Standard: K. Sasikiran, P. Harikrishna and K. Humpy won the mixed team gold in Doha in 2006.

Men's Team Standard: Pentala Harikrishna, Krishnan Sasikaran, Surya Shekhar Ganguly, Geetha Narayanan Gopal and Adhiban Baskaran won the bronze medal at the 2010 Guangzhou games. India's men's team won the silver medal at the 2022 Hangzhou Games.

Women's Team: The Indian Women's team won the silver medal at the 2022 Hangzhou Games.

CRICKET

Women's Cricket

Tests

FIRSTS IN TEST CRICKET

Category	Details
First captain	Shantha Rangaswamy was appointed as the first captain for the Indian cricket team
First match	India played against West Indies in 1976
First victory	India recorded its first victory against West Indies in November 1978
First century	Shantha Rangaswamy scored 108 against New Zealand on 8 January 1977
First double century	Mithali Raj scored 214 against England on 16 August 2002

Mithali Raj

A biopic on Mithali Raj was released in 2022 titled *Shabaash Mithu*

One-Day Internationals

FIRSTS IN ONE–DAY INTERNATIONALS

Category	Details
First captain	Diana Edulji was the first captain appointed in 1978
First match	The first match was played in 1978 against England.
First century	On 26 June 1999, Reshma Gandhi scored 104* (not out) against Ireland
First Asia Cup victory	The first Asia Cup victory was in 2004 against Sri Lanka
First to score over 7,000 runs	Mithali Raj has scored 7,805 runs in women's cricket between 1999–2022 in 211 innings. She holds the world record for this.

First to score 50 half-centuries	Mithali Raj has scored 64 half-centuries between 1999–2022
First to take 200 wickets	Jhulan Goswami has taken 255 wickets between 2002–2022
First to take 50 stumpings	Anju Jain has taken 51 stumpings in 62 Innings played between 1993–2005
First to score 800 boundaries	Mithali Raj has scored over 805 boundaries between 1999–2022
First to play 150 matches as captain	Mithali Raj holds the world record with 155 matches as captain

T20 International

FIRSTS IN T20 INTERNATIONALS

Category	Details
First captain	Mithali Raj was appointed captain in 2006
First match	The first match was played in 2006 against England
First hat-trick	Ekta Bisht took a hat-trick against Sri Lanka in 2012
First century	Harmanpreet Kaur put 103 runs on the scoreboard in 2018 against New Zealand
First Commonwealth Games medal	The Indian team settled for a silver medal at the 2022 Birmingham Games
First Asian Games medal	The Indian team bagged the gold medal playing the final against Sri Lanka at the 2022 Hangzhou Games
First to score 3,000 runs	Harmanpreet Kaur has a total of 3,195 runs between 2009–2023

First to play 100 matches as captain	Harmanpreet Kaur has played 103 matches as captain between 2012–2023

Harmanpreet Kaur

Harmanpreet Kaur has played 161 Women's T20I matches – the most in the world!

Men's Cricket
Tests

Indian cricket team 1932

FIRSTS IN TEST CRICKET

Category	Details
First match	India debuted against England on 25 June 1932 at Lord's cricket ground
First captain	C.K. Nayadu was the first captain in India's tour of England in 1932
First team	The squad that went for the first England tour included Lall Singh, Phiroze Palia, Jahangir Khan, Mohammed Nisar, Amar Singh, Bahadur Kapadia, Shankarrao Godambe, Ghulam Mohammad, Janardan Navle, Syed Wazir Ali, C.K. Nayadu, Maharaja of Porbandar, K.S. Limbdi, Nazir Ali, Joginder Singh, Naoomal Jaoomal, Sorabji Colah and Nariman Marshall
First to play for England and India	The senior Nawab of Pataudi, Iftikhar Ali Khan, debuted for England for the 1932–33 Bodyline series and later in 1946 played for India against England
First half-century	In the first Test match against England at Lord's in 1932 Amar Singh scored 51 runs
First century	Lala Amarnath scored 118 runs against England in 1933 at the Bombay Gymkhana Grounds
First match played in India	Between 5–8 January 1934, India played versus England at Eden Gardens in Calcutta (now Kolkata)
First victory	India beat England on 10 February 1952 at the M.A. Chidambaram Stadium, Chepauk, Madras
First Test side dismissed in the same day	In 1952, India was dismissed twice in a single day. The match was against England.

First Five-Test series to end in five draws	The India and Pakistan test series ended with five draws. The fifth match was held on 1 March 1955
First to score a double century	Polly Umrigar scored 233 runs in 1955–56 in a match against New Zealand
First to bat on all five days	M.L. Jaisimha during the India v. Australia test match in 1960 at Eden Gardens, Calcutta
First match interrupted by a solar eclipse	The Jubilee Test between India and England held on 16 February 1980 at Wankhede Stadium, Bombay (now Mumbai)
First to score centuries in first three Test matches	Mohammad Azharuddin playing against England in 1984–85
First Batsman to complete 10,000 runs	Sunil Gavaskar completed the 10,000 runs in March 1987 against Pakistan in Ahmedabad
First bowler to take all 10 wickets in an innings	Anil Kumble achieved this feat playing against Pakistan in 1999
First hat-trick	Harbhajan Singh claimed a hat-trick against Australia in 2000–01
First to score a triple century	Virendra Sehwag scored 309 in a match against Pakistan in 2004
First hat-trick in first over	Irfan Pathan dismissed Salman Butt, Younis Khan and Mohammad Yousuf in three consecutive deliveries on 29 January 2006
First to score 50 centuries	Sachin Tendulkar on 19 December 2010

Sachin Tendulkar (left)

Sachin Tendulkar was inducted in the ICC Hall of Fame in 2019. The other inducted cricketers are Diana Edulji, Virendra Sehwag, Rahul Dravid, Vinoo Mankad, Anil Kumble, Kapil Dev, Bishan Bedi and Sunil Gavaskar.

One-Day Internationals

FIRSTS IN ONE-DAY INTERNATIONALS

Category	Details
First captain	Ajit Wadekar was the first captain, appointed in 1974
First match	India played England on 13 July 1974 at Leeds.
First victory	India claimed its first victory in the inaugural Worl Cup against East Africa at Leeds
First to score a century	Kapil Dev scored 175* (not out) in 1983 during a match against Zimbabwe in the World Cup
First World Cup victory	India won the 1983 World Cup beating West Indies in the finals, under the captaincy of Kapil Dev
First Asia Cup victory	India won the Asia Cup for the first time in 1984 in the inaugural tournament

First to be dismissed for handling the ball	Mohinder Amarnath on 9 February 1986 against Australia
First hat-trick	Chetan Sharma in a match against New Zealand in 1987
First Batsman to complete 10,000 runs	Sachin Tendulkar on 31 March 2001 in a match against Australia in Indore
First ICC Champions Trophy	India was declared the co-winner along with Sri Lanka in 2002
First 400 runs in a World Cup match	Team India put up a score of over 400 on 19 March 2007 against Bermuda
First double century	Sachin Tendulkar scored the double century on 24 February 2010 against South Africa
First to score a century on World Cup debut	On 21 February 2011 in a match versus Bangladesh during the 2011 World Cup at Mirpur, Bangladesh, Virat Kohli scored a century in the ODI
First to win the World Cup on home ground	Team India was the first country to win the World Cup on home ground in 2011. The Finals were played against Sri Lanka at the Wankhede Stadium, Mumbai.
First to score 2,000 runs at the World Cup	Sachin Tendulkar completed 2,000 runs in the 2011 World Cup
First 50 centuries	Virat Kohli scored his 50th ODI century in a match against New Zealand in 2023

Virat Kohli

Virat Kohli made 765 runs in the 2023 World Cup which is the highest runs scored in a single edition of the World Cup.

T20 Internationals

FIRSTS IN T20 INTERNATIONALS

Category	Details
First captain	Virendra Sehwag was the first captain appointed for T20 Internationals
First match	India played against South Africa in 2006
First victory	India won with a score of 127/4 against Africa on 1 December 2006
First winner of the T20 World Cup	The Indian cricket team defeated Pakistan to become the first in the world to win this title in 2007

First half century	Robin Uthappa scored a half century in the league stage game of the 2007 T20 World Cup against Pakistan
First six sixes in an over	Yuvraj Singh hit six sixes in succession in one over which was bowled by Stuart Broad of the England team in 2007.
First century	Suresh Raina made the first century against South Africa on 2 May 2010
First hat-trick	Deepak Chahar dismissed Shafiul Islam, Mustafirzur Rahman and Aminul Islam of the Bangladesh team in succession in 2019
First to score 10,000 runs	Virat Kohli reached the 10,000 mark in 2021
First Asian Games gold	India won the gold medal at the 2022 Hangzhou Asian Games

GENERAL

FIRST RECORDED MATCH

The earliest record of Cricket in India goes back to 1721 when English merchants played a game at Cambay.

FIRST TOUR BY OVERSEAS TEAM

Led by George Vernon, his team played 11 matches in India and won eight, drew two and lost one to the Parsees in 1889–90. In 1892–93, Baron Hawke (7th) led a team that played four matches out of which they won three. The Association of Cricket Statisticians considers this the first team to play matches in India.

FIRST TOURNAMENT

An annual Cricket series between the Parsees and the Europeans was started in 1892 with two matches being played in Bombay and Poona (now Pune), Maharashtra. From 1907 to 1911, the tournament turned into a triangular contest when Hindus joined in. Then it became quadrangular with the entry of Mohammedans in 1912. A fifth team, 'The Rest', was added in 1937 and it became the Bombay Pentangular. The tournament was abandoned in 1945 after Mahatma Gandhi alleged that it had a communal character.

FIRSTS IN INTERNATIONAL CRICKET COUNCIL (ICC) AWARDS

Player of the year – Men: Rahul Dravid in 2004

Cricketer of the year – Men – Test: Rahul Dravid in 2004

Cricketer of the year–Men–ODIs: M.S. Dhoni in 2008

Cricketer of the year – Men – T20I: Suryakumar Yadav in 2022

Emerging cricketer of the year–Men: Irfan Pathan in 2004

ICC Spirit of Cricket award: M.S. Dhoni in 2011

Player of the year – Women: Jhulan Goswami in 2007

Cricketer of the year – Women – ODIs: Smriti Mandhana in 2018

Emerging cricketer of the year – Women: Renuka Singh in 2022

FIRSTS IN CRICKET

Category	Details
First cricket club	The Calcutta Cricket club was established in Calcutta by the britishers in 1792
First Indian cricket club	The Oriental cricket club was established by the Parsi community of Bombay in 1848
First cricketer to be knighted	Sir Gajapatiraju Vijaya Anand, popularly known as 'Vizzy' was knighted in 1936 for services to cricket
First Women's cricket Association	The Women's cricket Association of India was established in 1973 with Premala Chavan as its first president
First six sixes in an over	Ravi Shastri hit six sixes in a single over which was bowled by Tilak Raj. During the Ranji trophy season of 1984–85, he became the second person in history to achieve this feat
First TV dismissal	Sachin Tendulkar was declared out based on television evidence on 14 November 1992, in a match against South Africa
First Indian President of ICC	In 1997, Jagmohan Dalmiya became the first Indian president of the International Cricket Council (ICC)
First foreign coach	John Wright coached the Indian National cricket team from 2000–05
First cricketer inducted by the Indian Air Force	Sachin Tendulkar was presented with the honorary rank of Group Captain on 3 September 2010

First captain to win all ICC trophies	Under the captaincy of M.S. Dhoni, India won the T20I World Cup (2007), the ODI World Cup (2011) and the ICC Champions Trophy (2013)
First Cricketer to score 100 centuries in Test and ODIs combined	Sachin Tendulkar achieved this feat in 2012. This includes 51 centuries in Tests and 49 centuries in ODIs.
First cricketer to get MCC membership – woman	Anjum Chopra was presented with honourary life membership of the Marylebone Cricket Club (MCC), Lord's cricket ground, London in 2016
First woman cricketer to score 10,000 runs in international cricket	Mithali Raj achieved this feat on 12 March 2021 against South Africa. She was only the second woman in the world to hold this record. She has a total of 10,868 runs.

FIRST WISDEN AWARD WINNERS

These awards are given by the annual publication, *Wisden's Cricketers' Almanack* which is also known as the 'Bible of Cricket'. Here are the first recipients of the awards:

Cricketer of the year: Ranjitsinhji in 1987

Leading cricketer in the world: Virendra Sehwag in 2008

Leading woman cricketer in the world: Mithali Raj in 2017

First to win Player of the year thrice consecutively: Virat Kohli won it in 2016, 2017 and 2018

Ranjitsinhji: first Wisden cricketer of the year

CUE SPORTS

FIRST NATIONAL CHAMPIONSHIP – BILLIARDS

In 1931, the first National Championship was held in Calcutta, West Bengal, with only eight entries. M.M. Beg won the title.

FIRST NATIONAL CHAMPIONSHIP – SNOOKER

The first National Snooker Championship was held in 1939 in Calcutta, West Bengal. P.K. Deb won the title.

FIRST WORLD CHAMPION

Wilson Jones was India's first world champion after winning the World Amateur Billards Championship in 1958.

FIRST TO SURPASS 1,000 POINTS IN NATIONAL BILLIARDS CHAMPIONSHIP

Michael Ferreira became the first Indian to surpass the 1,000 point mark in 1978.

FIRST WORLD SNOOKER CHAMPION

Om B. Agarwal won the IBSF International Billiards and Snooker Federation World Snooker Championship at Dublin, Ireland, in 1984.

FIRST WORLD CHAMPION ON DEBUT

Geet Sethi became world champion on debut when he beat Bob Marshall, to win the 25th World Amateur Billiards Championship in 1985 in Delhi. He was also the first unseeded player to become world champion.

FIRST BILLIARDS AND SNOOKER HAT-TRICK

Geet Sethi achieved a hat-trick of three consecutive National Championship titles in billiards and snooker from 1985 to 1987. He also won the national titles for both sports in 1988.

The match between Bob Marshall and Geet Sethi reportedly lasted eight hours.

FIRST ASIAN SNOOKER TITLE

Yasin Merchant beat Udon Khaimuk of Thailand by eight frames in New Delhi on 15 July 1989 to win the Asian Confederation of Billiard Sports (ACBS) Championship.

FIRST ASIAN GAMES TITLE

At the 1998 Bangkok Asian Games, Ashok Shandilya won the gold medal. In the doubles, Ashok Shandilya and Geet Sethi won a gold, beating Devendra Joshi and Balachandra Bhaskar, who won the bronze.

FIRST WORLD LADIES BILLIARDS AND SNOOKER ASSOCIATION TITLE

In April 2012, R. Umadevi won her maiden, and India's first, World Ladies Billiards and Snooker Association title, beating the then world no. 13, Eva Palmius, 2–0 in the final at Cambridge, England.

R. Umadevi

FIRST WORLD GAMES SNOOKER TITLE

Aditya Mehta won the Quadrennial World Games snooker gold at Cali, Colombia, in July 2013.

India has won five gold medals in the sport at the Asian Games.

FIRST WORLD BILLIARDS TEAM TITLE

India 'B' won a gold while India 'A' bagged a silver in the inaugural World Billiards Team Championship in Glasgow, Scotland, in August 2014.

FIRST WIN AT THE WORLD LADIES BILLIARDS AND SNOOKER CHAMPIONSHIP

Chitra Magimairaj and Varsha Sanjeev won the senior gold medal and the U-21 gold medal, respectively, at the World Ladies Billiards and Snooker (WLBS) Championship in Leeds, UK, in April 2016.

FIRST SNOOKER TEAM WORLD CUP TITLE

Pankaj Advani and Manan Chandra won the International Billiards and Snooker Federation (IBSF) Snooker Team World Cup in 2018 in Doha, Qatar.

Pankaj Advani

FOOTBALL

FIRST HAT-TRICK IN INDIAN FOOTBALL

In the 1889 Trades Cup, Norman Pritchard scored a hat-trick for St Xavier's College, Calcutta, against Sovabazar Club.

FIRST INDIAN CLUB TO WIN A MAJOR TROPHY

Mohun Bagan of Calcutta, beat East Yorkshire Regiment of Ghaziabad 2–1 in the Indian Football Association (IFA) Shield tournament final on 29 July 1911 at the Calcutta Football Club Ground.

Mohun Bagan team with the IFA Shield

FIRST IN ENGLISH PROFESSIONAL CLUB

- The first footballer from the Indian subcontinent to play for a European club was Mohammed Salim from Calcutta. He played for the European club Celtic FC in 1936.
- The first to join an English club was Bhaichung Bhutia when he signed a contract to represent second division outfit, Bury FC, from 1999 to 2002.

- On 16 August 2015, Aditi Chauhan became the first Indian woman to play in the English league football as a goalkeeper for West Ham United.

FIRST INDIAN TEAM TO WIN THE DURAND CUP

Mohammedan Sporting won the Durand Cup in 1940 when it was first moved to Delhi and the final played at Irwin Amphitheatre (now Dhyan Chand National Stadium). Mohammedan Sporting beat Royal Warwickshire Regiment 2–1 in the final.

FIRST INTERNATIONAL MATCH

India entered the 1948 Olympics with seven barefoot players, under captain Talimeren Ao from Bengal, but lost to France 1–2. The lone goal was scored by Sarangapani Raman.

FIRST INTERNATIONAL TOURNAMENT WIN BY A CLUB

Mohammedan Sporting won the Aga Khan Gold Cup in Dhaka (then Pakistan, now Bangladesh) on 11 October 1960, defeating Makassar XI, Indonesia 4–1 in the final.

FIRST PROFESSIONAL COACH

Starting his career in 1963, Amal Dutta became India's first professional coach by coaching East Bengal. He also coached the other two big Kolkata clubs: Mohun Bagan and Mohammedan Sporting (Dhaka).

FIRST OLYMPIC REFEREE

Komaleeswaran Sankar became an Olympic referee when he was selected for the football tournament of the 2000 Sydney Olympics, one among the four match officials chosen from Asia.

India is the most successful team at the South Asian Football Federation (SAFF) championship with eight titles.

FIRST FIFA WORLD CUP REFEREE

Chosen to officiate at the 2002 World Cup in South Korea and Japan, Komaleeswaran Sankar was the first World Cup referee from India.

FIRST INDIAN TO BE NATIONAL COACH OF A FOREIGN COUNTRY

In July 2007, Syed Nayeemuddin was appointed national coach of Bangladesh. He was also the first Indian to coach a club side abroad, the Brothers Union of Bangladesh in 2004.

FIRST INDIAN TO BECOME A FIFA WORLD CUP MATCH COMMISSIONER

In a FIFA World Cup 2006 game, former All India Football Federation president Priya Ranjan Dasmunsi was the match commissioner. It was a group stage match between Australia and Croatia.

FIRSTS IN FOOTBALL

Category	Details
First club established	Calcutta FC in 1872
First Indian Football competition	Durand Cup was started in 1888 by Sir Mortimer Durand in Shimla
First Indian Federation	The Indian Football Association established in 1893
First hat-trick	R. Lumsden scored a hat-trick against Australia in 1938
First Olympic goal	Sarangapani Raman scored a goal in the 1948 London Olympics
First Asian Games title	The Indian team became champions at the Asian Games, winning a gold in 1951
First hat-trick after independence	Sheoo Mewalal scored a hat-trick in the 1952 Colombo Cup
First Asian team to reach Olympic semi-finals	Team India reached the semi-finals in 1956
First Asian to score hat-trick at the Olympics	Neville D'Souza scored a hat-trick against Australia at Melbourne in 1956
First South Asian Games Victory	India won the title in 1985
First SAFF Championship victory	India won this title in 1993
First National domestic league	The National Football League was established in 1996

First Nehru Cup victory	Team India won the Nehru Cup in 2007 beating Syria 1-0
First AFC Challenge Cup victory	Team India won the title in 2008
First player to win 100 caps	Baichung Bhutia won 107 caps between 1995–2009
First player to score 50 international goals	Sunil Chhetri scored his 50th goal against the Maldives in 2015. He had 93 international goals up till 2023
First professional football league for women	The Indian Women's League was established in 2016
First player to play in three continents	Sunil Chhetri has played in Asia, Europe and North America

Sunil Chhetri

GOLF

OLDEST CLUB

The Royal Kolkata Golf Club founded in 1829 is the oldest club outside Britain. The Kolkata Ladies Golf Club was established in 1891. The 'Royal' title was granted in 1912 to commemorate King George V and Queen Mary's visit in 1911.

FIRST PUBLIC GOLF COURSE

The Qutub Golf Course, New Delhi was established in January 2000 by the Delhi Development Authority. It began with nine holes and in 2002, further nine holes were commissioned to

Jyoti Randhawa was the first to top the Asian Tour Order of Merit in 2002.

Jeev Milkha Singh : first to play in a major

make it a genuine 18-hole course. The course offers a pay and play facility, making the sport accessible to public.

FIRSTS IN GOLF

Category	Details
First Indian Open winner	P.G. Sethi won the title in 1965
First international recognition	India was invited to the 1969 World Cup qualifying event. Ruda Valji and Shadi Lal were representatives of India.
First Normura cup victory	Indian squad of Raj Kumar Pitamber, P.G. Sethi, Vikramjit Singh, and Lakshman Singh was crowned Asia-Pacific Golf champions at the 1973 Normura Cup in Jakarta.
First Asian Games gold	The Indian team won the gold medal and Lakshman Singh won the individual gold at the 1982 New Delhi Asian games.
First to qualify for European PGA Tour	Jeev Milkha Singh was the first to qualify in 1998
First European – Asian tour victory	Arjun Atwal the Caltex Singapore Open in February 2002 and the Carlsberg Malaysian Open in February 2003.
First to top the Asian Tour Order of Merit	Jyoti Randhawa topped it in 2002
First to win on the Japanese PGA Tour	Jyoti Randhawa won the Suntory Open in 2003
First to gain qualification for the PGA tour	Arjun Atwal gained qualification for the full US Tour after making it through the qualifying school for the year 2004

First to gain a full 'card' on PGA Tour	Arjun Atwal gained a full card (exemption from playing qualifying rounds) after the 2005 season
First participation in the World Cup	Jyoti Randhawa and Arjun Atwal participated in the 2005 World Cup
First to play in three WGC events in a single year	Jyoti Randhawa achieved this feat in 2005
First Olympians	Aditi Ashok, S.S.P. Chawrasia and Anirban Lahiri participated in the 2016 Rio de Janeiro Olympics
First to win all three National titles	Amit Luthra is the first to win the Junior National (1979), men's National (1993, 1994) and Senior Nationals (2015, 2016)
Majors	
First to qualify for the British Open	Gaurav Ghei qualified for the event in 1997
First to play in a major	Jeev Milkha Singh made it to the 2002 US Open
First to play the PGA Championship	Arjun Atwal played the championship in 2005
First to play the Masters at Augusta	Jeev Milkha Singh played the Masters at Augusta, Georgia, US in 2007
First to make it to the Top 10 at a Major	Jeev Milkha Singh tied at the ninth position at 2008 PGA Championship
First hole-in-one at a Major	Anirban Lahiri was the first to make a hole-in-one at the Majors during Round 3 of the 2012 British Open

HOCKEY

FIRST HOCKEY CLUB

The first hockey club was established in Calcutta in 1855.

OLDEST TOURNAMENT

Men: Considered to be the oldest tournament, the Beighton Cup was started in Calcutta, West Bengal, in 1895. It was presented by T.D. Beighton, the legal remembrancer of the then Government of Bengal, the Cup was held initially in the form of local matches, evolving into a regular tournament. Its latest edition was held in December 2022.

Women: The oldest domestic tournament for women was the first National Championship held in 1947.

FIRST INTERNATIONAL APPEARANCE

Men: In 1926, the Indian Army team went to New Zealand to play 21 matches. They won 18, drew two, and lost one match. They scored 192 and conceded 24 goals.

Women: The women's hockey team made their first international appearance at the inaugural Hockey World Cup in 1974. They finished fourth in the tournament.

FIRST NATIONAL CHAMPIONSHIP

Men: Earlier known as the Inter-Provincial Championship, the first ever national championship was staged in 1928 at Calcutta.

Women: The Bombay Inter Provincial Hockey Association started in 1947 and started the first national championship for women.

FIRST MEDAL AT THE OLYMPICS

The Indian hockey team won its first Olympic gold medal in 1928, under the captaincy of Jaipal Singh Munda. From 1928 to 1956, the team was unbeaten, winning six gold medals. Since then, India has been adding medals to its Olympic tally, and currently, with a total of eight gold, one silver and two bronze medals, it is the single most successful team at the Olympic Games.

Indian Hockey Team 1936

FIRST HAT-TRICK IN SUCCESSION

Balbir Singh scored three goals in the semi-final against Great Britain at the 1952 Helsinki Olympics and netted five, including a hat-trick, against the Netherlands in the final.

Balbir Singh (center)

FIRST WIN AT THE ASIAN GAMES

Men: The men's national hockey team won the gold medal defeating Pakistan at the 1966 Bangkok Games.

Women: The women's national hockey team bagged the gold medal at the 1982 New Delhi Games.

FIRST MEDALS AT THE FIH HOCKEY WORLD CUP – MEN

Gold: India bagged the gold after defeating Pakistan at the 1975 Kuala Lumpur World Cup.

Silver: At the 1973 World Cup, held at Amstelveen, Netherlands, the Indian team settled for a silver after losing to the host team.

Bronze: India finished third after defeating Kenya at the 1971 World Cup in Barcelona, Spain.

Hockey is not the national sport of India. India does not have a national sport.

FIRST DOUBLE HAT–TRICK IN THE OLYMPICS

Mohammed Shahid scored seven goals, including a double hat-trick, against Thailand (11–0) on 24 September 1986 in the Seoul Olympics in South Korea.

FIRST COMMONWEALTH GAMES MEDAL

Women: The Indian women's hockey team won the gold medal at the 2002 Commonwealth Games in Manchester, UK. Led by Suraj Lata Devi, they defeated England 3–2.

Men: The men's hockey team won the silver medal at the 2010 New Delhi Games.

FIRST ASIA CUP WIN – WOMEN

The Indian women's hockey team won the Asia Cup for the first time, beating Japan 1–0 in the final at the National Stadium (now Dhyan Chand National Stadium), New Delhi, in February 2004.

FIRST JUNIOR ASIA CUP WIN

India won the fifth Junior Asia Cup in Karachi, Pakistan, in March 2004, beating the hosts 5–2.

FIRST DOMESTIC LEAGUE

Men: The first domestic league for men was the Premier Hockey League (2005).

Women: The Khelo India Women Hockey League for U-21 (2021) was the first domestic league for women.

FIRST FOREIGN COACH

Men: Gerard Rach from Germany, India's first foreign coach, was with the team at the 2004 Athens Olympics, and till January 2005.

Women: Herman Kruis from the Netherlands was the first foreign coach for the women's hockey team and took charge of the Asia Cup in Hong Kong in September 2007.

FIRST WOMEN PROFESSIONAL PLAYERS

Penalty corner expert Jasjeet Kaur Handa and Subhadra Pradhan played for HC Den Bosch club in the Dutch League in 2007.

FIRST ASIAN HOCKEY CHAMPIONS TROPHY WIN

Men: India won the inaugural edition of the tournament held in Ordos City, China, during August–September 2011, by defeating Pakistan 4–2 in the final via penalty strokes.

Women: Led by Deepika Thakur, team India won the Asian Women's Champions trophy held in Singapore in 2016, beating China in the final on shoot-out.

FIRST HAT-TRICK – WOMEN

Vandana Katariya scored an impressive hat-trick at the 2020 Tokyo Olympics against South Africa in a Pool A match.

Dhyan Chand scored 33 goals in three Olympic games – 10 in 1928, 12 in 1932 and 11 in 1936.

KABADDI

FIRST GOLD MEDAL AT THE ASIAN GAMES

Kabaddi was played for the first time in the 11th Asian Games in 1990 in Beijing, China. Pakistan, Japan, China, Nepal, Bangladesh and India.

Men: The Indian team bagged the gold at the inaugural games defeating Bangladesh.

Women: The women's team won the inaugural games at the 2010 Guangzhou Games defeating Thailand.

FIRST NATIONALS

Men: The first kabaddi Nationals for men were held in 1951 in Maharashtra and the host state won the title.

Women: In 1995, the first Nationals in kabaddi for women were held in Calcutta. Maharashtra won the title.

Junior: The first championships for junior boys and girls were held in 1974 and 1976 respectively at Asansol, West Bengal.

FIRST PARTICIPATION IN THE ASIAN JUNIOR CHAMPIONSHIP

The championship was held for the first time at Faridabad, Haryana, in January 2000, with teams from Bangladesh, Nepal, Sri Lanka, and Thailand. India won the gold.

FIRST WINS AT THE KABADDI WORLD CUP

Men: The men's team won the 2004 World Cup against Iran.
Women: The women's team won the inaugural World Cup in 2012 by defeating Iran.

FIRST PRO KABADDI LEAGUE

With eight teams participating, the first Pro Kabaddi League was held in 2014. Sixty games were played, with the Jaipur Pink Panthers winning the inaugural title, defeating U-Mamba 35–24.

FIRST TEAM TO WIN THREE CONSECUTIVE PRO KABADDI TITLES

Patna Pirates won three consecutive Pro Kabaddi League titles in 2016–17.

SHOOTING

FIRST GOLD MEDALS AT ASIAN GAMES

Category	Details
Men	Randhir Singh – Shotgun trap – 1978 Bangkok
	Jaspal Rana – 25 m centre fire pistol – 1994 Hiroshima

	Samaresh Jung, Vijay Kumar and Jaspal Rana – 25 m centre fire pistol team – 2006 Doha
	Jaspal Rana – 25 m standard pistol – 2006 Doha
	Ronjan Sodhi – double trap – 2010 Guangzhou
	Jitu Rai – 50 m pistol – 2014 Incheon
	Saurabh Chaudhury – 10 m air pistol – 2018 Jakarta – Palembang
Women	Rahi Sarnobat – 25 m pistol – 2018 Jakarta – Palembang

FIRST GOLD – ASIAN CHAMPIONSHIP

India's first gold in the Asian Championship was won by Dr Karni Singh who won an individual gold in the trap event in 1971 in Seoul, South Korea.

FIRST MEDAL HAUL – ASIAN CHAMPIONSHIP

India won two gold, one silver and two bronze medals in Jakarta, Indonesia, in 1983, in its first haul in the Asian Championship. Ashok Pandit and Mohinder Lal won the gold in the centre-fire pistol team event with a world record.

FIRST TEAM GOLD IN THE ASIAN CLAY CHAMPIONSHIP

Mansher Singh, Moraad Ali Khan and Manavjit Singh won India's first team gold at the Asian Clay Shooting Championship at Chengdu,

Shooting was omitted twice at the Olympics – once in 1904 and then in 1928.

China, in July 1995 with a tally of 357/375, equalling Kuwait's Asian record at the 1994 Hiroshima Asian Games in Japan.

FIRST GOLD – COMMONWEALTH GAMES

Men: Ashok Pandit won the gold in the free pistol event in Auckland, New Zealand, in 1990.

Women: Roopa Unnikrishnan clinched the gold in the rifle prone event in the 1998 Commonwealth Games in Kuala Lumpur, Malaysia.

FIRST NATIONALS

The first shooting national tournament was held in Delhi from 9 to 16 November in 1952.

FIRST OLYMPIC MEDAL

Rajyavardhan Singh Rathore won the silver medal in doubletrap shooting in the 2004 Athens Olympics in Greece.

FIRST INDIVIDUAL OLYMPIC GOLD MEDAL

Abhinav Bindra won India's first individual Olympic gold medal by claiming the honour in the men's air rifle event on 11 August 2008 in Beijing, China.

Abhinav Bindra (left)

FIRST MEDALS AT THE WORLD CUP

Category	Details
First Gold	Anjali Vedpathak-Bhagwat – 10 m air rifle – 2003 Milan
First pistol medal	Sonia Rai – women's air pistol – 2006 Resende, Brazil Bronze medal
First Gold – 10 m air pistol	Saurabh Chaudhary – 2019 Munich
First Gold – Air pistol – Mixed team	Heena Sidhu and Jitu Rai – 2017 New Dclhi
First Gold – Skeet	Mairaj Ahmad Khan – 2022 Changwon, Korea
First to win two Golds	Manu Bhaker won the 10 m air pistol gold and paired up with Om Prakash Mitharval for the 10 m air pistol mixed team at the 2018 Mexico World Cup

Manu Bhaker

Manu Bhaker is the youngest Indian to win a gold medal at the ISSF World Cup.

FIRST WORLD CHAMPIONSHIP GOLD

Ace shooter Abhinav Bindra won India's first gold medal in a World Championship in air rifle at Zagreb, Croatia, on 24 July 2006. Manavjit Singh Sandhu won the first shotgun gold medal in a World Championship by beating 124 shooters to the title in the trap event at Zagreb, Croatia, two days after Bindra's effort.

SQUASH

FIRST PROFESSIONALS

In the early 1990s, the first professionals were ArjunSingh (men) and Misha Grewal. The latter became a professional in 1993, and played the women's professional circuit in Asia, Europe, and the US. Her best rankings were second in Asia and 27th in the world.

FIRST MEDALS AT THE ASIAN GAMES

Category	Details
Men	
Singles	Saurav Ghoshal – Bronze – Doha 2006
	Saurav Ghoshal – Silver – 2014 Incheon
Team	Saurav Ghoshal, Sandeep Jangra, Harinder Pal Sandhu and Siddharth Suchde – Bronze – 2010 Guangzhou
	Saurav Ghoshal, Kush Kumar, Mahesh Mangaonkar and Harinder Pal Sandhu – Gold – 2014 Incheon
Women	
Singles	Dipika Pallikal – Bronze – 2014 Incheon

Team	Dipika Pallikal, Joshna Chinappa, Anwesha Reddy and Anaka Alankamony – Bronze – 2010 Guangzhou Dipika Pallikal, Joshna Chinappa, Aparajitha Balamurukan and Anaka Alankamony – Silver – 2014 Incheon
Mixed	
Doubles	Harinder Pal Sandhu and Dipika Pallikal – Gold – 2022 Hangzhou Abhay Singh and Anahat Singh – Bronze – 2022 Hangzhou

FIRST CHAMPION

Rajkumar Narpat Singh won the first squash Nationals in 1953 and made a hat-trick, holding the title for two more years.

FIRST JUNIOR AND SENIOR NATIONALS TITLE

Anil Nayyar won both the junior and senior titles in the Nationals in 1964, when he was 18 years old.

FIRST DOUBLES CHAMPIONS IN THE NATIONALS

Joshna Chinappa and Dipika Pallikal, representing Tamil Nadu, won the women's title and Saurav Ghosal and Harinder Pal Singh Sandhu,

Dipika Pallikal (right)

also representing Tamil Nadu, won the men's title at the first doubles event at the Nationals in 2004.

FIRST INDIVIDUAL MEDALS IN THE ASIAN CHAMPIONSHIPS

Bhuvaneshwari Kumari won the bronze in the 1990 and 1992 Asian Championships and Misha Grewal won a silver in the Asian Championship in 1996 at Amman, Jordan.

Bhuvaneshwari Kumari

FIRST TO WIN THE ASIAN JUNIOR TITLE – GIRLS

Joshna Chinappa was the first to win the Asian junior title (U-19) in 2003.

FIRST WIN AT THE ASIAN TEAM SQUASH CHAMPIONSHIPS

Women: The women's team won the championship in 2012 in Kuwait after defeating Hong Kong.

Men: Team Indian won the championship after defeating Kuwait in 2022 at South Korea.

Squash is a racket and ball game played with a hollow rubber ball by two or four players in a walled court.

FIRST JUNIOR WORLD NO. 1

Saurav Ghosal was the first Indian to be ranked junior world no. 1 when he won the British Junior Open in 2004.

FIRST TO WIN WORLD RANKING TITLES

In August 2003, Ritwik Bhattacharya became the first Indian to win back-to-back international Professional Squash Association (PSA) world ranking tournaments in New Zealand when he won the North Island Championship and the Royal Oak Open titles. In 2005, he won two more titles – the Esportiu Rocafort Squash Open in Barcelona, Spain, and the Rochester ProAm Squash Championship in New York, US. He has won four international squash titles.

FIRST INTERNATIONAL SUCCESS – WOMEN

Joshna Chinappa became the first Indian woman to claim a Women's International Squash Players Association (WISPA) title, defeating Malaysia's Low Wee Wern 11–8, 11–5, 11–3 in the NSC Super Satellite (no. 3) Squash Tournament final at National Squash Centre, Kuala Lumpur, Malaysia, in November 2008.

FIRST TO WIN WORLD DOUBLES TITLES

Since the inception of the tournament in 1981, India bagged its first gold medals in 2022. Dipika Palikkal became the first Indian to win two gold medals at the World Doubles Squash Championship winning the gold in women's and mixed finals. Dipika partnered Joshna Chinappa in the women's final and teamed up with Saurav Ghosal in the mixed doubles in the 2022 edition in Glasgow.

FIRST COMMONWEALTH GAMES GOLD

India bagged its first gold medal when Dipika Pallikal and Joshna Chinappa defeated Laura Massaro and Jenny Duncalf of England 11–6, 11–8 to win the women's doubles event in the Commonwealth Games in Glasgow, UK, in 2014.

SWIMMING

FIRST MEDALS AT THE ASIAN GAMES

Category	Details
Swimming	
100 m Freestyle	Sachin Nag – Gold – 1951 New Delhi
400 m Freestyle	Bimal Chandra – Bronze – 1951 New Delhi
100 m Backstroke	Kanti Shah – Silver – 1951 New Delhi
200 m Breaststroke	Jehangir Naegamwalla – Bronze – 1951 New Delhi
4 x 100 m Freestyle relay	Issac Mansoor, Bimal Chandra, Sambhu Saha and Sachin Nag – Bronze – 1951 New Delhi
3 x 100 m Medley relay	Kanti Shah, Jehangir Naegamwalla and Sachin Nag – Bronze – 1951 New Delhi
200 m Butterfly	Khajan Singh – Silver – 1986 Seoul
50 m Butterfly	Virdhawal Khade – Bronze – 2010 Guangzhou
50 m Breaststroke	Sandeep Sejwal – Bronze – 2014 Incheon
Diving	
3 m Springboard	K.P. Thakkar – Gold – 1951 New Delhi

	Ashu Dutt – Silver – 1951 New Delhi
10 m Platform	K.P. Thakkar – Gold – 1951 New Delhi
	T.T. Dand – Bronze – 1951 New Delhi

Water Polo

Team	Gold – 1951 New Delhi
	Silver – 1970 Bangkok
	Bronze – 1982 New Delhi

FIRST WOMAN TO PARTICIPATE IN THE ASIAN GAMES

Kumari Rima Dutta participated in the fifth Asian Games in Bangkok, Thailand, in 1966.

FIRST SWIMMER IN THE OLYMPICS

A stamp commemorating Arati Saha

Men: D.D. Mulji of Bengal was the first Indian swimmer in the Olympics, taking part in the 1928 Amsterdam Olympics.

Women: At the 1952 Helsinki Olympics, Dolly Nazir and Arati Saha represented India.

FIRST TO QUALIFY FOR TWO OLYMPIC EVENTS

Shikha Tandon of Bengaluru, Karnataka, qualified for the 50 m and 100 m freestyle events in the 2004 Athens Olympics, but did not win.

FIRST TO PARTICIPATE IN THE COMMONWEALTH GAMES

- Divers Dum Bahadur and Vasant Gadge were the first to represent India in the aquatics events at the 1978 Commonwealth Games in Edmonton, Canada.
- In 1982, for the first time, Indian swimmers participated in the Commonwealth Games at Brisbane, Australia. The team members were Wilson Cherian, Khajan Singh Tokas, T. Thoiba Singh, Sanjeev Chakraborty, Persis Madaan, Geeta Anand and Giselle Bharucha.

FIRST 100 M FREESTYLE – UNDER 1 MIN.

The first Indian swimmer to swim under 1 min. in the 100 m freestyle category was Basakha Singh, clocking 59.75 secs in 1971.

The butterfly stroke is swum on the chest with both arms moving symmetrically and the legs moving in the 'butterfly' kick movement. This is accompanied by movements of the hip and the chest.

FIRST 200 M FREESTYLE – UNDER 2 MINS

Virdhawal Khade of Maharashtra, who clocked 1 min. 49.86 secs, holds the record.

FIRST NATIONAL CHAMPIONSHIP

The first National Championship was held in Bombay, Maharashtra, in 1945.

FIRST TO WIN A MEDAL IN THE ASIAN INDOOR GAMES

Shikha Tandon won a bronze in the 100 m backstroke event at the Asian Indoor Games in Bangkok, Thailand, in November 2005.

FIRST PARA SWIMMER TO WIN BRONZE AT THE COMMONWEALTH GAMES

Prasanta Karmakar was the first Indian para swimmer to claim a bronze medal in the 50 m freestyle in the S-9 category at the 2010 New Delhi games.

FIRST VISUALLY IMPAIRED SWIMMER TO WIN A GOLD

Kanchanmala Pande won gold in the 200 m medley event in the S-11 category on 8 December 2017 at the World Para swimming Championship in Berlin.

FIRST INDIAN PARA SWIMMER TO QUALIFY FOR THE PARALYMPIC GAMES

Sharath Gayakwad was the first Indian para swimmer to qualify for the 2012 London Paralympic Games.

FIRST INDIAN PARA SWIMMER TO WIN GOLD IN THE PARA ASIAN GAMES

Suyash Narayan Jadhav won the gold medal in men's 50 m butterfly S7 (6 –7) category at the Para Asian Games held at Jakarta, Indonesia, in 2018 clocking 32.71 secs.

TABLE TENNIS

FIRST COMMONWEALTH MEDALS IN TABLE TENNIS

Category	Details
Men's singles	Chetan Baboor – Bronze – 2002 Sharath Kamal – Gold – 2006
Women's singles	Manika Batra – Gold – 2018
Men's doubles	Raman Subramanyan and Chetan Baboor – Bronze – 2002 Sharath Kamal and Subhojit Saha – Gold – 2010 Sharath Kamal and Anthony Amalraj – Silver – 2014
Women's doubles	Mouma Das and Poulomi Ghatak – Bronze – 2010 Manika Batra and Mouma Das – Silver – 2018
Mixed doubles	Sathiyan Gnanasekaran and Manika Batra – Bronze – 2018 Sharath Kamal and Sreeja Akula – Gold – 2022
Men's team	Chetan Baboor, Sourav Chakraborty, Soumyadeep Roy, Subhajit Saha and Raman Subramanyan – Bronze – 2002 Sharath Kamal, Shibaji Datta, Soumyadeep Roy and Subhajit Saha – Gold – 2006
Women's team	Kasturi Chakraborty, Poulomi Ghatak, Mouma Das, Nandita Saha and Shamini Kumaresan – Bronze – 2006

Poulomi Ghatak, Mouma Das, Shamini Kumaresan, Mamta Prabhu and Madhurika Suhas Patkar – Silver – 2010

Manika Batra, Mouma Das, Madhurika Patkar, Sutirtha Mukherjee and Pooja Sahasrabudhe – Gold – 2018

FIRST COMMONWEALTH CHAMPIONSHIPS

Team – Men: India won this title in 2004 and then again in 2015 and 2019.

Team – Women: The Indian team won this title in 2019.

Singles – Men: Sharath Kamal was the champion in the 2004 games.

Sharath Kamal

Singles – Women: Ayikha Mukherjee bagged the championship in 2019.

Doubles – Men: In 1997, Chetan Baboor and Subramaniam Raman won the title.

Sharath Kamal has won the Senior National Championship 10 times.

Doubles – Women: Pooja Sahasrabudhe and Krittwika Sinha Roy clinched the championship in 2019.

Doubles – Mixed: Sathiyan Gnanasekaran and Archana Kamath won the title in 2015.

FIRST PROFESSIONAL

Chetan Baboor played as a professional with Enig Club in Kalmar, Sweden, from 1998.

FIRST MEDAL AT THE ASIAN GAMES

At the 2018 Jakarta – Palembang Games, India won two bronze medals – In the men's team event and the mixed doubles event. The men's team included Anthony Amalraj, Harmeet Desai, Sathiyan Gnanasekaran, Sharath Kamal and Manav Thakkar. The mixed doubles team paired Sharath Kamal and Manika Batra.

FIRST GOLD MEDALLIST IN THE ASIAN CHAMPIONSHIP

Gool Nasikwala won the singles, doubles and mixed doubles gold medals in the 1952 Asian Championship in Singapore.

FIRST NATIONAL CHAMPION

Men: M. Ayub won the men's singles title in Calcutta in 1938.
Women: P. Lima won the women's singles in Bombay in 1939.

FIRST WOMAN TO PLAY IN TWO OLYMPICS

Mouma Das became the first woman player to qualify for two Olympic Games (2004, Athens and 2016, Rio).

FIRST ITTF PRO–TOUR TITLE

Sharath Kamal won the Egypt Open to become the first Indian to win an ITTF Pro-Tour event in July 2010.

FIRST INDIAN TO BE RANKED WORLD NO. 1 IN U–18

Manav Thakkar became the first Indian to be ranked world no. 1 in the boys' U-18 category in February 2018.

FIRST MEDAL IN ASIAN JUNIORS

India won the bronze medal in the 2006 Asian Junior Championship at Kitakyushu, Japan, in the girls' event.

FIRST TEAM MEDAL IN THE WORLD JUNIOR CHAMPIONSHIP

The Indian boys' team, comprising Soumyajit Ghosh, Harmeet Desai, and G. Sathiyan, won India's first- ever bronze medal in the 2011 Junior Championship held in Bahrain.

FIRST INTERNATIONAL LEAGUE

The first edition of the Ultimate Table Tennis (UTT) was held in July 2017 in Chennai, New Delhi, and Mumbai. Six teams took part the event and Falcons Club won the title by beating Shaze Challengers 14–9 in the final.

FIRST TO WIN ASIAN CUP MEDAL – WOMEN

Manika Batra (left)

Manika Batra became the first Indian woman to win a medal at the Asian Cup in 2022 as she defeated Japan's World No. 6 Hina Hayata in the bronze medal match. She also became the first Indian woman paddler to reach the semis of the continent.

FIRST PAIR TO WIN WTT CONTENDER TITLE

Manika Batra and G. Sathiyan became the first Indian pair to win WTT Contender title after beating Hungary's Nandor Ecseki and Dora Madarasz 3–1 (11–9, 9–11, 12–10, 11–6) in the final in Budapest in 2021.

TENNIS

FIRST GOLD MEDALS/TITLE IN TENNIS IN INDIA

Category	Details
Asian Games	
Men's Singles	Somdev Devvarman – 2010
Men's Doubles	Leander Paes and Gaurav Natekar – 1994
Men's Team	Zeeshan Ali, Asif Ismail, Gaurav Natekar and Leander Paes – 1994
Mixed Doubles	Leander Paes and Sania Mirza – 2006
Commonwealth Games	
Men's Singles	Somdev Devvarman – 2010
Grand Slam	
Wimbledon	Junior boys' – singles (1990), Mixed doubles (1999), Men's doubles (1999), Junior girls' – doubles (2003), Women's doubles (2015), and Junior boys' – doubles (2015)

French Open	Junior boys' – singles (1979), Mixed doubles (1997) and Men's doubles (1999)
US Open	Junior boys' – singles (1991), Mixed doubles (1999), Men's doubles (2002) and Women's doubles (2015)
Australian Open	Mixed doubles (2003), Junior boys' – Singles (2009), Men's doubles (2012) and Women's doubles (2016)

Leander Paes (left) and Mahesh Bhupathi (right)

Mahesh Bhupathi and Leander Paes won their first Grand Slam together when they won the Wimbledon men's doubles title in 1999.

FIRST WORLD PLAY–OFFS QUALIFYING TEAM – BILLIE JEAN KING CUP

Earlier known as the Federation Cup, the Billie Jean King Cup is a team event for women's tennis players. The Indian team progressed to the play-offs for the first time ever in March 2020, defeating Indonesia in the Asia–Oceania Group I event in Dubai, UAE, and finishing

Sania Mirza

second behind China. They lost the world group play-off tie against Latvia. The team comprised Ankita Raina, Rutuja Bhosale, Zeel Desai, Karman Kaur Thandi and Sania Mirza.

FIRST APPEARANCE AT THE DAVIS CUP

India played in the Davis Cup for the first time in 1921 against France in Paris and won 4–1. The Indian team comprised S.M. Jacob, Mohammed Sleem, A.A. Fyzee, and L.S. Dean.

FIRST SEEDED AT WIMBLEDON

Dilip Bose was the first seeded Indian player, at no. 15, in Wimbledon singles in 1950. He was a product of the Calcutta South Club, one of Asia's oldest tennis clubs.

FIRST INDIAN TO WIN TWO ATP CHALLENGERS SINGLES TITLES IN EUROPE

Sumit Nagal is the first Indian to win two ATP Challengers titles in Europe after he won the Tampere Open title in Finland in July 2023.

FIRST INDIAN TO WIN ATP CHALLENGER ON EUROPEAN CLAY

Sumit Nagal became the first Indian to win ATP Challenger on European clay after winning the ATP Rome Challenger in April 2023. He defeated Jasper De Jong in the final 6–3, 6–2.

WRESTLING

FIRST COACH OF THE YEAR AWARD

Late Yashvir Singh was the first Indian coach to be recognized as the Coach of the Year in 2010 by the Federation Internationale des Luttes Associees (FILA), the then apex body that governed wrestling.

FIRST TO WIN THE LAUREUS WORLD SPORTS AWARD

Vinesh Phogat is the first and only Indian wrestler to be awarded the Laureus World Sports Award 2019 in the comeback-of-the-year category. Phogat not only returned from her injury but also won the gold medal in both the 2018 Commonwealth Games at Gold Coast, Australia, and the 2018 Asian Games in Jakarta and Palembang, Indonesia.

FIRST JUNIOR WRESTLER OF THE YEAR AWARD

Deepak Punia (86 kg freestyle) became the first Indian wrestler to receive the Junior Wrestler of the Year title in 2019 from the UWW.

FIRST GOLD – ASIAN GAMES

Men – 90 kg freestyle category: Maruti Mane won the medal in the 1962 Asian Games in Jakarta, Indonesia.

Men – 52 kg Greco Roman category: Malwa Singh won the medal in the 1962 Asian Games in Jakarta, Indonesia.

Men – 100 kg Greco Roman category: Ganpat Andalkar won this title in the 1962 Asian Games in Jakarta, Indonesia.

Men – 100 kg category: Kartar Singh won the medal in the 1986 Seoul Asiad in South Korea.

Men – 65 kg freestyle category: Yogeshwar Dutt won the title in the 2014 Incheon Games.

Women – 50 kg freestyle category: Vinesh Phogat bagged the gold in the 2018 Asian Games in Jakarta, Indonesia.

Vinesh Phogat is the first Indian woman to win a gold medal in wrestling and to win back-to back Asian Games medals.

FIRST MEDAL – COMMONWEALTH GAMES

Men – 74 kg category: Rashid Anwar won a bronze medal at the 1934 Commonwealth Games held in London, UK.

Men – 100 kg category: Lila Ram won the first gold medal in the 1958 Games at Cardiff, Wales, in the heavyweight category.

FIRST AT THE OLYMPICS

Men: U. Zaw Weik playing in the 75 kg was the first to represent India at the Olympics, was placed 15th in the 1936 Olympics in Berlin, Germany.

Women: Geeta Phogat from Bhiwani, Haryana, was the first Indian woman wrestler to compete at the Olympics during the 2012 London Games.

FIRST OLYMPIC MEDAL

Men: Khashaba Dadasaheb Jadhav from Satara, Maharashtra, won a bronze in the bantam weight category (57 kg) in the 1952 Helsinki Olympics.

Women: On 17 August 2016, Sakshi Malik won a bronze for wrestling, in the women's freestyle 58 kg category in the Rio Olympics in Brazil.

Sakshi Malik (left)

FIRST WIN AT THE WORLD CHAMPIONSHIPS

Category	Details
Asian Wrestling Championship	
Men's Greco-Roman	Kartar Singh – 100 kg event – 1983
Men's Freestyle	Subhash Verma – 100 kg event – 1987

Women's Freestyle	Navjot Kaur – 65 kg event – 2018
Men's Freestyle team Champions	Team India – 2013
World Wrestling Championship	
Men's Freestyle	Sushil Kumar – 66 kg event – 2010

FIRST WINNER OF BOTH OLYMPIC AND WORLD CHAMPIONSHIP MEDALS

Sushil Kumar is the first Indian to win medals at both the Olympics and the World Championships. He won a bronze at the 2008 Beijing Olympics in the 66 kg freestyle category and a silver medal in the same category at the 2012 London Olympics. He also won a gold in the same category at the Moscow World Championship in Russia in 2010.

Sushil Kumar

AWARDS AND HONOURS

INTERNATIONAL AWARDS

FIRST TO WIN THE NOBEL PRIZE AND THE FIRST TO WIN THE NOBEL PRIZE FOR LITERATURE

Rabindranath Tagore (1861–1941) was the first Indian and the first Indian man to win the Nobel Prize. He won the Nobel Prize for Literature in 1913 for *Gitanjali*. With this win he also became the first non-European to win the Nobel Prize in Literature.

FIRST WINNER OF NEWBERY MEDAL

Dhan Gopal Mukerji (1890–1936), who was born in a village near Calcutta (now Kolkata), West Bengal and shifted later to the US, was the first Indian winner of the Newbery Medal for his novel, *Gay-Neck, the Story of a Pigeon,* in 1928.

FIRST WINNER OF THE NOBEL PRIZE FOR PHYSICS

Sir Chandrashekhara Venkata Raman (1888–1970) won the Nobel Prize in Physics in 1930 for the discovery of the light scattering effect that came to be known as the

Raman effect. The Raman effect was discovered on 28 February 1928, which is now celebrated as National Science Day in India. He was also the first Asian to win a Nobel Prize in the field of Science.

C.V. Raman is the paternal uncle to Subhramanyan Chandrashekhar, who won the 1983 Nobel Prize in Physics.

FIRST TO WIN THE PULITZER PRIZE

Men: Gobind Behari Lal (1889–1982), a science journalist in the US, won the Pulitzer Prize in 1937.

Women: Jhumpa Lahiri's (b. 11 July 1967) *Interpreter of Maladies* (Mariner Books/Houghton Mifflin) won the Pulitzer Prize for Fiction in 2000.

FIRST TO WIN THE RAMON MAGSAYSAY AWARD

Men: Vinoba Bhave (1895–1982) won the prestigious Ramon Magsaysay award for community leadership in 1958.

Women: Mother Teresa (1910–97) won the award for contributions to Peace and International Understanding in 1962.

A stamp commemorating Vinoba Bhave

FIRST GRAMMY AWARD

Men: Pandit Ravi Shankar (1920–2012) won the Grammy for Best Chamber Music Performance in 1968 for his album West meets East.

Women: Tanvi Shah (b. 1 December 1985) became the first Indian woman to win the Grammy when she shared the award for Best Song Written for Visual Media in 2008 for the song 'Jai Ho' from the film *Slumdog Millionaire*.

FIRST TO WIN THE NOBEL PRIZE IN PHYSIOLOGY OR MEDICINE

In 1968, Har Gobind Khorana (1922–2011) jointly won the Nobel Prize for Physiology or Medicine with Robert W. Holley and Marshall W. Nirenberg. He has also been awarded the Albert Lasker Award for Basic Medical Research, Padma Vibhushan, Louisa Gross Horwitz Prize and Willard Gibbs Award amongst others.

A Nobel Prize cannot be divided amongst more than three people.

FIRST WOMAN TO WIN THE NOBEL PRIZE AND THE FIRST TO WIN THE NOBEL PRIZE FOR PEACE

Winning the Nobel Prize for Peace in 1979, Mother Teresa (1990–97), became the first Indian woman to win the Nobel Prize. She founded the Missionaries of Charity in Calcutta to help the poor and the diseased. Although she was born in Albania, she acquired Indian citizenship in 1950 and received an honorary American citizenship in 1996.

FIRST WINNER OF THE RIGHT LIVELIHOOD AWARD

Ela Bhatt (1933–2022) was a social worker and lawyer who fought for the labour rights of self-employed women. She set up the Self-employed women's Association (SEWA) in 1972. The organization has over 25 lakh members across 18 states and has made significant achievements in establishing, health, death and maternity benefits.

FIRST WINNER OF THE WORLD FOOD PRIZE

This global award is given to outstanding individuals who have advanced human development by improving the quality, quantity or availability of food in the world. The first Indian winner of this award was agronomist, agricultural scientist and plant geneticist Dr M.S. Swaminathan in 1987.

FIRST WINNER OF THE UN HUMAN RIGHTS PRIZE

The United Nations (UN) Human Rights Prize is awarded in recognition of outstanding achievements in Human rights. It was established in 1966 and first awarded in 1968. In December 1988, the first Indian to receive the award was Baba Murlidhar Devidas Amte (1914–2008) for his work for the empowerment of people suffering from leprosy. He is also the only Indian winner of this prize till date.

FIRST TO WIN THE BOOKER PRIZE

Women: Arundhati Roy (b. 1961) won the Booker Prize in 1997 for her debut novel, *The God of Small Things.*

Men: Aravind Adiga (b. 1974) won the Booker Prize in 2008 for his novel, *The White Tiger*. Published in the same year, the novel is a take on India's class struggles through the lens of dark humour.

Arundhati Roy (right)

FIRST TO WIN THE NOBEL PRIZE IN ECONOMICS

> The award was initially called the Booker Prize for Fiction (1969–2001), then the Man Booker Prize (2002–19) until it was renamed the Booker Prize.

Amartya Kumar Sen (b. 1933) is an Indian economist and philosopher who was awarded the Sveriges Riksbank Prize in Economic Sciences in Memory of Alfred Nobel 1998. Hailing from Santiniketan, West Bengal, he graduated from University of Calcutta and went to Trinity College, Cambridge for his higher education including another Bachelor's degree. Among his many achievements, he was awarded the Bharat Ratna, National Humanitics Medal and the Johan Skytte Prize in Political Science among others.

FIRST TO WIN THE NOBEL PRIZE IN CHEMISTRY

Venkatraman Ramakrishnan (b. 1952) won the 2009 Nobel Prize in Chemistry jointly with Thomas A. Steitz and Ada E. Yonath. Among his many awards are the Fellowship of the Royal Society, Padma Vibhushan, and the Heatley Medal of the British Biomedical Society. In 2012, he was also knighted for his services in molecular biology as part of the British honours system.

A total of 615 Nobel awards have been conferred to 989 laureates across all categories (including Economics) between 1901 to 2022.

FIRST NOVEL IN AN INDIAN LANGUAGE TO WIN THE INTERNATIONAL BOOKER PRIZE

Tomb of Sand by Geetanjali Shree became the first Indian language (Hindi) novel to win the prestigious International Booker Prize in 2022. The original in Hindi, *Ret Samadhi* was published by Rajkamal Prakashan, and the translation was published by Tilted Axis Press and Penguin Random House India. The prize money of £50,000 (₹46 lakh approximately) was shared between Shree and her English translator, Daisy Rockwell.

NATIONAL AWARDS

FIRST GALLANTRY AWARDS

The Government of India, instituted the Param Vir Chakra, the Maha Vir Chakra and the Vir Chakra as the first three gallantry awards on 26 January 1950. All three are wartime gallantry awards. The Ashok Chakra, the Kirti Chakra and the Shaurya Chakra (formerly called – Ashok Chakra class I, Ashok Chakra class II and Ashok Chakra class III respectively) are peacetime awards instituted on 4 January 1952.

Param Vir Chakra: Major Somnath Sharma – Indian Army
Ashok Chakra: Havildar Bachittar Singh and Naik Narbahadur Thapa – Indian Army
Maha Vir Chakra: Brigadier Rajinder Singh – Indian Army
Kirti Chakra: Captain Joginder Singh Gharaya, Havildar Amar Singh, Naik Hardial Singh, Sepoy Sewa Singh, Sepoy Daryao, Major Gurucharan Singh, Sowan Prithi Singh, Flight Lieutenant Ulrich Anthony D'Cruz, Sergeant Ram Chandra Dua, Sergeant Dev Raj Singh, Flight Sergeant O. Sundaressiya and Shri B.B.L. Datt – Indian Army (7), Indian Air Force (4) and Civilian (1)
Vir Chakra: Major T.G.N. Pai and Second Lieutenant R. Kanikasamy – Indian Army
Shaurya Chakra: Major P.S. Gahoon, Second Lieutenant M. Thulasiram, Subedar Kartar Singh, Jemadar Samandar Singh, Lance Naik Bishan Singh, Lance Naik Milkha Singh, Sepoy Shankar Dass, Lieutenant Colonel R.A. Shebbeare, Major S.L. Menezes, Major A.T. Stephenson, Subjedar Major Dhan Singh, Havildar Naranjan Singh, Lance Daffadar Sultan Singh, Rifleman Bakhtawar Singh Bhandari, Sepoy Harchand Singh, Sepoy Ricchpal Singh, Niak Jograj Singh, Sepoy Ram Singh and Rifleman Til Bahadur Gurung – Indian Army (19)

FIRST BHARAT RATNA

The Bharat Ratna is the highest civilian honour of the country and is awarded for exemplary service to any field of human endeavour. The first winners were:

Men: C.V. Raman, Sarvapalli Radhakrishnan and C. Rajgopalachari were the first Bharat Ratna awardees in the year 1954.

Women: Former prime minister, Indira Gandhi won the prestigious Bharat Ratna in 1971, becoming the first Indian woman to win the accolade.

S. Radhakrishnan

The Bharat Ratna has been awarded to 45 people till date.

FIRST PADMA VIBHUSHAN

The second-highest civilian honour in India, the Padma Vibhushan is awarded for distinguished and exceptional service. The first winners were:

Men: Satyendra Nath Bose, Nandalal Bose, B.G. Kher, Zakir Hussain, V.K. Krishna Menon and Bhutanese Jigme Dorji Wangchuk were the first recipients of the Padma Vibhushan in 1954.

M.S. Subbulaksmi

Women: Social worker Janaki Devi Bajaj was the first woman recipient of the award in 1956.

FIRST PADMA BHUSHAN

The third-highest civilian honour in India, the Padma Bhushan is awarded for distinguished service of a high order. The first winners were:

Men: Kodandera Subayya Thimayya, Satya Narayana Shastri, Sukumar Sen, Jamini Roy, P.S. Rau, V. Narahari Rao, Maharaj Palden T. Namgyal, A.L. Mudaliar, V.N. Menon, V.L. Mehta, Josh Mahilabadi, Hussain Ahmed Madani, K.S. Krishnan, A.N. Khosla, Amarnath Jha, R.R. Handa, Maithili Sharan Gupt, Radha K. Gupta, Jnan C. Ghosh, M.I. Ganapati, Shanti Swaroop Bhatnagar and Homi Bhabha were the first to be awarded the honour in 1954.

Women: M.S. Subbulakshmi was the first recipient of the honour in 1954.

FIRST PADMA SHRI

The fourth-highest civilian award, the Padma Shri was first awarded in the year 1954. Here is a list of the first winners:

Name	Field
Asha Devi Aryanayakam	Public Affairs
Amalprava Das	Public Affairs
Mirnamayee Ray	Public Affairs
Perin Captain	Public Affairs
Achamma Mathai	Public Affairs
Machani Somappa	Public Affairs
Bir Bhan Bhatia	Medicine
Mathura Das	Medicine
Ramji Vasant Khanolkar	Medicine
K.R. Chakrovarty	Science and Engineering

Akhil Chandra Mitra	Science and Engineering
Surinder Kumar Dey	Civil Service
S.P.P. Thorat	Civil Service
Tarlok Singh	Civil Service
Apa Saheb Bala Saheb Pant	Civil Service
Bhag Mehta	Civil Service
K. Shankar Pillai	Literature and Education

FIRST RECIPIENTS OF THE SAHITYA AKADEMI AWARD

Men: Makhanlal Chaturvedi (1889–1968), a Hindi poet, was the first person to receive this award for *Him Tarangini* (Hindi) in 1955.

Women: Amrita Pritam (1919–2005) received the award in 1956, the year after its inception, for *Sunehre* (Punjabi), a collection of poems.

Amrita Pritam

FIRST ARJUNA AWARD

The Arjuna Awards for outstanding performance in sports and games is one of the prestigious sports honours in the country. The award was first instituted in 1961 and the first winners were:

Name	Sport
Gurbachan Singh Randhawa	Athletics
Nandu M. Natekar	Badminton

Sarbjit Singh	Basketball
Buddy D'Souza	Boxing
Manuel Aaron	Chess
Salim Durani	Cricket
P.K. Banerjee	Football
P.G. Sethi	Golf
Sham Lal	Gymnastics
Ann Lumsden	Hockey
Prithipal Singh	Hockey
Ramanathan Krishnan	Lawn Tennis
Prem Singh	Polo
Karni Singh	Shooting
K.S. Jain	Squash
Bajrangi Prasad	Swimming
J.C. Vohra	Table Tennis
A. Palanisamy	Volleyball
A.N. Ghosh	Weightlifting
Udey Chand	Wrestling

FIRST RECIPIENTS OF THE JNANPITH AWARD

The Jnanpith Award is presented annually by the Bharatiya Jnanpith to an Indian author for their contribution to literature. The first winners were:

Men: G. Sankara Kurup (1901–78) won the award in 1965, for his anthology of poems, *Odakkuzhal*.

Women: Ashapurna Devi (1909–95), received the award in 1976 for her novel *Pratham Pratishruti* (1965).

A stamp commemorating G. Sankara Kurup

FIRST WINNERS OF THE DRONACHARYA AWARD

Officially known as the Dronacharya Award for Outstanding Coaches in Sports and Games, it was instituted in 1985. It is presented annually by the Ministry of Youth affairs and Sports. The first winners were:

Men: Balchandra Bhaskar Bhagwat (Wrestling), Om Prakash Bhardwaj (Boxing) and O.M. Nambiar (Athletics) received the award in 1985.

Women: Hansa Sharma (Weightlifting) received the award in 2000.

FIRST WINNERS OF THE SARASWATI SAMMAN

The Saraswati Samman was instituted by the K.K. Birla Foundation in 1991. Award winners receive ₹15 lakh along with a citation and a plaque. The first winners are:

Man: Harivansh Rai Bachchan for Autobiography in four volumes (Hindi) in 1991.

Woman: Balamani Amma for Nivedyam (Malayalam) in 1995.

A stamp commemorating Harivansh Rai Bachchan

FIRST WINNER OF THE MAJOR DHYAN CHAND KHEL RATNA AWARD

The Major Dhyan Chand Khel Ratna Award (formerly known as the Rajiv Gandhi Khel Ratna Award) was instituted in 1992 and is the highest sporting honour in the country. The first winners were:

Men: Viswanathan Anand was the first recipient of the award for his contribution to Chess in 1991–92.

Women: Karnam Malleswari was the first woman to receive the award. She won the award for her contribution to Weightlifting in 1994–95.

In 2023, the Major Dhyan Chand Khel Ratna Award was bestowed on Badminton players, Satwiksairaj Rankireddy and Chirag Shetty.

Karnam Malleswari

FIRST WINNERS OF THE TENZING NORGAY NATIONAL ADVENTURE AWARD

The Tenzing Norgay National Adventure award is the highest adventure sports honour in the country. Awarded annually by the Ministry of Youth Affairs and Sports, they were first announced in 1994. Here are the first winners:

Men: Baldev Kanwar, Nima Norbu, Rajeev Sharma, A.K. Singh and Hukum Singh won the award.

Women: Chandraprabha Aitwal, Kunga Bhatia, Gurmayum Anita Devi, Radha Devi, Dicky Dolma, Suman Kutiyal, Savita Martolia,

Bachendri Pal (left)

Rita Gombu Marwah, Bimla Negi, Sarla Negi, Bachendri Pal, Harshha Panwar, Rita Patel, K. Saraswati, Deepu Sharma, Rachel Thomas and Santosh Yadav won the award.

FIRST SAHITYA AKADEMI BHASHA SAMMAN AWARD

The Bhasha Samman Awards are given annually for contribution towards the development of a language. The first of these awards were given in 1996 to:

- Dharikshan Mishra for Bhojpuri,
- Bansi Ram Sharma and M.R. Thakur for Pahari (Himachali),
- K. Jathappa Rai and Mandara Keshava Bhat for Tulu (Karnataka), and
- Chandra Kanta Murasingh for Kokborok (Tripura).

FIRST RECIPIENTS OF THE MAJOR DHYAN CHAND AWARD FOR LIFETIME ACHIEVEMENT IN SPORTS AND GAMES

Popularly known as the Major Dhyan Chand Award, the award was instituted in 2002 and is awarded annually by the Ministry of Youth Affairs and Sports to honour lifetime achievements in Sports. Here is a list of the first winners:

Men: Shahuraj Birajdhar (Boxing) and Ashok Diwan (Hockey) won the honour in 2002.

Women: Aparna Ghosh (Basketball) was awarded in 2002. She is the only woman Basketball player to receive this honour.

MISCELLANEOUS

FIRSTS IN THE WORLD

Category	Details
First Tandoor ovens	Remnants of clay ovens or tandoors have been found at the sites of the Indus Valley Civilisation, dating back to 2600 BCE
First drainage system	The Indus valley civilization had a sophisticated drainage system around 2600 BCE
First pappadams	As per scriptures of Hinduism, pappadams existed about 2500 years ago
First veterinary hospital	In the reign of Ashoka the great (r. 268–232 BCE), the first veterinary hospital was established in India to work on the tenets of the *Shalihotra Samhita*, one of the earliest treatise on veterinary medicine
First listing of protected species	Ashoka is believed to have built a list of protected species as part of the legislation. The oldest such list is found in the 5th pillar edict in 242 BCE, which was also probably a revised list
First Stupas	The earliest stupas have existed in India from around 5th century BCE. The construction of

	Buddhist Stupas began on a large scale during the reign of Ashoka
First to espouse 'money is everything' philosophy	The *Arthashastra,* composed between 3rd century BCE–3rd century CE mentioned three pursuits of life – wealth, charity and desire. It also emphasised that money was the way to achieve the other two pursuits as well
First laws against cruelty	The *Arthashastra* mentioned fines for people who inflicted pain on quadrupeds
First casinos	The idea of casinos was first mentioned in *Arthashastra*, where the operation was defined as being undertaken and supervised by the superintendent of gambling who was responsible for providing equipment and accommodation and could levy five per cent of the winnings as revenue
First social stratification based on 'caste'	*Manusmriti* dated back to 1st to 3rd century CE is a part of scriptures and *Dharmsastras* of Hinduism. It acknowledges and justifies the caste system that divides Hindus into four castes based on their 'Karma' and 'Dharma': Bhramins, Kshatriyas, Vaishyas and Shudras. The caste system was legally abolished in 1950
First sex manual	The Kama Sutra set in 2nd–3rd century CE is believed to be the earliest sex manual in the world
First to give the atomic theory of time	The Jain sect of philosophers in Northern India conceptualised time as a string of countless

	atoms and movement takes place in tiny steps. This theory was present around 200 CE
First general theory of Quantam Physics	The first general theory of Quantum Physics was applied to all material phenomena by Jain philosophers around 400–500 BCE
First practice of Yoga	Believed to have originated around 400 CE, Yoga was a spiritual Hindu practice to detangle the spirit from the entanglements of the lived human experience. Patanjali's *Yoga Sutras* is believed to be the first text on Yoga
First to refine sugar	Sugar plantations was established by around 1000 BCE. Refinement of sugar is believed to have taken place during the Gupta empire. Although *Arthashastra* also contains mentions the description of a Sugar mill
First merry-go-round	Prince Bhoja of Malwa describes a rotating mechanical amusement ride called *Rathadota*
First parachute	The Indian text *Prabhavakacavita* mentions two brothers who jumped off a tall tower and landed safely with the help of two special 'umbrellas'
First ice cream	Dairy-based ice desserts were first developed by the Mughals in the 1500s
First kulfi	The Mughals were the ones to invent kulfi – a sweet dairy-based dessert prevalent in India
First rust-proof iron	The Iron pillar at the Qutub Minar complex in Delhi was constructed around 400 CE. The pillar has since then stood in the open and has not shown any sign of rust

IMAGE COPYRIGHT INFORMATION

NOTE: CCA-SA refers to the Creative Commons Attribution-Share Alike Wikimedia Commons/ International Wikimedia Commons licences; Public Domain/PD: All public domain photographs have been sourced from: Wikimedia Commons/Public Domain; PIB: Press Information Bureau; GODL: Government Open Data Licence – India; GoI: Government of India

GOVERNANCE, POLITICS AND NATIONHOOD

4: PD–US; **5**: PD; **10**: PD–India; **12**: PD–India; **17**: CC0 1.0 Universal Public Domain Dedication; **18**: **top**: GODL–India/GOI; **bottom**: GODL–India/India Post; **20**: GODL–India/President's Secretariat

DEFENCE

25: GODL–India/India Post; **26**: PD–UK/Royal Air Force; **29**: GODL–India/India Post; **34**: by courtesy of PIB; **36**: by courtesy of PIB; **40**: GODL–India/Ministry of Defence; **41**: GODL–India/Indian Navy; **42**: GODL–India/Ministry of Defence; **43**: GODL–India/Integrated Defence Staff

STATES AND UNION TERRITORIES

47: Pexels.com/Canva Studio; **49**: Pexels.com/Alejandro Barrón

EDUCATION

56: PD–US/Colesworthey Grant; **57**: PD–India; **58**: PD–US; **62**: PD–India; **65**: PD; **67**: CCA–SA 4.0 International/Smuconlaw/ https://commons.wikimedia.org/wiki/File:National_Law_School_of_India_University,_Bangalore,_India_-_20130524-01.JPG

TRANSPORT

73: PD–US/Lambert Weston and Sons; **74**: PD; **76**: PD–US/ Western Railway; **77:** PD–India; **79:** PD–India; **82**: PD/ Ollietheecopreneur; **86**: CCO 1.0 Universal Public Domain Dedication/Fly2Blue;

STRUCTURES

91: GODL–India/Prime Minister's Office; **94**: PD/David Castor; **95**: GODL–India/Ministry of Culture;

BUSINESS AND ECONOMY

103: PD–India; **104**: **top**: GODL–India/Post of India; **bottom**: PD–India; **106**: PD–India; **111**: GODL–India/India Post

SCIENCE, TECHNOLOGY AND SPACE

116: PD/British Museum; **118**: PD–US, India, Sweden/Nobel Foundation; **120**: GODL–India/Post of India; **125**: PD–India; **128**: GODL–India/Indian Air Force; **129**: Free licensed image catalogued by Johnson Space Center of the United States National Aeronautics and Space Administration (NASA) under Photo ID: JSC2002-E-25323; **131**: GODL–India/Mars Orbiter Mission Data Archive; **134**: GODL–India/Indian Space Research Organisation

MEDICAL SCIENCE

136: CCA–SA 3.0 Unported/Alokprasad at en.wikipedia/ https://commons.wikimedia.org/wiki/File:Shushrut_statue.jpg; **137**: PD/ L.vivian.richard at English Wikipedia; **138**: PD–India; **140**: CCA–SA 4.0 International/Vishnoi M/ https://commons.wikimedia.org/wiki/File:AIIMS_-New_Delhi%27s_Ward_Block.jpg; **143**: GODL–India/Ministry of Railways; **144**: CCA–SA 2.0 Generic/World Economic Forum/ https://commons.wikimedia.org/wiki/File:Naresh_Trehan_at_the_World_Economic_Forum_on_India_2012.jpg

CINEMA AND PHOTOGRAPHY

147: PD/Henry Brispot; **150**: PD–India; **152**: PD–India; **155**: PD–India; **157**: PD–India; **158**: PD–US; **159**: PD–India; **162**: **top**: PD–India; **bottom**: Fair Use/Theo's little bot; **163**: CCA-SA 4.0 International/Markgoff2972/https://commons.wikimedia.org/wiki/File:Ravi_Shankar.jpg; **164**: Fair Use/Kailash29792; **165**: Fair Use/Theo's little bot; **166**: **top**: PD–India; **bottom**: Fair Use/Kailash29792; **167**: **top**: PD–India; **bottom**: Fair Use/Kailash29792; **170**: PD; **172**: PD/g.p. jacomb-hood, Ralph Lake; **173**: GODL–India/Ministry of Information and Broadcasting; **175**: CCA–SA 4.0 International/Vikramjit Kakati/ https://commons.wikimedia.org/wiki/File:Raghu_Rai_pix_by_Vikramjit_Kakati.jpg

THE ARTS

181: PD/Rembrandt Peale; **183**: PD–US; **186**: by courtesy of Shubhali Chopra; **193**: **top**: CCO 1.0 Universal Public Domain Dedication/Gary Todd; **bottom**: PD; **194**: PD–India; **195**: PD–India; **196**: GODL–India/India Post; **208**: GODL–India/

President's Secretariat; **209**: Pexels.com/Oktay Köseoğlu; **210**: GODL–India/Ministry of Information and Broadcasting; **211**: Shutterstock.com; **214**: PD; **217**: CCA–SA 2.0 Generic/ Knowtex/ https://commons.wikimedia.org/wiki/File:Grand_Palais_%26_Kapoor_-_Night_of_Museums_2011_(2).jpg

LIBRARIES AND MUSEUMS

220: by courtesy of Shubhali Chopra; **225**: by courtesy of PIB; **226**: by courtesy of PIB

MEDIA AND COMMUNICATIONS

230: PD–India; **235**: GODL–India/India Post; **237**: GODL–India/India Post; **239**: GODL–India/President's Secretariat; **242**: CCA–SA 3.0 Unported/Shrutuja Shirke/ https://commons.wikimedia.org/wiki/File:Airtel.JPG

SPORTS

247: GODL–India/Ministry of Youth Affairs and Sports; **249**: CCA-SA 4.0 International https://commons.wikimedia.org/wiki/File:Sheetal_Devi_(Para-archer).png; **253**: GODL–India/President's Secretariat; **254**: GODL–India/Prime Minister's Office; **256: top left**: GODL–India/Prime Minister's Office; **top right**: GODL–India/Prime Minister's Office; **bottom**: GODL–India/Ministry of Youth Affairs and Sports; **263**: GODL–India/GOI; **264**: GODL–India/Ministry of Youth Affairs and Sports; **265**: CCA–SA 2.0 Generic/Wolfgang Jekel/https://commons.wikimedia.org/wiki/File:Viswanathan_Anand_(2016)_(cropped).jpeg; **266**: CCA–SA 3.0 Unported/Stefan64/https://commons.wikimedia.org/wiki/File:DGukesh23b.jpg; **268**: CCA–SA 3.0 Unported/Harrias/https://commons.

wikimedia.org/wiki/File:Mithali_Raj_Truro_2012_square.jpg; **270**: **top**: CCA–SA 4.0 International/Bahnfrend/https://commons.wikimedia.org/wiki/File:2016%E2%80%9317_WBBL_ST_v_PS_17-01-21_Kaur_(03).jpg; **bottom**: PD–India; **273**: GODL–India/GOI; **275**: GODL–India/President's Secretariat; **280**: PD–US/George Beldam; **282**: GODL–India/ministry of wcd of gov of India; **283**: GODL–India/President's Secretariat; **284**: PD–India; **288**: Shutterstock.com/daykung; **289**: Shutterstock.com/Isogood_patrick; **293**: PD–India; **294**: PD; **300**: GODL–India/President's Secretariat; **301**: GODL–India/Rajya Sabha Tv; **303**: GODL–India/GOI; **304**: CCA–SA 4.0 International/Tpsn98290/ https://commons.wikimedia.org/wiki/File:Bhuvneshwari_Kumari.jpg; **307**: GODL–India/India Post; **311**: GODL–India/Ministry of Youth Affairs and Sports; **313**: GODL–India/President's Secretariat; **315**: PD; **316**: Shutterstock.com/Paul Cowan; **319**: GODL–India/President's Secretariat; **320**: GODL–India/Ministry of Youth Affairs and Sports

AWARDS AND HONOURS

322: GODL–India/India Post; **325**: Shutterstock.com/lev radin; **328**: **top**: PD–US/White House; **bottom**: PD–India; **330**: PD–India; **331**: GODL–India/India Post; **332**: GODL–India/India Post; **333**: **top**: GODL–India/GOI; **bottom**: GODL–India/President's Secretariat;

INDEX